Political Freedom

The Problems of Philosophy
Their Past and Present
General editor: Ted Honderich
Grote Professor of the Philosophy of Mind and Logic,
University College, London

Other books in the series

Private Ownership
James O. Grunebaum

Religious Belief and the Will
Louis P. Pojman

Mind–Body Identity Theories
Cynthia Macdonald

Practical Reasoning
Robert Audi

Personal Identity
Harold W. Noonan

If P, then Q:
Conditionals and the
Foundations of Reasoning
David H. Sanford

The Infinite
A. W. Moore

Thought and Language
Julius Moravcsik

The Nature of Art
A. L. Cothey

Explaining Explanation
David-Hillel Ruben

Scepticism
Christopher Hookway

Weakness of the Will
Justin Gosling

Rationality
Harold I. Brown

The Rational Foundations of
Ethics
T. L. S. Sprigge

Moral Knowledge
Alan Goldman

Knowledge of the External
World
Bruce Aune

Human Consciousness
Alastair Hannay

The Implications of Determinism
Roy Weatherford

Political Freedom

George G. Brenkert

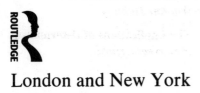

London and New York

First published 1991
by Routledge
11 New Fetter Lane, London EC4P 4EE

Simultaneously published in the USA and Canada
by Routledge
a division of Routledge, Chapman and Hall, Inc.
29 West 35th Street, New York, NY 10001

Typeset in 10/12pt Times by
Selectmove Ltd, London
Printed in Great Britain by
Biddles Ltd, Guildford, Surrey

British Library Cataloguing in Publication Data
Brenkert, George G.
  Political freedom – (The Problems of philosophy)
  1. Equality & freedom. Sociopolitical aspects
  I. Title II. Series
  323.01

Library of Congress Cataloging-in-Publication Data

Brenkert, George G.
  Political freedom / George G. Brenkert.
  p. cm. – (Problems of philosophy)
  Includes bibliographical references and index.
  1. Liberty. I. Title. II. Series: Problems of philosophy
(Routledge (Firm))
JC585.B645 1991
323.44 – dc20

ISBN 0–415–03372–1

To A.L., J.K., and H.B.P.

Contents

Preface   ix

Part 1

1 Political freedom and political philosophy   1

2 Conservative freedom   31

3 Liberal freedom   65

4 Radical freedom   101

Part 2

5 Political freedom as empowerment   139

6 Political freedom, involvement, and democracy   171

7 Freedom, enablement, and resources   205

Notes   243
References   263
Index   275

Preface

As this book was being completed cries for political freedom broke out over Eastern Europe. Though this book was not written with those countries specifically in mind, it is my hope that it will be relevant to their circumstances. It would be ironical, however, if the revolutions in Eastern Europe and their apparent eagerness to adopt 'Western' ways convinced those in the West that there is little left to do within their own political systems. I believe that to be false. This is not to say that I do not believe that citizens, for example, of Great Britain and the United States do not enjoy a great deal of political freedom. But there is much more to be done. It was with the incomplete and inadequate state of political freedom in Western countries in mind that this book was written.

The problem of political freedom takes many forms. Should laws against public demonstrations by extremist groups, e.g., the Nazis or the Red Brigade, be passed? What limits, if any, should be imposed on publications, television programs, record albums, or art forms which are sexually explicit, anti-state, or anti-religious? What forms of electronic monitoring of its citizens may the governing institutions of a society adopt? Do workers have political rights within the corporations for which they work? Do communities have a responsibility to define a view of the good life and foster its realization in its members? These are not idle issues. They are not simply conundrums for scholars. They are not merely parlor games.

Roughly stated, these problems concern the forms of determination in which individuals stand to each other and to various institutions within a political society. Their resolution is crucial to political and human life, for they define the basic relations involving power, authority, and coercion among individuals. Few, if any, can escape the influence of the answers given.

Herein lies our problem. There have been countless different "solutions" offered to the problems of political freedom over the past two millennia. Which answers should we adopt? How are we to know what is political freedom? I have not written this book as a "how to" account of political freedom. It does not provide recipes for political action. Instead, it is philosophical in that it attempts to deal with various basic conceptual and theoretical issues at the heart of political freedom.

As I see it, our task is twofold. First, we must understand those past answers which influence our present views of political freedom. By looking backward we can more easily see where we presently stand and the directions in which we must go. However, to discuss even the most prominent past proposals in a single book requires some principle of selection and organization.

I have resolved this difficulty in the first part of the book by concentrating on modern Western political thought. This does not mean that I think that the reflections of Plato and Aristotle are irrelevant to present questions. However, I have given precedence to modern thinkers. Further, rather than simply present a brief discussion of a large number of thinkers, I have focused on a very few of those modern thinkers who have greatly influenced our thought. Even that I have done within what I call "models of freedom." My intention has been to capture the major views of political freedom which today orient our relations to each other and to our political institutions.

There are, I think, three different models (conservative, liberal, and radical) of political freedom which play prominent roles within our political lives. The models themselves are abstractions, but only in the sense that none of them has been proposed by a single thinker. They are not abstractions in that they daily influence our lives. Thus, I think these models should be familiar and useful in understanding modern thought on political freedom. My argument is that each model is subject to important limitations and internal problems. The upshot of recognizing this is that we are forced to formulate a different view of political freedom which would be more adequate to our time.

A word should be said on how I constructed these models. As just suggested, they are the result of a twofold abstraction from the history of political thought. On the one hand, they are abstracted from the works of some of the most prominent political thinkers. On the other hand, they are also abstracted from political movements that are identified as "conservative", "liberal," and "radical." Thus, it goes without saying that the particular views of this or that political thinker or political movement may diverge from the models which I have created and to which I have linked such thinkers or movements. Conservatism, liberalism, and radicalism are complex movements. In order to grasp some of the main themes which form the warp of modern discussion of political freedom I believe this abstraction to be important.

In the second part of the book I present a more adequate model of political freedom. In developing this new view, which I call "freedom as empowerment," I have drawn on various aspects of the models I have previously examined. I can only assert dogmatically at this point that the account we need is one which does not simply attempt to isolate a space for each individual from the rest of society, but one which ensures his or her integration into society. Not freedom from politics, but freedom to live within the political setting is what political freedom requires.

My intention in undertaking these two tasks has been to write one book – not two books, one historical and one contemporary, simply glued together. In addressing abstract philosophical questions, I have tried to keep in mind the problems of political freedom as they arise out of real, practical contexts. By proceeding in this manner I have sought to avoid the conclusions of some, currently writing, whose accounts openly imply that threats do not limit individual freedom, that withholding information and censoring books do not restrict one's freedom, or that the access one has to material and cognitive resources is not part and parcel of one's political freedom. Such conclusions by various contemporary philosophers suggest to me the abstract, unworldliness of their views. How successful I have been in developing an alternative view, the reader will have to judge.

I appreciate the patience of Routledge in my preparation of this manuscript. It was an undertaking larger than I anticipated at the outset. The patience of my family has also been significant. I would like to thank James Bennett, Frank Cunningham, Thomas Donaldson, Robert Evans, James Gould, Roger Paden, N. Scott Arnold, John Hardwig, Hugh LeFollette, and Richard Norman. Each of these individuals has been generous with his time in agreeing to read parts of this text and to make suggestions for its improvement. They offered much good advice; too much of it, I suspect, they may believe I did not take. However, I greatly appreciated and benefited from their help. I hasten to add the usual, but important, comment that problems and difficulties remaining are due to the author.

Part I

1 Political freedom and political philosophy

The first step to the understanding of men is the bringing to consciousness of the model or models that dominate and penetrate their thought and action.

(Berlin 1981: 159)

I PROBLEMS OF POLITICAL FREEDOM

Debate over political freedom is at the center of much of our public life. Here are three familiar examples.

Conservatives argue that a free society would instil traditional religious, moral, and social values in each individual. Thus, in the name of freedom, the selling of pornographic material ought to be banned as injurious to the moral fiber of society. Liberals contend that a free society would maintain certain minimal standards of non-interference, while letting individuals do what they choose. Thus, they conclude that the sale of pornographic material ought *not* to be banned among consenting adults. Finally, radicals claim that pornography oppresses women. Since a free society would not permit the oppression of its members, the sale of pornography ought to be banned.

Liberals contend that political freedom requires that all adult citizens be permitted to participate in the political process through voting and office holding. Only in this way can individuals control government power and protect their private affairs from unwarranted political intrusion. Radicals agree that freedom requires participation in the affairs of society. They claim, however, that participation does not have simply an instrumental importance and that it *cannot* be found within a society whose public affairs are political in nature. Conservatives maintain that people may be free not only within a political society but may also be politically free even if their access to voting and office holding is limited by various substantive conditions, such as property holding or literacy.

Liberals and conservatives argue that a person's material resources are irrelevant to whether or not he or she is free. Having a certain amount of wealth may make one's freedom more valuable, but does not alter the fact that one can be free even if poor. However, radicals reject this view, claiming instead that a free society would provide the material circumstances whereby individuals could realistically acquire the freedom others say they have. Material resources, they argue, do not simply make one's freedom more valuable, like a glossy shine on one's auto, but are part and parcel of freedom itself.[1]

Obviously such examples could be multiplied endlessly. Four features of these disputes are noteworthy. First, they involve practical problems which are unavoidable. Whether stores are permitted to sell pornographic materials, citizens allowed to participate in political processes, or material resources provided to the poor are questions which, though subject to compromise and disguise, must be addressed. Secondly, these problems are of considerable importance. How they are resolved affects the daily lives of people, even those who profess indifference to political issues. Thirdly, these disputes appear to continue endlessly. Thus, they raise the question whether one set of responses to these disputes can be said to be better or more rational than others. Contrariwise, must we simply look to "the likings and dislikings of society, or of some powerful portion of it"? (Mill 1956: 10). Finally, such disputes concerning political freedom are not unique. They also arise in our discussions of justice, democracy, and equality, as well as power, family, and class.

Accordingly, it seems that we face a dilemma. We cannot avoid saying something about disputes over political freedom, but the endlessness of such disputes raises the question whether we can say anything meaningful. It is not surprising then that so many despair of political disputes, try (unsuccessfully) to avoid them, or treat them simply as matters of subjective opinion. If we are to discuss political freedom, we need to know not only why we have these disputes but also whether there are routes we might take to reduce or resolve them. Only if these questions are satisfactorily answered would it make sense to discuss which view of political freedom we should adopt and how we should respond to particular problems of political freedom.

In the following chapter, I argue that though political disputes are not subject to any final resolution and hence may continue endlessly, this is not a reason to despair or conclude that they are simply matters of opinion. Instead, because reason and evidence are fully appropriate in them, political disputes may be genuine disputes. They are not simply empty expressions of emotion. We can show which views are better than others and hence on what side the preponderance of reason lies. Accordingly, it makes sense to ask which political views we ought to adopt. Though the remainder of this chapter seeks to convince the reader of these views, the larger proof I offer lies in the chapters that follow.

II POLITICAL DISPUTES AND ENDLESS DISPUTES

There have been a host of explanations why political disputes continue endlessly. Some are cognitive in nature: people are intellectually rigid, factually misinformed, conceptually confused, and/or begin with different assumptions about human nature. Other explanations portray the language of politics as either simply expressive of emotions or as having suffered a breakdown such that it is no longer able to sustain rational or objective argument.[2] Finally, there are psychological and evaluative accounts that point to the role of self-interest, the need for power or dominance, and different risk assessments.

Quite clearly several of these factors may play a significant role in our political disputes. Misinformation, conceptual confusion, and self-interest, for example, often stand in the way of resolving particular controversies. Theoretically, however, each of these could be eliminated such that political disputes could be resolved. On the other hand, claims that political language is simply emotive or that it can no longer sustain rational argument have been shown to be unacceptable.[3]

It does not follow that we need not worry about the endlessness of our disputes. Far from giving soothing assurances at the outset, I think it is important to see that the problem is actually more difficult than often thought.

Quite standardly it is held that at the crux of each political dispute is a concept (core meaning or "exemplar") around which various interpretations or conceptualizations occur. For example, Lukes suggests that the core concept of power is that A affects B in a "nontrivial or significant manner" (Lukes 1974: 26). Berlin says that "the essence of the notion of liberty, both in the 'positive' and the 'negative' senses, is the holding off of something or someone" (Berlin 1969: 158).[4]

This core meaning can, however, be interpreted or applied according to diverse criteria. For example, Gallie suggests that at the core of the concept of democracy is "a demand for increased equality" (Gallie 1956: 184). Criteria according to which this core concept has been interpreted include: "the power of the majority of citizens to choose (and remove) governments"; the "equality of all citizens . . . to attain to positions of political leadership and responsibility"; and "the continuous active participation of citizens in political life at all levels" (Gallie 1956: 184f). These criteria might be variously linked to the core meaning of "democracy" to produce different conceptualizations of this concept.

On this view, then, disputes concerning these concepts are over the criteria by which the core meaning is to be interpreted. The core meaning, as distinct from the different conceptualizations, anchors the debate. Though debates over these criteria may be endless, there is at least a focus around which the debate rages which ensures its unity. Disputants are not simply talking about different issues. This core meaning is one of the factors which allows for rational discussion over the political issues at stake. Accordingly, if we can settle upon the core meaning of the concepts used in our political disputes, we can begin to seek a resolution of these disputes.

However, this standard view of the disputes surrounding political concepts is mistaken. It treats the matter as less complicated than it really is and, thus, incorrectly identifies the reason why political disputes continue endlessly.

When we engage in political disputes, for example over freedom, we may not be able to identify some single core meaning which is then variously interpreted or conceptualized. In fact, what seems more likely when we dispute over freedom, justice, or equality is that we have not only different conceptualizations but also have different concepts in mind. The complexity of these concepts stems from the fact that each of them does not have a self-same core meaning which is interpreted according to different criteria. Rather, more radically, there are various different meanings identified with "the" concept in question. In this sense, for example, the words "free" or "freedom" seem simply to be different umbrella terms which apply ambiguously at times to these different meanings or concepts.

For example, the following have been identified with freedom: lack of coercion, the presence of opportunities, the ability to do what one wants, self-determination, rational action, and self-realization. It is not obvious, however, that one could plausibly argue that all are conceptualizations (though in different ways) of some self-same concept (or core meaning) of freedom. Rather, they seem to constitute more than one, and perhaps several, concepts of freedom. Similarly, it seems unlikely that merit, equality, desert, and entitlement are all criteria for a single concept of justice. Instead, different concepts of justice focus on these different "criteria." This is not to say that the meanings constituting these different concepts of justice or freedom do not overlap. I think they do. But there is not a self-same (core) meaning which defines the basic concept of freedom or justice.[5] Thus, the complexity which attaches to such concepts is much greater than many think.

To defend this view two things must be done. On the one hand, reasons must be given why we need not assume that there is some common core of meaning at the crux of such disputes. On the other hand, we must also explain what unifies such debates; why they can, nevertheless, be coherent.

The view that there must be a common core meaning to each concept around which various conceptualizations are formed assumes that this core is analytically tied to the concept, all other criteria or meanings being merely synthetically linked. Thus, for example, it might be argued that "freedom is the lack of coercion" is an analytic statement, one which captures the core meaning of "freedom." As such, its denial would be contradictory. However, "freedom requires material means" or "freedom is the ability to determine one's own destiny" are synthetic statements. Their truth or falsity would depend upon what empirical connections they have with individuals lacking coercion.

The problem with this view is the following. It has been plausibly argued that its underlying assumption, that there is a sharp analytic-synthetic distinction, stems from a faulty view of language. Though this point cannot be argued here, Quine and Putnam, among others, have shown that this sharp distinction "breaks down when we confront concepts with multiple and variable criteria" (J.N. Gray 1978: 390). With such concepts as freedom, justice, and politics, it seems doubtful that there is some uncontested central or core meaning. Instead, there may be a number of different meanings which are variously identified with "the" concept in question. Thus, even though Berlin suggests that "the essence of the notion of liberty, both in the 'positive' and the 'negative' senses, is the holding off of something or someone" (Berlin 1969: 158) his suggestion quite clearly focuses on negative freedom (the lack of coercion), rather than positive freedom (self-mastery or self-determination). Others, such as McCloskey, speak unabashedly of multiple concepts of freedom. Even Berlin is ambiguous in that sometimes he claims there are two different concepts of freedom, while at other times he claims there are simply two different conceptualizations of freedom.[6]

It is pointless then to dispute which of the various different meanings or concepts of freedom is the "true" one. One need simply look in the *Oxford English Dictionary* to see that freedom has (and has had) a number of different meanings. The attempt to reduce these to one schema, formula, or core meaning is mistaken. Lippman made the point some time ago, that we cannot simply reject other meanings of "freedom" as inappropriate. To try to do so is to misrepresent a process of conceptual legislation as one of neutral semantic description.[7]

Further, even if we agreed on "the" meaning of "freedom" it would be open to others to reject that account, because (they might contend) it simply reflects how the word's meaning has been corrupted within the current political context. Accordingly, if someone showed that there was one concept that all people used, it would still be arguable whether we should continue to use that concept.

Hence, the view that disputes involving political concepts focus on some core meaning or concept which receives different interpretations or conceptualizations should be given up.[8] The common core which many have sought to identify for concepts such as freedom or justice not only need not be particularly helpful in guaranteeing the unity of debate over that concept,[9] but also it may prevent people from recognizing the internal complexity of the concept involved. Attempts to identify one such common core have the effect of making such disputes overly abstract and Procrustean.

III THE FOCUS OF DEBATE

If such disputes are not about the same common exemplar or core meaning, how can disputes regarding political freedom be coherent? Would we not be dealing with apples and oranges? Wouldn't our arguments simply pass one another? I think not.

Rather than trying to identify the core meaning of political concepts such as freedom, we need to characterize the general space or area within which questions concerning each of our basic political concepts arise. Thus, for example, freedom concerns how, to what extent, and in what ways our lives (or those of certain institutions) are determined by restraint, coercion, power, authority, and the individual him or herself.[10] In short, freedom occupies a certain area, space, or dimension in our lives concerning the forms of determination in which an individual stands to others and to various institutions.

This is a formal characterization of freedom. It refers to a space that may be filled in various ways. The identification of this aspect of our lives is not itself a concept of freedom. However, questions concerning this area are questions concerning freedom. Clearly, within this area there may be different concepts of freedom as well as different interpretations of those concepts. Prior to experimentation and discussion, there is nothing absurd or contradictory in any one of a number of possible formulations of the concept.[11] Thus, it is not so much the content of the concept, but the context into which it fits that may form a fairly constant point of reference.

Perhaps an example will help. Suppose two people are arguing over whether to put a chair, a stool, or a couch in the corner of a room. On one level chairs, stools, and couches form three different concepts. Of course, on a more general level they could be said to be instances of the same concept, i.e. things on which people may sit. But this general statement hardly uniquely identifies chairs, stools, or couches. It is not the core meaning of any of them. What unifies this debate and makes it genuine is that one or the other of these pieces of furniture is to be fitted into this space which calls for something on which people may sit. To place a couch in this space is, *ipso facto*, to exclude placing either a chair or stool there. To defend the chair is to defend a different set of relations to others than a couch would permit. Still, the debate remains unified and genuine.

Similarly, in our lives problems concerning restraint, authority, power, and the determination of individual action inevitably arise. This space concerns freedom. Defenses of liberal or conservative views of freedom are defenses of rather different responses to the problems surrounding these concepts. They define different relations among individuals. Nevertheless, even if there is no core meaning or concept (on one normal level), debate over how to arrange or orchestrate these various features of our lives can still remain genuine. In this sense, then, I suggest that even though the meanings of the term "freedom" may differ, they have a common logical space (cf. Swanton 1985: 818, 822).

Suppose, however, that it is objected that if it is a "space" that defines the common area of disputes over freedom, and hence renders such disputes genuine, then someone could claim that total domination also fits into this space and hence can be seen as an instance of freedom. Similarly, it might be objected that the "space" or "area" of freedom, at least as so far characterized, might even be said to define a space within which politics might find residence. In short, the objection is that I have defined a space which, though it should uniquely allow in only freedom (albeit in its many forms), also allows domination and perhaps also politics. How significant is this notion of a "space"?

What these objections suggest is that this notion of spaces needs further characterization and refinement. Before proceeding, however, two comments are appropriate. First, that domination should fit within the space reserved for freedom is not as preposterous as it might initially seem. Historically, freedom has also been identified with the following: the recognition of necessity, following the moral or natural law, morally virtuous action, and submission to one's leader. Again, it is hard to imagine that there is any one thing which all these claims have in common, other than being different resolutions of the problems which arise with the determination of individual conduct in light of coercion, power, force, and authority. Further, it is not preposterous that what some identify as freedom others would identify as domination. This possibility ought not to be proscribed by this initial, methodological chapter. We should not suppose that the various uses of "freedom" have simply one thing in common.

Secondly, however, though the space within which different concepts of freedom may be found seems open in that it allows for different concepts of freedom, it cannot be so open that anything is let in. Such a promiscuous approach would render "freedom" meaningless. Undoubtedly "freedom" and other basic political concepts are troublesome concepts to work with. But they are not simply empty expressions. Even the above minimal characterization of freedom's logical space does not allow *any* meaning to be attributed to "freedom." Specifically, it characterizes freedom as a relation between or among different individuals, not simply the condition of a single individual. It rules out treating freedom as a question of aesthetics or a problem concerning the nature of knowledge. Nevertheless, we need to know how to characterize this space more fully if we are to avoid the above objections.

We can do this by drawing on ingredients of "freedom" as suggested by reference to various concepts of freedom that have been historically prominent. Thus, to call something "free" or part of "freedom" might include reference to the following:[12]

1   The interests and goals an individual has are subject to the individual's own determination.
2   Individuals are not subject to coercive force or constraint imposed by other individuals.
3   The desires and beliefs of individuals are not manipulated by others.
4   Individuals self-consciously and knowingly do what they wish to do.
5   Rights protect individuals from opposed individual and institutional forces.
6   Individuals are not only not forced, but also are able to do various things.
7   Different opportunities are available so that individuals may do various things rather than just one thing.
8   Individuals are not subject to irrational passions and desires.
9   Individuals live according to values with which they identify.

There is nothing about these ingredients which makes any one of them logically necessary for a concept of freedom constructed within this space. Further, they cannot all be said to be logically necessary for some such concept since some may conflict with others.[13] Finally, the list could be altered. It might be added to or some might even be dropped.[14] Some of them might be changed, though some could change more easily than others. They do, however, relate to the determination of an individual's behavior. As such, they set boundaries to our use of the word "freedom." Proponents of different concepts of freedom fasten on subsets of these ingredients. Accordingly, though their concepts may not have the same meanings they fall within the same logical space. Thus, debates over these concepts may be meaningful.

At the same time, this approach allows that the debate over concepts such as freedom may range along a wide spectrum of answers. It does not imply, as do accounts that attempt to identify core meanings, that large numbers of people who dispute over freedom are conceptually confused. Rather, on my account, they may be conceptually clear, though substantially opposed. This is more faithful to our situation.

But why should just these ingredients be listed? They are not simply haphazardly chosen or selected by observing sample utterances of the ways in which people today use the word "freedom." What then makes these ingredients hang together?

The reason is that each of these ingredients has historically been picked out as important to freedom. By "important" I mean that they have gained adherents, altered the ways people think about freedom, or influenced the action of significant groups of people.[15] Their connection with freedom has been viewed as crucial by thinkers and practical people. These are the ingredients to which people have returned over and over, and connected with freedom. In short, there is an appeal to historical convention. If people and society had been different, then the ingredients would be different. Accordingly, if the development of technology, population centers, anonymity in cities, opportunities, traditional forms of behavior, etc. had been different, the ingredients that give form to the logical space attributed to freedom would be different.

The conventions appealed to are not, as some have held, simply linguistic conventions or conventional rules of discourse. The preceding ingredients do not simply reflect linguistic convention (though this is partially the case) so much as various ways of life, i.e. practical answers to such questions which have come to have theoretical import. As MacIntyre has urged, we must look to "the continuity of institutionalized argument, debate, and conflict" (MacIntyre 1973: 5).

Thus, what binds these ingredients to freedom are our forms of life as well as our language uses of them. We continue to solve problems of freedom in multiple and conflicting ways, which may themselves be problematic. Still, the solution to our question is practical as well as theoretical. Accordingly, the debate over freedom is unified not from within by some core notion, but from without by language uses, historical arguments, and forms of life associated with "freedom." In short, freedom does not have an endoskeleton, but an exoskeleton. There is not some unchangeable or unique essence which lies at the heart of the debate over political freedom that unifies it. Rather there are some roughly drawn boundaries that unify it. Within this space, genuine debate may rage. Nevertheless, because of the nature of its skeleton or boundaries, the edges will be vague and indeterminate; but this is what we experience. This is why changes can and do take place. It also means that there may be different foci within this broad range which different people pick out as "the" concept of freedom. Accordingly, the meaning we attribute to "freedom" will be the result of our discussion, not something which we can simply declare at the outset. Too often, philosophy has proceeded in the opposite direction.

This answer does not purport to pick out any particular concept of freedom. What it does is to offer an account of the context within which questions of freedom arise. It portrays a context which provides a basis for saying that when people dispute over questions of freedom they are talking, even though they do not appeal to a common meaning or core concept, about the "same" thing. Even though this may be only roughly the case, it is still sufficiently so for argument and discussion. Opponents both wish to fill the same space, and their answers are, practically as well as theoretically, incompatible. Their answers cannot both occupy the same space or be realized at the same time. To adopt one answer is to exclude, or greatly restrict, the possibility of accepting any other answer. Thus, conservative freedom and liberal freedom cannot be realized at the same time and place both because of the different concepts involved and because those concepts of freedom have different practical implications.

The upshot of the preceding is, then, that there may be genuine disputes over our central political concepts even though those concepts do not contain a common core meaning. We should not be surprised that there is not a single concept of freedom concerning which various different and conflicting interpretations are made. As noted above, this is suggested by the multiple entries under "freedom" in the *Oxford English Dictionary*. It is true that many do claim that there is one concept of freedom, but such accounts involve conceptual legislation as well as various normative assumptions. They are not simple descriptive revelations of the single core meaning of freedom.

Thus, the problem of disputes over political freedom relates to why we ought to adopt this or that concept, rather than simply this or that conceptualization of some single concept. The problem is both fundamental and difficult.

IV THE ENDLESSNESS OF POLITICAL DEBATES

Granted that different ingredients may be used to constitute prominent political concepts within the same logical space referred to by a common umbrella term, why do people not come, nevertheless, to the same concept of freedom? How are we to understand the apparently endless debate involving these concepts? There are several interconnected reasons.

To begin with, political concepts such as freedom involve an appraisiveness which contributes to these differences and disputes. This is not to say that these concepts are simply appraisive in the manner of "good" or "wrong." They are not merely general terms of appraisal. They do not simply express, signify, or make known our approval of some valued condition.

Still, some of them are appraisive in the sense that their explication directly involves normative or evaluative concepts. For example, if political justice is a form of fairness or treatment according to one's merits, then our very explication of justice involves concepts which are themselves directly normative. The same would be true if freedom is defined by various rights or virtuous action.

However, our political concepts are not always appraisive in this sense. For example, at least some liberals view freedom simply as the lack of constraint. This they understand to be a wholly descriptive state of affairs, though it is also one they value. But their valuing it does not make freedom, for those liberals, an evaluative (or appraisive) concept.[16] Analogously, they might say, the nature of diamonds as a form of carbon can be wholly captured by a descriptive statement. It does not follow, however, because they are highly valued, that diamond is an appraisive concept.

Nevertheless, even though not all our political concepts are directly appraisive, it does not follow that appraisiveness does not play a role in the endless debate over them. The selection of the descriptive characteristics of such concepts depends, even if only indirectly, on normative or evaluative considerations in two senses. First, even if freedom is simply the lack of interference, we must know which obstructions of a person's actions are "interferences." It seems unlikely that even the most silly and unimportant obstructions reduce one's freedom. A person who complained that his freedom was reduced by a door which was innocently left closed and which he could easily open on his way between two rooms would be thought to be joking – simply because the nature of the obstruction is so minimal. But to make these determinations we must appeal to some evaluative or normative standards.

Secondly, simply the identification of a descriptive characteristic with freedom involves selecting it out of a number of other possible characteristics (some appraisive and some not). This selection involves various values and norms on the basis of which it is held to be the correct or appropriate one. Our political concepts (as our scientific concepts) must be accepted or adopted, they are not simply given to us as the products of a virgin birth. Appraisiveness plays a role even in such apparently descriptive political concepts.

Accordingly, we might hold that political concepts such as "democracy," "politics," and "freedom" may either be appraisive concepts themselves or be "bounded by normative considerations" (cf. Connolly 1974: 20; 30f). In some cases, we must look beyond the concepts themselves and the conditions they capture to identify the normativity or appraisiveness that surrounds them. Hence, when we speak of such concepts being subject to normative interpretations, the normativity is sometimes external to the concept. To speak of such normativity is simply to say that the lines according to which we draw this or that concept's boundaries cannot be neutrally or simply descriptively drawn.

It has been objected, however, that the presence of appraisiveness or normativity would contribute to the endless debate with such concepts only if the criteria involved (whether internal or external) were themselves endlessly contestable (cf. J.N. Gray 1978: 392; Swanton 1985: 820–1). On the contrary, if we had a touchstone by which normative criteria or selections could be judged, then we might be able (theoretically) to bring political (and other) debates to an end.

But this does not seem possible. Because the various ingredients of normatively bounded political concepts may be differently selected by diverse individuals without theoretical inconsistency, there is reason to believe that we lack such a touchstone. For example, in discussing political freedom conservatives may emphasize the role of traditional rights, liberals may pick out the importance of the lack of coercion and radicals may point to self-determination. Each of these views may be by itself coherent. Similarly, democracy might be linked to "the power of the majority of citizens to choose (and remove) governments," to "the equality of all citizens, irrespective of race, creed, sex, etc., to attain to positions of political leadership and responsibility," or to "the continuous active participation of citizens in political life at all levels" (Gallie 1956: 184-5). Each view may point with justification to historical and philosophical grounds for linking particular characteristics with political freedom or democracy. Further, various interpretations of each of these "ingredients" may also be offered without inconsistency. For example, the participation required by the third view of democracy above might be taken to require active involvement of citizens in planning and decision making, or simply the knowledgeable responses of citizens to situations their representatives face.

My point is that without further substantive argument there is nothing improbable or absurd with these various alternative interpretations and selections. Any practical inconsistencies or tensions that develop with each interpretation may be attributed to other parts of a larger system within which the particular interpretation of the political concept is always held. For example, practical problems or untoward consequences may be attributed to chance and accounted for through a variety of reasons. Thus, it is impossible to evaluate any particular account of freedom, justice, or community, outside of a larger system within which it fits.

Consequently, the endlessness of political debate is due to the possibility that, prior to substantive argument, the ingredients of our basic political concepts may be variously selected as parts of larger systems of views within which they are embedded. Only from these larger perspectives can we assess the merits and the difficulties that attach to these views. The problem of the endless debate over appraisive or normative characteristics is then the problem whether there is some (single) perspective or standpoint from which such debates may be resolved. Accordingly, it is important for understanding the endlessness of political debates to look to the larger systems within which our political concepts are embedded.

V   EMBEDDEDNESS, MODELS, AND FORMS OF LIFE

The political concepts over which we endlessly dispute due to their evaluative nature, their complexity, and variable ingredients are embedded in various models and forms of life by which we understand our world. There are two parts to this further characteristic.

First, our concepts do not float about some intellectual landscape unattached to the real world. They play a role in our world and grow out of that world. This means that they come embedded in a host of other assumptions, views, values, attitudes, concepts, and beliefs which together form what I shall call, a model. It is because they play a more or less integrated role within certain models that they have the meaning and import they do.

Thus, some claim that positive views of freedom are incoherent if they are wrenched out of a rationalist philosophical psychology in which they have been historically embedded (cf. J.N. Gray 1978: 387). Again, some maintain that Hobbes held the views on individualism he did because of his nominalist views (Greenleaf 1972a: 22). To debate simply about the concept is a futile abstract exercise. In short, this or that account of a particular concept is meaningful only within a larger context. To get at this larger context is to discuss such concepts within models, rather than simply as abstract concepts.

For example, in order to understand the liberal view that political freedom requires letting Nazis march before City Hall, it would be necessary to raise questions regarding the nature of formal versus substantive rules, the nature and origin of individual wants, the self-sufficiency of individuals, and the role of the state versus the individual. It would not be sufficient to speak simply of freedom as the lack of constraint. Negative freedom makes sense only within certain assumptions about individualism and the questionable power of the state. Hence, liberal freedom is embedded in liberal society. The concept of freedom does not stand apart from the society(ies) in which it is found. It has a functional role in those societies. Thus, debates over this or that freedom, or even over more general aspects of freedom are essentially tied up with other parts of a more global view. In this debate, some ingredients of freedom are tied more closely with freedom than other ingredients.[17] Since there is nothing absurd initially about linking freedom to some of these ingredients rather than others, people dispute over different concepts of freedom. It is for this reason that it is so difficult to change the minds of others on specific issues. Their particular views are bound up in various models of freedom.

Obviously there may be a lack of constraint under any form of life. But to fasten on the lack of constraint as the necessary and sufficient condition of *freedom* is to implicate a particular form of life with a particular historical ancestry and other assumptions about humans and society. Thus, lack of constraint (i.e. negative freedom) for people within another model, which emphasized group unity (interconnectedness and cooperation) and the beneficence of the ruling power, might be an expression of alienation or rebellion, not of freedom.

In defending this view I reject the attempt to focus on concepts as single, neutral "entities." Such a view of concepts is a form of conceptual atomism. It suggests that concepts such as freedom can be separated from the conceptual network within which they exist. It portrays a structure with various uniquely identifiable parts, which are, however, interchangeable with other structures. Such conceptual interchangeability or uniformity does not exist. Concepts cannot be shifted interchangeably from one model, perspective, or tradition to another, as parts might be in the assembly-line production of two different car models.

On the contrary, to adopt a particular concept is to pick it out of the range within the area sheltered by the umbrella term "freedom." This is to pick out a form of behavior, which is connected with other assumptions, values, and views. More generally a whole history of events, arguments, and historical experiences lie behind the assumptions and values which envelope the particular concept. That is why negative freedom does not simply belong to this or that theorist and it is reasonable to look more broadly in seeking to understand such a concept of freedom. Negative freedom does not stand nakedly against our other concepts and beliefs, but is clothed within them.

It might be objected that the same concept can be held by people within different political models. For example, it has been argued that both libertarians and socialists adhere to the same negative concept of freedom, even though politically they are at odds. The difference is that socialists give a much broader interpretation of the nature of constraint than do libertarians. It is from this difference, it is argued, that the political disagreements (in part) stem, not from different concepts of freedom.

I do not deny that some socialists, or even radicals, have used a negative concept of freedom in their work. What this shows is the power a dominant model may have to influence people who seek to formulate diverse political views. In this way political views are transformed. Thus, many American conservatives have as much, if not more, in common with libertarians, as they do with traditional conservatives.

However, what I deny is that the complex history of political freedom can be understood simply by means of negative freedom. There are at least three concepts of freedom which have played central roles in this history. Further, each concept is embedded within a model within which it can only be understood. Indeed, such models are themselves embedded within larger systems or paradigms by which a society operates (cf. Wolin 1968: 149). Finally, I think I can show that the prominent political representatives of the models I will discuss have not operated with the same concept, but with distinct concepts of freedom.

On the other hand, I do not claim that the model to which concepts such as freedom are linked must enjoy a full-bodied existence. It may be going out of existence, like the life that Don Quixote sought, or not yet realized like the one various utopians have described. However, since our concepts structure our experience, our experiences will reflect them. And since some such experiences become dated – they no longer relate to present conditions – the concepts and models involved may become antiquated. Still, any tendency to view our concepts as independent of such experiences is wholly abstract and dubious.

Secondly, the role that such concepts play in their models is a constitutive one, in that the particular perspective that the model captures is created through these concepts. This is not meant to suggest, however, that models are simply the passive results of their constitutive concepts. As Abraham Edel notes, "different types of models develop their own concepts in terms of their own demands" (Edel 1969: 378). There is a dynamic interconnection between models and their concepts, rather than a one way relation. Similarly, there is a dynamic relation between a model and the circumstances within which it is held and defended. It is for this reason that the concepts and their models admit of considerable modification, which "cannot be prescribed or predicted in advance" (Gallie 1956: 172).

The concepts that constitute a model help to define our view of the world, the questions to be asked, and the answers to be given. They do this inasmuch as they impinge primarily, though not wholly, on a self-constituted reality. Only at the borders of these models do they impinge on "facts" of the world which they share with other models. To this extent, they create their own world and reality, as well as constitute a reality in the world.

It is this further characteristic of concepts such as freedom that ultimately renders them endlessly debatable. We are forced, thereby, to view them in broader contexts which are themselves partisan and non-neutral (cf. J.N. Gray 1978: 394). They are (partially) constitutive of this model. This is more easily accepted if one remembers that such concepts do not pick out "things," but rather capture complex forms of relations or interaction among humans. That these relations presuppose certain conditions and are most "at home" in certain contexts or models should not be surprising.

It should be clear from the preceding that a model of freedom is not simply another way of speaking about a concept, or "the" concept, of freedom. Models include concepts but are not the same as any one concept. By "model" I do not mean simply an abstract formula.[18]

Instead, by each model of freedom I try to capture a context from which emerges (and which involves) a way of thinking and viewing freedom which is not reducible to some other view and which arguably plays a role in actual political debates. The formulation of such models is constructive and creative in the sense that they do not exist "out there" as distinct objects. They are interpretative vehicles, not simply identifiable with the view which some political philosopher has proposed. Thus, political freedom is not what political thinkers have said about political freedom, though too often this is how it is viewed. Instead, it is a group of beliefs, attitudes, values, and insitutions formed in response to a number of problems – involving coercion, power, material resources, etc. relating to the forms of determination in which individuals stand to each other and to various institutions within a political society – on which political thinkers have commented. We tend to transpose the proper object of our discussions. The carts get in the way of the horses.

Still this is not to say that what political philosophers have said does not play an important role in any particular model. My comments above on the focus of the debate indicate this. Indeed, if we view political freedom through such models then it follows that we may look to past thinkers as contributors to present models of thought and ways of living, rather than simply as individuals engaged in their own unconnected projects. In some cases, ironically, it may be because of what they do not say or what they unwittingly assume along with other political philosophers of their time that they contribute to present models. It is an exaggerated individualism which requires that we seek to understand each past thinker by him or herself, rather than as part of a movement of ideas and society. As such, the consideration of the views of past thinkers is not simply an antiquarian's holiday, a little bit of antique hunting in the area of the history of ideas, but an attempt to view them in a philosophical manner as having contemporary significance.[19]

From the preceding, it follows that these models can be adjudicated only to a limited extent. The contestability of concepts within such different models is due to the fact that these concepts play roles within different forms of life (with different assumptions and commitments) for which there are no wholly external "objective" referents. They create or constitute the very "object" in question. They impinge on non-social "reality" only indirectly and at the edges. Thus they can fail only in the most blatant sense when people cannot or will not live in these ways – though people have proven that they will live in a vast variety of ways. Similarly, they fail if they are self-defeating or self-destructive. They fail to the extent that they are swept away by historical and technological changes.

Gray claims, for example, that

> an essentially contested concept is a concept such that any use of it in a social or political context presupposes a specific understanding of a whole range of other, contextually related concepts whose proper uses are no less disputed and which lock together so as to compose a single, identifiable conceptual framework.
>
> (J.N. Gray 1977: 332)

The spirit of this is correct, even if its expression is overly rigorous. That such concepts form "a single, identifiable conceptual framework" is correct if this does not imply that it is utterly unique and stands without overlapping in any way with other frameworks. In fact our models do overlap, because our life experiences overlap we share many important features of a roughly common life. Thus, though the means we have to criticize those who view the world from within other models is limited, we are not wholly without means to evaluate their views and actions. Accordingly, though the present point concerning the embeddedness of concepts is an important one to make, it is also important not to overstate it.

These models involve various assumptions, commitments, and views which are utterly basic to them but which are not (wholly) shared by other models. If justification and explanation is always dependent upon certain bases then one can appreciate that the basic concepts and forms of social and political life people defend will be different. However, inasmuch as these models and concepts cannot wholly be abstracted from overlapping experiences and mutually recognized facts, they cannot, by the same token, insulate themselves from rational appraisal and criticism.

The upshot of the above argument is that to understand the endlessness of debate over political freedom we must consider such concepts and conceptions of political freedom not by themselves but as they cluster together into models of freedom. I have rejected the suggestion that such concepts are themselves necessarily evaluative, although evaluative considerations enter into their constitution. Neutrality is a figment of the imagination; evaluation is inevitable. The moment we select among the various complex features of a concept we have taken a stand which may be opposed by others. To analyse political freedom is (however unwittingly) to take an evaluative stand. Analysis is always justification. Conceptual clarity is philosophical advocacy. Conceptual inquiry is conceptual legislation; this cannot be neutrally done (as liberal views of legislation maintain). This conclusion has two further implications.

First, to proceed in this manner is, in effect, to push us back to a more traditional sense of political philosophy. Political philosophy in the traditional sense is an inquiry concerned not solely with elucidation of concepts, but with the critical examination of presuppositions and assumptions, the questioning of the order of priorities and ultimate ends, as well as the consideration of empirical connections between patterns of thought and the ways of life of specific social groups. This way of proceeding encourages us to look to the various traditions, demands, and arguments embodied in such models. It allows us to look not only at what individuals positively say about political freedom, but also at the background conditions and forces which play out their roles given what such views do *not* say.

Secondly, the endlessness of political debate does not imply that objectivity is out the window. We have not yet seen how reason can enter in. However, to the extent that we examine, as just suggested, the fuller context out of which these debates arise, isolate the various strands of thought which exist within them, and identify the strains and tensions within each view, we can develop a rational argument which evaluates the models of freedom which dominate our lives. This approach I take to be dialectical in a traditional and philosophical sense. It is to the role that reason can play in disputes involving such concepts that we must now turn.

VI MODELS AND ENDLESS DEBATE: THE PROBLEM OF RATIONALITY

The challenge posed by allowing that there may be endless debate over political concepts is radical relativism. If disputes over freedom may continue endlessly, how is it possible to claim that one view of freedom is superior to, or more rational than, another view. At stake is the rationality of debates using such concepts.

I think that we can rationally defend one view as superior to other views, that is, as the view which the preponderance of reason supports, even though we must recognize that there are different concepts and conceptions of (political) freedom and that we cannot show that one view is the best view. Obviously, I do not imply that the argument which establishes this will be able to win over everyone. This is implausible. Quite correctly, Gallie says that

> if the notion of logical justification can be applied only to such theses and arguments as can be presumed capable of gaining in the long run universal agreement, the disputes to which the uses of any essentially contested concept give rise are not genuine or rational disputes at all.
>
> (Gallie 1956: 188)[20]

But what, then, can we hope for and what can we do?

What we cannot do is simply dispute over whether this or that meaning of "freedom" as identified in various uses of ordinary language is the correct or true meaning of "freedom." Our problem is one of identifying a concept of freedom which for theoretical and practical reasons we should use in discussing political freedom. We cannot do this by appealing to ordinary language. Nor can we confine ourselves simply to questions of the "internal" nature of this or that concept of freedom. Finally, since we have rejected the suggestion that the same exemplar or common core lies behind all views on political freedom, we cannot appeal to such a common core or exemplar in order to show the rationality of a person's continued use of, or conversion to, a particular concept.

Instead, we must look at the various concepts of freedom within the models in which we find them, that is with the other assumptions, views, and concepts to which they are linked. What is striking about such models is their coherency. They "hang," more or less roughly, together. A person holding a certain view of freedom can be expected to have certain other views – sometimes because of logical entailment, but at other times simply because such views (for various historical and practical reasons) hold together. Thus, for example, we expect a conservative to have certain views on tradition, but also on law, order, and religion.

In order to study and evaluate these models, our approach leads us to examine the inner lines which tie the various views together; to examine their stress points; their dependencies on certain social settings; the conditions under which they might break down or collapse; their inner consistencies or inconsistencies. Also, we must look to their external stress points. Such models have a touchstone in the "real world," by which I do not imply that there is a world "out there" wholly independent of various descriptions. Rather the "real world" places various practical limitations on what this or that model may accomplish. It may bring it up short. This is the truth in Tawney's comment that "the only sound test of a political doctrine is its practical effect on the lives of human beings" (Tawney 1953: 87).

Among the questions we must ask are the following: which values does the model actually support? How useful is this model in understanding and explaining present desirable and undesirable features of society? How fruitful or suggestive is it for responding to changes in society? Is it in tune with social, political, economic, and psychological "realities"? How comprehensive is each model? How broad is the range of our political experience that it can encompass? Which model is most adequate given our knowledge of society? What view does it take of humans and how sensitive is it to human concerns? Does the model make dubious assumptions about the nature of the self and its relation to society?

For example, it might be argued that the notion of each individual being able to do everything by him or herself – such extreme views of self-reliance or self-sufficiency – is simply irrational in today's society, even though it may not be possible to convince any particular person otherwise. The psychological toll, the economic demands to sustain it, and the social implications for human relations within a society may be argued to be greater than the value they support. Thus, when the implications and consequences of their views are portrayed to them, people have grounds to consider revising their views toward some more consistent and rational view. Of course, people may continue to advocate and live by an extreme individualistic point of view. But the psychic, economic, and practical consequences may be overwhelming when viewed in terms of significant groups of people in a modern, complex, and interdependent society.

In such discussions, evaluative, conceptual and empirical or contingent considerations are relevant. The point of the discussion is not to reject this or that concept and the models they are embedded in because the models do not conform to "the facts" and, hence, are false. As it was argued above, there are no simple "facts" to which such a model or paradigm might conform. Instead, we seek an appreciation of the role of a particular political concept as it is embedded in a broader model. In so doing, we can take a much broader and more pragmatic approach. By showing the tensions, problems, and discrepancies that arise with the use of a particular concept and model, we undermine rational acceptance of that concept and model. Parekh's comment is appropriate:

> facts do not falsify a social and political theory in a way that the discovery that there is no cat in my r)oom falsifies t.he assertion that there is. Rather they impugn the validity of a theory by showing how in the course of explaining them it is forced to become more and more muddled, incoherent, ambiguous, bizarre. Facts destroy a social or political theory not so much by falsifying it as by undermining its integrity and credibility, by making it incoherent.

> (Parekh 1973: 82)

What Parekh says here about explanatory political theories is also true of normative political models, paradigms, and theories. As such, claims of incommensurability are overblown. We deal on both practical and theoretical levels when we debate and evaluate our political concepts and their models.

In so proceeding we provide good reasons that some views are better than others. We need not accept the view that different models of freedom are simply the expression of different classes. If some people or classes refuse to recognize an arguably better model there is little more we can do. There are limits to reason. But reality (if we are correct) may also catch up with them – or pass them by. Some views, political as well as scientific, must simply die out. It was not arguments which killed chivalry but changed conditions. Similarly, various scientific views do not disappear because they have been conclusively refuted; they fade away due to changed circumstances.

This may not seem sufficient to some since it allows for debate to continue. However, this reaction to lack of agreement on our basic normative concepts and judgments should be balanced by our recognition of the disputability which arises over some of our basic naturalistic concepts. Scientists and philosophers have debated endlessly over such basic notions as mass, number, cause, and time. Very rarely are we able conclusively to prove or disprove a position either in scientific or political questions. Further, in both cases judgments must be made as to the sufficiency of the evidence for the view in question. Since reasonable individuals may, in such cases, judge differently, there may not be a "natural" or conclusive end to discussion.

It might be responded that there is a difference between scientific and political debate in that in the case of science there is something "there" against which we can make (or not make) progress. Whereas in the case of the normative aspect of our political debates it is unclear what there might be against which we could test the normative views we hold. Thus, any "progress" or objective measure of better or worse seems questionable.[21]

Certainly the constitutive role that political concepts play in our political models reinforces this viewpoint. However, similar claims have been made for scientific concepts. Further, we should neither exaggerate the unity of scientific opinion nor underestimate the unity of moral and political opinion. Very few individuals believe that the unmotivated killing of an innocent person is morally or politically right. Further, there is little political debate today over chattel slavery or the sacrifice of women and children to appease the community's gods. We should not allow endless disputability to deter us from believing that genuine, even if endless, debate is possible in either realm.

The reason we can rationally argue that some models are better than others is that, though each model contains a different concept of freedom, they overlap in various ways and the people who hold them share certain common experiences. Even though people inhabit different worlds their worlds are not wholly other. We can translate the languages of different cultures, even significantly different cultures, although we may not be able to capture every nuance or detail of meaning. If the worlds which people of different cultures inhabited were wholly incommensurable this would not be possible. But they are not. Their referents are not wholly other, though they may differ importantly. People within one model (or paradigm) can imagine (within limits) what others experience and claim as virtues of their model.

In short, our differing political views or models share various similarities as well as have numerous differences. Even though different ingredients are selected and form different larger views, still there is overlap among the views and experiences, such that those who hold one view can recognize and (within limits) understand the views and experiences of others. Conservatives, liberals, and radicals can mutually agree on instances of political freedom, exploitation, or injustice. Though they would disagree on extensions beyond these cases and though they may agree on the basis of different concepts, still their experiences and views do overlap in some areas. Thus, there is room for debate. Rational argument and objectivity are possible among such views.[22]

Accordingly, we might be able to give a number of examples of what are instances of political freedom on which virtually everyone would agree, e.g. uncoerced voting, non-libellous expressions of one's political views, etc. In this sense, those who use different concepts of freedom can and do recognize that their use is contested by others, and have at least some appreciation of the criteria by which others apply their own concepts (cf. Gallie 1956: 172).

It might be responded, however, that these agreed-upon examples and jointly recognized criteria require interpretation, and that though there is overlap between models this is on a level which does not include various basic assumptions. Both responses may be true. Conservatives and liberals may hold rather different assumptions about the nature of society or human beings. Still such assumptions need not be seen as always basic. In some contexts they may be basic, in others they may not be. Hence, we need not always begin with the basic views of individuals. We might begin with particular cases upon which we agree.

It is mistaken, that is, to think that a person may be most closely attached to the basic premises from which his or her political views are derived. It may be that they are more closely attached to some of the derived views rather than the premises (assuming that we retain such an image). And if there is agreement on these derived views among those who subscribe to different models, then we may move people away from a model they hold by focusing on these mutual agreements.

Thus, it may be possible to criticize assumptions which people of different political views hold; we need not simply treat them as sacrosanct or critically untouchable. It is mistaken to adopt the image of differing basic axioms from which incommensurable political systems are derived. This Euclidean view of morality and political philosophy is no longer acceptable. Accordingly, we may abandon the image of political views being deductively supported by a few axioms or assumptions. An Archimedean point does not exist, and is not needed, for the justification of our political claims.

We tend, in part, to hold such erroneous views because of a mistaken view of reason. Though they cannot be elaborated on, there are two parts to this claim. First, we tend to assimilate reason to a logical deductive model according to which for something to be rational it must be rational for all people and follow from the same basic premises. On this view it is further assumed that only if we can finally resolve these problems can we also view them as subject to rational debate. That is, it is held that only if there is a single solution can we speak of rationality.

Though this is a legitimate view of one aspect of reason, it is also an overly narrow view. Reason can function within the overlapping and incomplete premises noted above. People with different political views do not need to give up all attempts to reason together.[23] Their reasoning can lead them to modifications and alterations in their own views, as well as the views of others. Thus, we need not expect reason to lead us all to the same view, even though we are all rational and have jointly reasoned. On the other hand, some views might be supported by reasons and yet still conflict with other views similarly supported.

Secondly, we tend to think of rationality as something that can be achieved by this or that individual. On the contrary, rationality is the result of dialogue beginning from incomplete and only partially overlapping premises. It is, an important sense, a social achievement. The rational view will be the result of an ongoing discussion which is open to all participants, and responsive to the kinds of questions listed above (Hardwig 1973). Accordingly, the rational view cannot be certified simply by one's own self-inspection. It can be determined only through discussion with others. This means that rationality – both individually and politically – can develop only within certain minimal relations of trust and community, as well as access to information and intellectual exploration. It also means that, at any given time, there will be legitimately different accounts of what is rational.

Hence, what I give in the following is only a proposal, a place for beginning. I do not claim finality for it. Still, I believe that it is in the correct direction; modifications will hopefully strengthen it, rather than undercut it. To reason in this way regarding political freedom is to engage in a study which is dialectical in a meaningful and important sense.

In short, the justification or legitimation of this or that model of freedom is not the same as simply showing the rationality of such a model as a means to some end. Because we often take such means/ends rationality as an ideal, we assume we require some single joint major principle. This is mistaken. Consequently, we may not be able, logically or deductively, to argue a person out of his or her view. This is the truth behind the recognition that debate over some concepts and ideals may be endless. But we can show opponents the implications, presuppositions, "contradictions," and consequences of their own views. In this way, we may show that some views are more fully supported by reason than others.

It is important concerning the account just defended to emphasize the role of the history of political views in justifying a model of political freedom. If I am correct about the notion of models of freedom, then it is through some such model (or models) that each of us presently understands our own situation. Only if we know at the outset where we presently stand, to what we are committed, what the stresses and tensions are within our present views, as well as what alternative views are, will it be possible to go beyond them when we consider the limitations of each model and whether a different model is needed. Simply to present a new model would leave ungrounded and unmotivated the model to be deployed.

The argument here is not simply historical or psychological. It is philosophical in that an understanding and justification of a new and different model can only be accomplished by appealing to these past models, and by drawing on various elements from them. A new model will be justified to the extent it can show the limitations of past accounts, show that it can succeed where other accounts fail, and show that it takes account of the circumstances in which we find ourselves.

Thus, rational debate over models of freedom seems possible; we are not confronted simply with a sea of subjectivity. It is, or should be, possible to argue that some particular model of freedom is more reasonable and, as such, has the preponderance of reason on its side. At the same time, I have admitted, this is not to say that this can be demonstrated with any logical certainty or that the argument to be laid out will thereby convince all who come to know it.

VII THREE MODELS OF POLITICAL FREEDOM

I suggest that three rival models of political freedom have dominated modern political thought: conservative, liberal, and radical. These designations are familiar and should be so. The models they name are, quite obviously, abstractions from the views of particular individuals as well as political movements. But this is to assert neither their lack of importance nor their irrelevance to the views from which they are culled. Indeed, since conservatives, liberals, and radicals often intensely disagree amongst themselves, one tends only to see difference and opposition when looking to the particular views that people actually hold. Nevertheless, there are certain family resemblances which are strong enough to group the competing views of political freedom under these three headings.

Within these three models we may identify three distinct concepts of freedom. There are not, as I have already argued, only one or two concepts of freedom. Accordingly, differences among the various views on freedom are not to be explained by a variation in the value attributed to freedom or in an account of the source of its value.

In my presentation of these models (in following chapters), I have tried not to play Procrustes with the views of those upon whom I have drawn – though some clipping, cutting, and "forming" have been inevitable. I note where individuals, whom I have claimed to be part of a tradition or model, differ from that model. But I think it is important to see such individuals as part of a larger picture, one to which they have contributed, rather than simply formulating isolated statements which may or may not be related to other historical thinkers and movements.

Almost certainly some will criticise these models for being "abstractions." I have not denied that they are abstractions, but I reject this as a criticism. I would further admit that the lines by which I construct them might be differently drawn. Nevertheless, the fact that individuals holding these views tend to group themselves under the above headings is at least initial justification for their use. Further, I contend that the way in which I draw these concepts and models is helpful and interesting. Viewing these concepts of freedom within their broader political views reminds us of the practical nature of this problem. To deal with these "abstractions," then, may be refreshing as well as useful.

The content of these models can only be indicated with the greatest of brevity here. It will, however, serve to remind us that the various accounts of the problem of political freedom are remarkably different. Thus, conservatives such as Edmund Burke, Alexis de Tocqueville, and Michael Oakeshott link political freedom with tradition, law, order, and a government which openly defends various religious and moral beliefs. Conservative freedom is characterized by a set of traditional rights which disperses power. Such freedom is part of a natural and virtuous order. It is oriented primarily towards the past and unbegrudgingly acknowledges the importance of the political realm.

Liberals such as John Locke, John Stuart Mill, and Isaiah Berlin emphasize that security and the protection of the individual are crucial to political freedom. Liberty, for them, is the lack of coercion of the individual by government and society. Within certain broad bounds, individuals are to be left to pursue their own ends.[24] These boundaries, however, hedge in freedom. The freedom which liberals seek is simply the lack of coercion or constraint. Such freedom is oriented primarily toward the present and only begrudgingly recognizes the importance of politics. The freedom liberals seek is found most characteristically in the private realm.

Radicals such as Karl Marx, Vladimir Lenin, and Herbert Marcuse believe that people's freedom is negated or restrained by the oppressive and irrational nature of the capitalist system, that individuals may have to be forced to be free, and that a different social, economic, and political system must be devised. Radicals, or so I shall present them, seek to defend a view of freedom in which individuals, conceived as communal beings, exercise self-determination. Radical freedom is, then, oriented primarily towards the future and seeks to escape from politics altogether.

The judgments and views constituting these different models are not simply arbitrary, on the one hand, or wholly similar on the other hand. Each model emphasizes various aspects of human experience which seem important. Conservatism focuses on tradition, customs, virtue, community, and order. Liberalism emphasizes the lack of interference, the individual, rights, and self-reliance. Radicalism stresses subtle means of manipulating individuals, self-determination, rationality, and community. In short, those who have held these different models have not been simply confused, ill-willed, or mis-informed individuals. They have been responding to conditions within themselves as well as within society – hence these models of freedom have appealed to significant numbers within the political spectrum.

The connection of such views with the preceding labels should be familiar. Once such models are filled out, the philosophical problem becomes, as discussed above, what we are to make of them. What strengths and weaknesses does each have? The point that needs to be emphasized is that our interest in these models is not simply an historical interest, but essentially a philosophical interest. I shall argue that each of them is significantly defective. In their place, I shall defend (in Part 2) a different model of freedom, one which I believe is superior to any of these three models.

VIII CONCLUSION

At the crux of political debates over freedom, justice, and community lie concepts over which we endlessly debate. These concepts are internally complex and lack any core meanings which necessarily and sufficiently define them. Nevertheless, debate over such concepts remains possible because of historically associated and conventionally linked meanings. Such debates are also endless due to an appraisiveness which either directly or indirectly characterizes the central concepts, the variable interpretations that can be given of such concepts, and the embeddedness of such concepts in larger conceptual models. These models constitute various formulations of our political reality.

Though these concepts and their models differ in basic ways from each other, they also overlap in various aspects. This means that though debate involving these models and their central concepts is interminable, it need not be irrational. Those who use one model can understand and recognize the meaning and nature of different models used by others. Though it is not possible to say which model is ultimately "the best" one, it is possible to say that some models are superior to others. This involves examining them both internally and externally. We look to their inner lines of stress, tensions, and contradictions. We also examine how they are situated within various views of history, human nature, and society. To do so should tell us whether some models are superior to other models also available to us. If some ordering of these views were impossible, then practical difficulties would not be theoretically resolvable and the discussion of such issues would seem to lack any point. They could, then, only be resolved by force and conflict. This is the limit of philosophy. On the other hand, if such argument can be given, it follows that each person cannot "simply" have his or her own view – some views may be more correct or plausible than other views.

Toward these ends, in the following chapters I explore three different prominent models of freedom and their concepts of freedom. In doing so, I argue that various problems and limitations of each model call for a new model of freedom.

2 Conservative freedom

Liberty, the only liberty I mean, is a liberty connected with order;
that not only exists along with order and virtue, but which cannot
exist at all without them. It inheres in good and steady government,
as in its substance and vital principle.

(Edmund Burke in Millar 1941: 99–100)

I INTRODUCTION

Conservatives have often asserted their attachment to liberty in rather
profuse terms.[1] Edmund Burke claimed that "[liberty] is not only a
private blessing of the first order, but the vital spring and energy
of the state itself" (Burke 1901, II: 229). Alexis de Tocqueville
claimed that "nothing is more fertile in marvels than the art of being
free" (Tocqueville 1969: 240). Michael Oakeshott suggests that an
"emphasis on liberty" is "the distinctive feature of the tradition within
which he allies himself" (Oakeshott 1962a: 39).[2]

But the conservative view of freedom is nothing if not complex.
Conservatives have opposed large-scale government, central planning, and government responsibility for welfare. Burke, widely
characterised as the founder of conservatism, defended a *laissez-
faire* economy, as have other conservatives after him. Such positions
coincide with those of classical liberals, who unambiguously view
freedom as the highest value.[3]

However, conservatives have also censored what can be published
or read, rejected the demand for "one man, one vote," opposed
women's liberation movements, defended school prayer, and attacked
various alternative (e.g. homosexual) "life styles." These positions
appear to restrict, not enlarge, freedom. And some conservatives
might agree. This is not because they do not value freedom, but
because they hold more highly other values, such as law, order

and tradition.[4] Still, other conservatives have claimed that these positions are not simply compromises with other values, but are directly required by conservative political freedom itself.

Accordingly, various accounts have been given of conservative freedom. Though some claim that conservatives and liberals share the same negative concept of freedom (freedom is simply the lack of constraint) (Meyer 1964; Harbour 1982), others claim that conservatives defend a positive concept of freedom, e.g. one focused on self-control or self-determination – a concept which is frequently linked with radical views (cf. Parry 1982).[5] And yet others maintain that conservatives adhere to a concept of freedom which combines both negative and positive concepts (Scruton 1983).

Thus, the nature of conservative political freedom is a matter of some perplexity. Adding to these woes is the fact that conservatives tend to be rather reticent when it comes to explicitly defining the concept of freedom with which they work.[6] Instead, they prefer to use it, while avoiding any explicit statement of its nature. Few conservative accounts formulate any general definition of freedom such as we commonly find in liberal and radical works.

These questions and problems can be resolved, I believe, by the conservative model of freedom which I develop in this chapter. Central to this model is a concept of political freedom which is not reducible to familiar negative and/or positive concepts of freedom. In brief, conservative political freedom consists in those traditional rights and liberties by which power is dispersed in ways such that it is not exercised arbitrarily by members of society.

This concept of freedom is not a negative concept of freedom in that it does not simply spell out an arena within which the individual is free from interference from others. Thus, conservatives and liberals cannot be said to share the same concept of freedom, but simply give it different interpretations. Something more fundamental separates them. On the other hand, it is not a positive concept of freedom in that it does not specify who or what controls a person's actions. It does not focus on self-mastery or self-government. Rather, it consists in a set of concrete, historically inherited interrelations (rights) within which members of a political society live freely.

I do not claim that those conservatives who have contributed to this account of conservative freedom agree on all the particulars. I do claim that this concept of freedom is distinct from other concepts of freedom, that it is part of an approach to the problem of political freedom which various people have taken (however unclearly), and that these people have been conservative. There is a sense, then, in which this concept of freedom uniquely finds its "home" in conservatism. Further, I think that this concept of freedom is tied to conservatism as a political view, rather than simply a natural psychological attitude.[7] It is with the former, not the latter, than I am concerned.

In developing this conservative model of freedom I wish to argue that it contains a number of serious problems and dilemmas, though it also contains a number of important reminders and insights for us when we think about and seek to further political freedom. Ultimately, however, I think that this model is inadequate. Though conservative freedom sets out to defend a practical, concrete, and non-theoretical account of political freedom, it ends up with *ad hoc* defenses of the status quo. It is unable satisfactorily to identify the traditions and rights, required by its own account, for political freedom. Thus, a fundamental tension or contradiction lies at the heart of conservative political freedom. Consequently, conservatism as a political view tends to collapse into conservatism as a natural psychological attitude. Ultimately, the problem is that its basic concept of freedom is both impotent and empty. It is this that leads to the various different interpretations it has received and to its inadequacy.

II THE CONCRETENESS OF CONSERVATIVE FREEDOM

It is important at the outset to understand the reluctance of conservatives to formulate a model of freedom abstractly, independent of particular societies. In general, they refuse to formulate abstract definitions of political freedom such as "freedom is the lack of (political) coercion."[8] They decline to specify universal principles of freedom which can then be applied to each society to determine its level of freedom.[9] They oppose the construction of hypothetical social contracts or original positions from which we might deduce the nature of political freedom. Consequently, the nature of conservative freedom is, at least at the outset, less clear than other models.

Part of this reluctance is simply the realistic view that freedom can only be realised in concrete, practical contexts and consequently will vary from place to place. Thus, Burke says that "abstract liberty, like other mere abstractions, is not to be found. Liberty inheres in some sensible object; and every nation has formed itself some favorite point, which by way of eminence becomes the criterion of their happiness" (quoted in Canavan 1959: 63). But though this understanding of the conservative objection to abstract views is important, it does not itself explain why abstract definitions or principles of freedom could not be formulated. As such, it does not explain why "it is of the nature of conservativism to avoid abstractions" (Scruton 1980: 17).

Oakeshott suggests what is at issue when he mocks those who say

> we must be clear . . . about what we mean by "freedom." First let us define it; and when we know what it is, it will be time enough to seek it out, to live it and to die for it. What is a free society? And with this question (proposed abstractly) the door opens upon a night of endless quibble, lit only by the stars of sophistry.
>
> (Oakeshott 1962a: 39)

For conservatives the problem of political freedom is not one of defining a word or even analyzing a concept of freedom. Contrariwise, we are often told that we must first be clear about our concepts or the words we use. Then, we can proceed to use these clarified meanings to construct justifiable political theories about, for instance, political freedom. And only later can such theories be used as our guides in the battle for political freedom.

Conservatives complain that this reverses matters. Conceptual analyses and theorizing independently of attending to the actual historical circumstances and traditions of each society (i.e. how society actually operates) may result in theoretical neatness but false simplifications or generalizations concerning complex matters. They squeeze out the complexities of our lives, our society and traditions, and treat them as unimportant (cf. Oakeshott 1962b: 123). Burke, for instance, speaks of freedom in at least three senses: that of spontaneous action, of the lack of restraint, and as a set of rights and liberties, which members of a society enjoy. What is striking is that Burke and conservatives (more generally) rarely attempt, as liberals (for example) do, to reduce these different meanings to a single meaning which is the heart of their theory and from which they deduce the nature of political freedom.[10] Instead, quite plausibly, they recognize them as different legitimate meanings.[11] The real question we face, conservatives insist, is not "Which meaning of 'freedom' is the true one?", but "What aspects of our society contribute to (political) freedom?"

Further, such abstract, generalized accounts are misleading in that their abridgment omits parts of the whole knowledge which is used in political activity (Oakeshott 1962b: 125). For example, the nature of political freedom is not a question of theoretical or ideological knowledge (such as is involved in constructing some state of nature or social contract position) but rather one of practical knowledge and experience. It is a question of looking to the free way of life we know which has developed through experiments and adjustments over the centuries. Thus Oakeshott urges that "the purpose of the inquiry is not to define a word, but to detect the secret of what we enjoy ['a free way of living'], to recognise what is hostile to it, and to discern where and how it may be enjoyed more fully" (Oakeshott 1962a: 40). Only when we see what is inherent in political freedom, as we know it, will we understand what political freedom is and what we must fight for. Otherwise, we end up with wild-eyed dreams and ideals about freedom which are either impossible or dangerous to realize in present society while destroying the very freedom we seek.

Quite similarly, Tocqueville contrasts two different kinds of generalization, which might be called aristocratic and democratic. The former "results from the slow, detailed, and conscientious labor of the mind"; through it "the sphere of human knowledge" is widened (Tocqueville 1969: 440). The latter, however, "springs up at once from the first quick exercise of the wits and begets only very superficial and uncertain notions" (Ibid.). "Democratic man," Tocqueville adds, "likes generalizations because they save him the trouble of studying particular cases" (Ibid.).

It is in a like spirit that Burke characterises as "destructive to . . . freedom" the speculations of

> people who have split and anatomized the doctrine of free government, as if it were an abstract question concerning metaphysical liberty and necessity and not a matter of moral prudence and natural feeling. They have disputed whether liberty be a positive or a negative idea; whether it does not consist in being governed by laws, without considering what are the laws, or who are the makers.
> (Burke 1901, II: 228)

Accordingly, conservative opposition to abstract accounts of freedom arises from a view concerning the relation between analysing concepts or word meanings, formulating theories, and getting to know what some real object, condition, or experience is. If we focus on our concepts and linguistic intuitions independently of the institutions wherein they are presently realised, if we attempt to generalize without looking to the particulars, we are going to miss what we are really interested in, namely political freedom. Instead, the emphasis in our inquiry should be on the "arrangements" according to which we live a free life, rather than on the meanings of our words, concepts, or abstract theories.

The point here is not that we should not analyse the concepts we use, but we must take great care in how we go about it. The object of our inquiry should direct how we go about that inquiry. Since political freedom is constituted by a set of practical arrangements in a society, it is to these practices we should look, not simply to our idea or concept of freedom. Thus, Oakeshott maintains that to arrive at "an intelligible concept" of freedom or politics, etc. we must consider that concept within "an already existing tradition of how to attend to our arrangements" (Oakeshott 1962b: 123).[12] From abstract definitions of words we cannot deduce what freedom is.

Now it might be protested that we must know what we mean by such concepts as political freedom *before* we try to study them in our real political life. Conservatives could agree. Surely we must use our words and concepts to understand our experiences and participate in this free way of life. But these words and concepts have grown out of that way of life; they are rooted in it. More broadly, Oakeshott claims that any system of ideas is not, in fact, "the quasi-divine parent of political activity, but its earthly stepchild." It is a system of ideas abstracted from the manner in which people have been accustomed to go about the business of attending to the arrangements of their societies (Oakeshott 1962b: 118, 118–19, 120). These abstractions are secondary to our daily arrangements.

Thus it is only because we already have an idea of political freedom *within* our real political life that we can perform the abstractions we do when we arrive at accounts of the meaning or nature of political freedom.[13] If we refrain from attending to this knowledge, we run the risk of formulating impossible dreams and empty ideals. In short, our concepts grow out of our practical life – not the other way around.

Now surely conservatives are correct to warn us about abstract speculations concerning practical matters. All too often, political philosophers fail to appreciate the historically limited nature of the concepts and ideas with which they work and the practical, rather than the theoretical, nature of the problems they confront. However, this conservative reminder (that our understanding of "freedom" grows out of the arrangements of our society) carries particular significance for our purposes only because conservatives conjoin it with a second view already suggested above, viz. these arrangements embody freedom. When we turn from our concepts and abstract theories to focus on the arrangements within our society we are not looking to the dead remains of the past, but to its wisdom. When we look to these arrangements we look to what we, as a people, know about freedom on the basis of considerable experience. To disdain this is to reject one's heritage, freedom, and ultimately oneself.

Thus, conservatives contend not only that we understand the meaning of our concepts prior to our theorizing about them, but also that the truths of morality and freedom are already (at least implicitly) known to us and embodied in our free society. Burke claims that "we think that no discoveries are to be made in morality; nor many in the great principles of government, nor in the ideas of liberty, which were understood long before we were born" (Burke 1973: 99).

Oakeshott captures these points with his example of cookery:

> the cookery book [i.e. a set of concepts and principles] is not an independently generated beginning from which cooking can spring; it is nothing more than an abstract of somebody's knowledge of how to cook: it is the stepchild, not the parent of the activity.
>
> (Oakeshott 1962b: 119)

Similarly, our knowledge of the concepts and principles of political freedom is not something which we can generate prior to our knowledge of a free way of life and the arrangements it involves. We must attend to the latter in order to formulate the former. The point is that we are not ignorant. We can (and must) begin by turning to what we already know.

It is a Cartesian vanity, then, which leads people to refuse that which is given to them by the history and tradition of their society, and to attempt to rebuild the whole of moral and political knowledge by pretending to purge their consciousness and begin again (cf. Oakeshott 1962a: 38). Our situation is more like that of Meno's slave than Descartes by the fireside. We do not need to construct (or reconstruct) our knowledge of political freedom from some null base or some absolutely certain set of axioms. Indeed, we cannot. Rather we must recall what we (or the species) already dimly know. To analyze words and concepts independently, not to see their connection with our ways of life, is (false) abstractionism. Intellectual integrity does not require that we wipe the slate clean but simply see what is before our eyes.

Now given the preceding two views it is understandable why conservatives urge that to understand the nature of political freedom we must look to the form it takes within each society (Tocqueville 1969: 315, 504). In doing this, it should be noted, conservatives advocate yet a third view: what is important in a society's arrangements are the details and the nuances, not some hidden essence which must be abstracted from our social and political arrangements. The various concrete historical patterns of behavior which are the object of our inquiry are "not susceptible of the distinction between essence and accident." "Knowledge of [such traditions] is unavoidably knowledge of [their] detail: to know only the gist is to know nothing" (Oakeshott 1962b: 128–9). Thus, again, conservatives hold that the kind of knowledge involved in understanding political freedom is different from that which is centrally involved in word or conceptual analyses or in the formulation of theories.

An important implication of this view, conservatives hold, is that the contrary (liberal or radical) quest for some underlying and hidden essence reflects a disvaluation of, if not an alienation from, appearances. This disvaluation is expressed in some liberal and radical literature by disgust with the historical concreteness of man's being.[14] Thus, Burke held, Hart claims, that the defense of what the philosophies called "appearances" or "masks" is the defense of society itself, that the reality of society consists of appearances, of "roles," not simply of "hidden" essences (Hart 1967: 226). The search for some "natural man" behind these is a search for a mythical being (Hart 1967: 225–7).

Nevertheless, surely there are problems with these views. Though conservatives are correct to insist that political theories or models of freedom must draw on past experience, this does not mean that they must remain wedded to that experience. It is false that accounts of political freedom (or of cooking) are "nothing more than an abstract" of what we or others already know. They can, and have, gone beyond how "we are accustomed to conduct our affairs" (Oakeshott 1962b: 120). The question is whether they are justified in doing so. With this in mind, the conservative view that the results of historical experimentation ultimately accord with morality and freedom seems unduly optimistic. Slavery, the oppressive treatment of women and ethnic minorities, as well as the exclusion from political decisions of those politically capable raise legitimate doubts about the coincidence of historical experiments and morality. Finally, surely people need not be alienated if they reject at least some of the historical appearances that surround them. Indeed, doing so may be a sign of maturity and moral insight.

Conservatives are not without responses to these charges. However, we must first look to the concept of political freedom conservatives use so as to understand these responses. Afterwards we can explore their answers to the preceding objections.

III CONSERVATIVE POLITICAL FREEDOM: CONCRETE RIGHTS AND LIBERTIES

When we look to our actual political experience, rather than the a priori musings of our intellects, we find that political freedom is practically constituted by various concrete rights and liberties enjoyed by the members of a free society. For example, Burke held that, for Britain, at least, Habeas Corpus and the Common Law play a central role in permitting or constituting a free political system (Burke 1901: 193, 197). Among the inherited and hence real rights of man Burke mentions the following: a right to live by the rule of law; a right to justice; a right to the fruits of their industry; and to the means of making their industry fruitful; "a right to the acquisitions of their parents; to the nourishment and improvement of their offspring; to instruction in life and to consolation in death" (Burke 1973: 71).

Tocqueville and Oakeshott identify a somewhat more restrained list of rights. For the English, Tocqueville mentions trial by jury, "liberty of speech and freedom of the press, personal freedom, and the conception of rights and the practice of asserting them" (Tocqueville 1969: 674-5). Oakeshott lists the rights of association, to own private property (including a proprietary right over one's personal capacities and labor [Oakeshott 1962a: 46]), and to freedom of speech (Oakeshott 1962a: 43). The most important of these, Oakeshott holds, are the rights to association and private property (Oakeshott 1962a: 44ff). Freedom of speech is not as crucial as the others since "the major part of mankind has nothing to say" (Oakeshott 1962:43; cf. 43ff).

There are many questions which such lists raise. Are these rights and liberties the only ones constituting liberty? What is the significance of the fact that the preceding lists are not the same? Why do these rights pick out freedom, rather than justice or some other political concept? How are hierarchies among such rights determined?

There are no simple or short answers to these questions. Neither are there any neat theoretical answers. The practical answer is that we can know what are the rights and liberties which members of a free society must have only by looking to customs and traditions of a society, not to some abstract universal principles.[15] The wisdom of the species, conservatives contend, is buried in these customs and traditions, and the small experiments which they embody.

Four aspects of this appeal to customs and traditions are especially relevant here. First, the legal rights and liberties of a society may be simply a dead letter, a lifeless corpse, if they are not animated by the ways that people actually and habitually live – in short, if they are not part of the customs and traditions of the people of that society. It is with reference to such customs, habits, and traditions that conservatives (and others) speak of the "spirit of freedom" (cf. Tocqueville 1969: 63). They are the heart of conservative freedom.

Secondly, the status of the rights conservatives do accept is that of prescriptive rights, i.e. rights which have been guaranteed to individuals from time immemorial. To speak of the "prescriptive nature" of these rights is, for conservatives, to claim that the rightness of these ways of acting grows out of their reaffirmation over many successive generations. In this sense, that something is customary or traditional lends it an aura of rightness. Hence, it is not simply due to the inevitability or reoccurrence of various relations that conservatives recognize certain rights.

Thirdly, the rights which constitute conservative freedom come attached to various responsibilities and obligations that individuals, as members of historical societies, owe to one another. Any understanding of freedom simply in terms of individual rights unattached to responsibilities or obligations results in the tendency to make demands on society while denying what one owes to others (Tocqueville 1969: 72). Abstract understandings of rights leads to liberalism, not conservatism (cf. Harbour 1982: 85–6, 103–4).

Fourthly, the customs and traditions of each society are unique. Inasmuch, then, as freedom is bound up with customs and traditions, it is not transferable in precisely the same form from society to society. Ortega y Gasset comments that

> each authentic institution is untransferable. . . . Where begin and where end those political entities which language . . . puts before us as independent and self-sustaining objects, calling them by the definite names of "tribunate of the people," "parliament," "freedom of the press"? None of these institutions terminates in a clear-cut line. They all reach back into the particular collective life where they originated and whence they receive their indispensable supplements, their strength and their control.
>
> (Ortega y Gasset 1946: 47)

Thus, political freedom will look different from society to society.[16] Hence, the particularity of conservative freedom. This, conservatives argue, is not a deficiency of conservative freedom but one of its strengths.

Accordingly, when we look to the customs and traditions of Anglo-Saxon countries we find the following particular implications and interpretations of the above rights and liberties.

First, the rights held by people who are politically free need not include the right of each person to vote in general or special elections (Tocqueville 1969: 504). Nisbet claims that "one will search the history of conservative thought in vain for anything resembling a 'one man, one vote' philosophy" (Nisbet 1986: 40). Burke comments: "It is said, that twenty-four millions ought to prevail over two hundred thousand. True; if the constitution of a kingdom be a problem of arithmetic" (Burke 1973: 64).

However, the constitution and political freedom of a kingdom are not matters of arithmetic. They form a practical matter. To gain knowledge and understanding of them requires years of experience, training, and commitment (Oakeshott 1962b: 113). These conditions can only be met, conservatives contend, by those citizens who can devote themselves to politics. This will usually require additional (financial) conditions which cannot be met by the masses. Thus, for Burke the people (the public) "consisted of some four hundred thousand free men, possessed of leisure or property or membership in a responsible body which enabled them to apprehend the elements of politics" (quoted in Kirk, 1986: 18–19). Hence, conservatives have generally advocated rule by an aristocracy or elite, and feared any rule by the masses. Any pure form of democracy is dangerous to political freedom. Accordingly, given the importance of practical experience and the desirable role of the elite, any right to vote for all people can only be met with skepticism and reluctance by conservatives. At best, it is a measure they will agree to if more desirable measures cannot be met.

Secondly, political freedom is compatible with a society which is both hierarchical and unequal. Indeed, historical experience leads conservatives to believe that hierarchy and inequality are necessary for political freedom. This is true not only among various classes, but also between males and females (cf. Tocqueville 1969: 601). Since the classes and the sexes differ, they require different protections and treatments. Political freedom does not require that they have the same (political) rights. This view of the incompatibility of freedom and equality is one aspect of the conservative view of freedom upon which virtually every conservative agrees.[17]

Thirdly, speech may be curtailed when it attacks or questions the basic values and morals of a society or simply proves offensive to people (cf. Devlin 1965). Now if political freedom is the set of rights and liberties that individuals enjoy in a society, then we need not conclude that the freedom of individuals has thereby been diminished. Certainly, for liberals this amounts to the subordination of the freedom of individuals to other values, such as the harmony or order of society. But such subordination of individuals, conservatives contend, enhances the freedom in society. Individual rights are not absolute; they are derivative from and subordinate to other obligations, roles, statuses, etc. Thus, for conservatives, it does not contravene a person's freedom to prohibit him from selling pornographic literature, using narcotics, or soliciting sex. To engage in such activities would not be to act freely so much as to act with license. If this strikes a person as strange, then it merely reveals the extent to which that person is not conservative, but liberal or libertarian. The conservative view does allow that people should be tolerant of other views and activities, but certainly it does not allow the breadth of tolerance (or indifference) that liberals accept.

Finally, conservatives tend to agree that historically we have learned that the right to property is essential for political freedom. "Separate property from private possession, and Leviathan becomes master of all" (Kirk 1986: 9). The connection of freedom and private property is one of the canons of conservative thought (cf. Kirk, 1986: 9). Private property plays a vital role in assuring that power is dispersed and that, given its importance to its owners, such power is not capriciously or arbitrarily exercised.

The preceding details, drawn from the customs and traditions of Anglo-Saxon countries, fill in the content of conservative political freedom. Attention to non-Anglo-Saxon countries would presumably tell a different, though related, story. In drawing out these details we have been following the conservative view that the practical political experience of each society must determine the nature of the rights and liberties which constitute political freedom within that society.

IV THE CONSERVATIVE CONCEPT OF FREEDOM

The concept of freedom conservatives use within their model of freedom can be elicited from the preceding section. I noted earlier that conservatives recognize a number of different senses of freedom. I also indicated that the question that concerns conservatives is not, "Which is the real meaning of 'freedom'?", but "According to which meaning do we live as members of politically free society?" This is a practical question, one to which a partial answer is given in the preceding section.

Accordingly, when we reflect on the nature of political freedom as we actually experience it in our society, we see that it is bound up with the rights and liberties possessed by members of a society. This is crucial to the meaning of "freedom" for conservatives. It is this concept of freedom which is implied when Burke (and other conservatives) says that he seeks an ordered freedom, a political freedom constituted and defined by various inherited rights, laws, and liberties enjoyed by the members of an historical society. This is freedom in its basic political sense. In this way, our answer to the practical question leads us to the conceptual answer. The latter depends on the former, not the other way around. Similarly, Oakeshott says that

> the freedom which we enjoy is nothing more than arrangements, procedures of a certain kind: the freedom of an Englishman is not something exemplified in the procedure of *habeas corpus*, it *is*, at that point, the availability of that procedure. And the freedom which we wish to enjoy is not an "ideal" which we premeditate independently of our political experience, it is what is already intimated in that experience.

(Oakeshott 1962b: 121)

Thus, the conservative concept of freedom is captured simply by the various rights and liberties held by members of each society. It is these which compose, as Burke says, a manly or rational liberty, a virtuous liberty. It is in this sense that Burke says that "Liberty . . . is a *general* principle, and the clear right of all the subjects within the realm, or of none" (Burke 1901: 198). Such is the liberty found in and constituted by an ordered state.

However, this can only be a first part of the characterization of conservative freedom. Simply to identify conservative political freedom with various rights does not tell us why some rights (of the many that we have) are tied to freedom, rather than, say, to justice, or some other value. Conservatives must specify those rights which define political freedom and are identified by tradition.

Their answer is that political freedom is defined by those particular rights and liberties which form relations in which people are not subject to despotic and arbitrary power. For example, Oakeshott speaks of the dispersion of power as essential to freedom. Though he variously identifies the relation between the dispersion of power and freedom, Oakeshott holds that dispersion of power defines or characterizes the rights which constitute political freedom.[18]

Burke is also seriously concerned with the presence of arbitrary power in society. For example, he also claims that the ordered state which Britain enjoys involves a dispersion of power (Burke 1973: 262). But this set of laws and the order it brings about must have a particular shape. Hence, he comments that "liberty is in danger of being made unpopular to Englishmen. Contending for an imaginary power, we begin to acquire the spirit of domination, and to lose the relish of honest equality" (Burke 1901: 243). That is, freedom requires a way of living and acting that does not seek after imaginary powers in an attempt to dominate; a dispersion of power is important. Similarly Tocqueville remarks repeatedly on the connection between liberty and the multiplying of functions in society whereby the power of authority is dispersed and not concentrated in one person or a small group of individuals (cf. Tocqueville 1969: 72, 184).

Thus, the conservative concept of political freedom would seem to consist of those rights and liberties enjoyed by members of a society which disperses power and does not exercise that power arbitrarily. It is this meaning or concept of freedom which is basic to conservative political freedom.[19]

Now is this sense of "political freedom" a legitimate and distinct sense of "freedom"? Is it a unique concept of freedom? To begin with, it virtually restates the first entry under "freedom" in the *Oxford English Dictionary* (*OED*). This first entry for "freedom" is: "Not in bondage to another" and its first submeaning is that of "not bound or subject as a slave is to his master; enjoying personal rights and liberty of action as a member of a society or state." This is different from the second main meaning, i.e. "release, loose, unrestricted" (*OED*). Thus, freedom in its first sense simply refers to a set of rights, protections, guarantees which constitute and define one's position in an ordered society. This sense of "freedom" thus appears to be distinct and legitimate. It is also an open-ended concept. It refers to a status or position which individuals share as members of a society in which arbitrary power is not exercised and individual rights are respected. However, it does not further specify what those rights or roles and statuses are.

This account of freedom also makes sense of the etymology of "free." According to the *OED* "free" derives from the sense of "dear" which was attributed to members of a household as opposed to the slaves. That is, this sense is status attributing. So the understanding of freedom arrived at here is coherent with the etymological roots of "freedom". It encompasses the idea of persons being members of some group, society, or community in which their status or position is secured.

It should be recalled, as I have noted above, that the present meaning of "freedom" is not the only one conservatives recognize. Conservatives also speak of freedom in the sense of spontaneous action. As such, freedom is the vitality of humans. This is freedom in a basic ontological sense. Understood as a capacity to act independently of natural causation, i.e. in the sense of free will, it is what distinguishes humans. But it is also an abstract and dangerous force. It is what Tocqueville calls "wild freedom" (Tocqueville 1969: 28), or "liberty of corrupt nature" (Ibid.: 46). Conservatives are ambivalent towards this sense of freedom. Freedom in this sense must be tamed to be realized. As Burke says, its perfection is its fault (Burke 1901: 229). In this wild, ontological sense, it is appropriate for conservatives to be non-committal as to whether it is advantageous or not (Ibid.). It makes sense to say that this liberty is a good to be improved on (Burke 1969: 229). By itself, it is unacceptable and impossible to live by. It "must be limited in order to be possessed" (Burke 1901: 229). But when limited it is not only "a private blessing of the first order" it is also "the vital spring and energy of the state itself, which has just so much life and vigor as there is liberty in it" (Ibid.).

This is also a basic sense of freedom, one distinct from political freedom. Their distinctness is evident in that prior to limitation, people could experience freedom in this ontological sense outside of society. It is not, quite clearly, simply a set of rights. Further, it is not merely a lack of restraint, but an energy, a spontaneity, a vital spring within people. Neither is it self-determination, a concept of freedom suggesting consciousness and even rationality. It is simply a basic ontological thrust. Only if this is tamed is it compatible with political freedom. However, this is not to say that political freedom is simply a modification of this. Admittedly, Burke says that "liberty . . . must be limited in order to be possessed" (Burke 1901: 229). But the rights which constitute political freedom are not simply protections of such wild freedom; they are substantial transformations of this spontaneous activity. As such, ontological freedom and political freedom are distinct. Neither one is reducible to the other.

V THE UNIQUENESS OF CONSERVATIVE FREEDOM

It is important to contrast conservative political freedom with several other concepts of freedom to further demonstrate its independence. For example, if conservative freedom involves the dispersion of power (subject to various assumptions) to individuals, and power involves the ability to do or accomplish various things, then, it might be thought that conservative freedom is a form of self-determination. Further, since such power is not to be exercised arbitrarily, it might be thought that what conservatives are defending is a view of freedom as rational self-determination. Accordingly, some have claimed that what is really involved in conservative freedom is some form of positive freedom. It might be said that Burke suggests this view when he speaks of "the full rights of men, each to govern himself" (Burke 1973: 73).

It is false, however, to think that the heart of conservative political freedom lies in each individual rationally and reflectively determining his or her own path. This might be a liberal or radical view, but it is not the conservative view. Conservative freedom is quite compatible with individuals living (not necessarily reflectively either) in various ways which accord with tradition and custom. As Burke puts it, the individual is weak, but the species is wise. Individuals must look to the customs, rituals, and traditions of a society. They must seek there for "intimations" as to the content of freedom. A sympathy with what is natural and essential in society is enjoined, rather than some individual process of rational reflection to determine (*à la* Kant) the universal laws of reason by which a person is to act. In the harmony of such living and acting with social customs individuals experience freedom.

It is for these reasons that Burke criticises the destruction by the French of the principle of obedience and their advocacy of self-government for each person (soldiers included) under the notion of the rights of man (Ibid.: 237). He comments that

> we are afraid to put men to live and trade each on his own private stock of reason; because we suspect that this stock in each man is small, and that the individuals would do better to avail themselves of the general bank and capital of nations, and of ages.
>
> (Ibid.: 100)

Conservative political freedom is, then, not one of individual self-determination, let alone autonomy, but primarily a social or community freedom of which they partake. In this sense, the individual is not the primary bearer of freedom as is the case with liberals. The individual cannot provide the historical continuity and bases required for political freedom; only the community or society can do this. Accordingly, conservative freedom is a thoroughly political concept: individuals are free only as they exercise their historical rights within a political society.[20]

It might be maintained, however, that the conservative concept of freedom is actually simply a version of negative freedom (i.e. the lack of constraint). To speak of rights which disperse power, it will be said, is simply to speak about preventing some people from forcing other people to do something other than they want. Thus, to speak of the dispersion of power (or arbitrary power) is simply another way of speaking about freedom in the sense of a lack of constraint.

It may be admitted that this is part of the conservative concept. Or rather, it is one of the consequences of this view. But to say that this is simply what "freedom" means for conservatives is unwarranted. When Burke and Oakeshott use the word "freedom" it is not possible simply to substitute for it "lack of coercion" or some such other phrase. When the liberal or radical seek some more basic and general meaning of "freedom" – e.g. lack of coercion or self-determination, the reason is to gain some criterion, some means, to test whether this or that right is appropriately part of a free society. But conservatives reject this. The meaning of "freedom" and the nature of political philosophy are thereby misconceived.

To begin with, though at least part of the point of conservative freedom in dispersing non-arbitrary power is to moderate the number of restraints and amount of coercion one suffers, this is not the central point. The dispersion of power is not simply a negative act – the scattering of power to the winds or an attempt to eliminate power (Tocqueville 1969: 601). It is also a positive act, viz. an extension of power to members of society (within certain assumptions about humans and society, e.g. the need for differentiation). As such it is also the assertion of the importance of power and authority for freedom. Freedom, that is, does not simply lie in the lack of arbitrary power or in the lack of concentrated power. It is not simply freedom from these forms of power. Only power can limit power, and therefore though it must be dispersed, we must not (and cannot) seek to escape from it in order to be free (cf. Rossiter 1955: 366).[21] Thus, Burke comments that "in all monarchies the people must in effect themselves, mediately or immediately, possess the power of granting their own money, or no shadow of liberty could subsist" (Burke 1964: 63). Liberty requires such power, not simply freedom from the king's power.

Secondly, the rights and liberties which are part of conservative freedom are not simply guarantees of the lack of constraint or coercion. As opposed to liberal views of rights, conservatives hold that individual rights stem from roles and relations involving reciprocal obligations which define a system within which we live. The rights of freedom are not simply "free standing rights" which merely impose obligations on others.[22] They impose duties and obligations on oneself as well.

The point is that one cannot properly speak of such rights without speaking, at the same time, of the duties and obligations one also has within the various relationships which are thereby defined. The right of voluntary association is at one with "the duty of not forming or joining any association designed to deprive, or in effect depriving, others of the exercise of any of their rights, particularly that of voluntary association" (Oakeshott 1962a: 44). Though many conservatives suggest that it is these duties, not the rights, which are primary in such relationships, it would seem more appropriate for them to hold that it is the reciprocal relationship which is basic, not either one of its parts. Thus, Burke's condemnation of the French Revolution was not simply that they had removed too many restraints. It went more deeply than this to the destruction of various basic relationships which define a free society. Accordingly, conservative freedom is actually constituted by a set of reciprocal relations among people. It is for this reason that freedom and moral responsibility are bound up together for conservatives.

Now behind these claims are two crucial assumptions. First, there is the underlying attitude that it is all right for people to be commanded and to stand in reverence, awe, or respect of others. Conservatives do not maintain, as liberals tend to believe, that people must do what they do on their own; that they must be independent of all others; that it is demeaning to them to be commanded or stand in reverence and awe of other people. Instead, on the conservative model, knowing one's place and identifying with it, not envying but respecting those around one, being in awe of those above one are important to one's well-being and freedom. The attitudes of reverence, veneration (Kirk 1952: 198), and humility (Burke 1973), conservatives hold, are important human attitudes. Many conservatives give this a further theological twist: "the principle of homage and service to what is above one has it culmination and final justification in fealty to God, the true sovereign and supreme exemplar" (Babbitt 1924: 101).

Accordingly, since people by nature need to respect others, need discipline, seek to be reverent, respectful, to honor and be in awe of other people, a freedom which links rights and obligations, liberties and duties, will not necessarily be experienced as reducing one's freedom. Humans are not simply rational, conscious machines seeking only their own good and hence seeking freedom simply in release from other people. This is the implicit liberal view of humans; it is false, simplistic, and dangerous. Conservative freedom, on the contrary, is found in the rights and obligations one shares with others.

Secondly, customs and traditions are not viewed as external to individuals, but as constituting part of the identity of individuals. Thus, for individuals to follow such traditions and customs is not for them to be acting under some compulsion, but to be acting out various values and beliefs which make them who they are. Only if this is understood can we properly understand the comments of conservatives like Ortega y Gasset who claim that "people are free – in the political sense – when they live under institutions they prefer, no matter what those institutions are" (Ortega y Gasset 1946: 32). Or Burke's comment that "If any ask me what a free government is, I answer, that, for any practical purpose, it is what the people think so, – and that they, and not I, are the natural, lawful, and competent judges of this matter" (Burke 1901: 227). The arrangement of rights and obligations (and their related customs, traditions, and laws) which define political freedom within a political society are not, for the most part, "a burden to be carried or an incubus to be thrown off, but an inheritance to be enjoyed" (Oakeshott 1962b: 113). Though they may indeed impose restraints on people, conservatives hold that restraints and freedom are not necessarily antithetical. Surely freedom in the sense of spontaneous action is antithetical to restraints, but not the political freedom which has grown with the customs and traditions with which people identify.[23]

With the conservative notion of freedom, then, there is certainly "freedom from," but that is only one aspect of political freedom. To identify liberties and rights with "freedom from" is like characterizing the structural beams of a building as merely the means whereby the building does not collapse; i.e. their nature is to provide freedom from collapse. This is silly, however, since they not only hold up the building but also are part of the building, they define its form and appearance and they (partly) determine the nature of the internal movement within the building. In short, they are not simply to be understood as providing "freedom from collapse." Neither is conservative freedom simply negative freedom.

Thirdly, conservatives claim that their view of freedom provides for a naturalness and harmony between individuals in society. Burke and other conservatives speak repeatedly of their views in terms of following nature (Burke 1973: 89, 94, 99). As free people, individuals naturally occupy different roles and relations; they respect and admire each other. Class conflict is minimized in following the various rights and liberties. There are not conflicts or obstructions. There is, then, a sense of harmony, ease, and unfetteredness. But (again) it is mistaken simply to see negative freedom.

For example, we might speak similarly of how freely a person skates or dances, meaning that he or she does it with an ease, a naturalness, that is striking and attractive. "A skillful musician is 'freer' to play his instrument than a novice" (Hart 1967: 234). Likewise, in speaking of the importance of habit (and hence customs and traditions) to conservatives, Hart notes that "habit performs complex tasks with greater ease and efficiency than does the conscious reason" (Ibid.). He proceeds to say that:

> there is a sense, indeed, in which it is really habit, paradoxically enough, that renders one free, since freedom actually is experienced only as a quality of an activity. One is free to do this or that; one is not "free" in an abstract way apart from activity.
>
> (Ibid.)

Such comments concerning conservative freedom do not reveal an underlying negative freedom. It is not the unfetteredness, or lack of coercion or fetters, which is primary here. The person whom we compliment as dancing with great freedom we do not compliment for dancing simply without obstructions or fetters, but for the naturalness and the harmony of bodily motions. The unfetteredness is, as it were, a spinoff of what is crucial. It is obvious that this could be confused with simply the lack of restraint, but that is to miss what is crucial for what is secondary. As Burke says "the *effect* of liberty to individuals is, that they may do what they please" (Burke 1973: 20; emphasis added). The point is that the "doing as one pleases" is a consequent of liberty, not liberty itself. It is mistaken to take the consequent for the underlying principle. Similarly, Burke charges others with "see[ing] nothing in that [revolution] of 1688 but the deviation from the constitution; and they take the deviation from the principle for the principle" (Ibid.: 34).

The problem with liberals is that they forget the order within which it is possible, *qua* free, to do as one pleases or not be restrained. As such, their view of freedom is superficial; they mistake a surface phenomenon for the depth phenomenon. They mistake the consequence of liberty for liberty itself.

Finally, the argument here has not been that negative freedom is not a legitimate meaning for "freedom," or that conservatives are not interested in the level of coercion in society. Rather, the argument has been that "freedom" is not used simply in this negative sense when conservatives speak about "political freedom." It is only part of their understanding of political freedom. Thus, the conservative concept of political freedom is unique. It is not freedom in any of its other senses: ontological, negative, or positive.

VI CUSTOMS, TRADITIONS, AND FREEDOM: PROBLEMS

Conservative freedom is not only unique in the sense that it is not reducible to other concepts of freedom it is also unique in its formality. By this I mean that from the concept of conservative freedom one can draw little guidance as to what is or is not freedom. We can derive from this concept only the most general guidelines as to whether this or that society is a free society, since it does not tell us which rights and liberties such a society must have. Thus it leaves rather open the form of government compatible with conservative freedom. However, if the argument in preceding sections is correct, the function of such a concept is not to provide these answers.

As we have seen, we must, instead, turn to the traditions and customs of each society to fill out conservative political freedom. It is these customs and traditions which tell use which rights free individuals have such that power is dispersed and not arbitrarily exercised. These rights evolve, we have seen, through a process of many small experiments which embody the wisdom of the species. To ask simply about this or that dispersion of power is to ask an abstract question since the choice has already been made through countless experiments over thousands of years.

However, though traditions and customs may be crucial in filling out conservative political freedom they amount to a very problematic answer. For example, it would seem that traditions and customs will not only differ between countries, but also within a country. Further, these different traditions and customs may conflict. They require interpretation. Yet, conservatives have disagreed over these interpretations. Cowling, for instance, notes important differences between Burke and contemporary British conservatives (Cowling 1978: 10ff). To which traditions or customs should we then appeal? Are conservatives committed to defending the institutions and relationships of their society which have attained the status of tradition and custom even though those institutions and relationships are of a liberal nature? Since the conservative view of freedom lacks a substantive ideal, these questions and details are crucial. Unless they can be resolved conservatives will lack a coherent model of political freedom.

Secondly, some customs and traditions seem simply antiquated. Liberals and radicals complain that they are the inflexible, dead hand of the past which prevents the full realization of freedom. Conservatives reject this view, but must allow (as most conservatives do) that society, its customs and traditions, do (and must) change.

Burke spoke of principles which would allow for gradual change. Indeed, Burke says that a state must have "two principles of conservation and correction" (Burke 1973: 33). "A state without the means of some change is without the means of its conservation" (Ibid.). Thus, conservatives must specify some means of determining which customs, conventions, and traditions (or which aspects of them) are to be retained, and which allowed to wither away. The reason is that they have no other choice, since times and conditions change.

Thirdly, it is crucial that the group can be identified which has the appropriate customs and traditions. Cowling expresses these concerns in a way which only lightly obscures the racism which such group identification may give rise to. Thus, he speaks of the British loss of a national identity due to alien communities and the efforts that are required to recapture such an identity (Cowling 1978:16). The problem here is how to draw the boundaries between one society and another (cf. Parry 1982: 414f). What constitutes the identity of a society? These questions arise when the community of ideas that constitutes a society of any sort is disputed or not widely recognized (Devlin 1965: 9).

Only if conservatives can satisfactorily answer these questions will they have not only a unique concept of freedom but an acceptable model of freedom. However, the solution to these problems is not obvious. Some conservatives argue that customs and traditions carry within themselves the reason for following them. Scruton claims that:

> the customary act is the one for which the answer to the question "Why are you doing that?" is "it is what is done". In that answer many things are embodied: the thought that their acting alike is reasonable; an indifference to time, and a consequent sense of what it would be like to act likewise at any other time.
>
> (Scruton 1983: 194)

But this cannot help here. On the one hand, it seems false. There are simply too many customs or traditions which do not seem reasonable: e.g. denial of the vote to women, exclusion of blacks from political office, etc. Second, as noted above, some customs and traditions will conflict with others. We must pick some over others. The reason which customs and traditions carry within themselves cannot be a conclusive, legitimizing reason. At most it could be a prima-facie reason.

Accordingly, some conservatives have suggested distinguishing what is primary and what is secondary to a society and its customs. For example, Wilson claims that "conservatism is not necessarily a defense of the *status quo*; in no case could it be a defense of everything as it is, but it is a defense of primary elements in the social structure, with concessions made on secondary problems" (Wilson 1941: 39f). Conservatives focus on "the basic patterns" in a society. However, Wilson does not say how we are to determine these elements and basic patterns. The most he says is that conservatives try "to sense those changes which would free the masses, and they have opposed them as they were able" (Ibid.: 37). But this renders the question simply one of intuition or feelings.

Perhaps Burke is thinking along these lines when he claims that the needed principles of correction and conservation involve acting in accord with "the spirit of our constitution" (Burke 1973: 34). But, again, how are we to know what this is? Simply to say that it is "the idea of inheritance [which] furnishes a sure principle of conservation, and a sure principle of transmission; without at all excluding a principle of improvement" (Ibid.: 45) is not terribly helpful. Kirk suggests that Burke held that "history demonstrates that [the true natural rights of men] are the rights desired by the *true* natural man, man civilized and therefore mature, the civil social man" (Kirk 1951: 448). But this merely raises the problem of who are the mature "civil social" men and what to say when (as does happen) they disagree.

Oakeshott is aware of the objection that, for instance, Britain might be considered two societies with two different sets of traditions (Oakeshott 1962b: 135). He gives three answers. First, he claims that the absence of homogeneity does not necessarily destroy singleness (Oakeshott 1962b: 135). This may be true, but it does not tell us what that "singleness" is or how to identify it.

Secondly, he argues that "what we are considering here [in Britain] is a legally organized society and we are considering the manner in which its legal structure (which in spite of its incoherences cannot be supposed to have a competitor) is reformed and amended" (Ibid.). But reference to legal structure is hardly the same as identifying a society constituted by its own customs and traditions. Within the legal structure of the Soviet Union there are a number of societies with their own customs and traditions which, on conservative grounds, should be viewed as distinct.

Thirdly, Oakeshott says that by a "single community" he means a collection of people who commonly recognize a "manner of attending to its arrangements" (Oakeshott 1962b: 135; cf. 123). But this simply raises the question, once again, of how they recognize such arrangements. Thus, Oakeshott's answers are not particularly helpful.

We could, of course, identify a coherent sense of conservative political freedom (and a means to resolve political disputes concerning freedom) just in case we all agreed on the central customs and traditions of our society. But this has two striking limitations. First, this would plausibly occur only within very small groups. Thus, just as radical freedom is sometimes criticized for being applicable only to small intimate groups of people, a similar criticism might be brought against conservative freedom. It will be meaningful and useful only to the extent we are dealing with relatively homogeneous populations with commonly recognised traditions which are interpreted, with some uniformity, in similar ways. But this preserves both conservative and radical freedom by condemning them to irrelevance. Secondly, even for small groups this answer would leave open the question as to what was the basis of those customs and traditions. In short, why should we believe that they are justified?

VII A NATURAL MORAL ORDER: NATURAL RIGHTS AND NATURAL LAW

A different, seemingly more powerful answer to these problems is the view that those customs and traditions are the important, primary, and justified ones which accord with an underlying natural moral order. In general, conservatives tend to maintain that there is an objective morality (cf. Burke 1973: 99).[24] In this sense, it might be said that what drives conservative freedom is a sense of, and a demand for, moral order within society.

This moral order would serve as the basis upon which the needed distinctions between primary and secondary, legitimate and anti-quated, customs or traditions could be made.[25] Only in this sense could we understand that "t;he *essence* of social conservatism is preservation of the ancient moral traditions of humanity" (Kirk 1986: 8; emphasis added). Further, by linking freedom with a natural moral order, conservatives would be defining a freedom in accord with nature itself.

There is, however, considerable lack of agreement over how conservatives view this natural moral order. Some see natural rights; others see natural law. Some see neither.

For example, Kirk claims that Burke accepted natural rights (Kirk 1951). Burke does speak of natural rights on a number of occasions: "a conservation and secure enjoyment of our natural rights is the great and ultimate purpose of civil society" (cited in Ibid.: 444). Tocqueville also seems to accept that there exist some natural rights (Tocqueville

1969: 104, 562). Thus, in linking freedom with enjoying rights in a society which disperses power and does not exercise arbitrary power, conservatives could be defining an order in accord with various natural rights. An appeal to natural rights might anchor or explain the claims conservatives make about customs and traditions.

However, not all conservatives agree. Oakeshott says that "freedom . . . is not a 'human right' to be deduced from some speculative concept of human nature" (Oakeshott 1962b: 121).[26] Casey says quite bluntly that "English conservatism . . . has never based itself upon the supposed 'rights of man' . . ." (Casey 1978: 82). Other conservatives seem ambivalent on the matter. For example, Kirk wavers between claiming that the conservatives are opposed to natural rights and the view that they are only opposed to some absolute interpretation of them (Kirk 1986: 22).

Similarly, some claim that the idea that there is an eternal (natural) moral law which is objective and unchanging is important to conservative views. Burke's views are linked with natural law by several commentators.[27] However, Huntington agrees with Mannheim that conservatives cannot accept a theory of natural law as a set of transcendent and universal moral principles (Huntington 1957: 459). Mannheim himself holds that "the key problem for conservatism was opposition to natural law thought" (Mannheim 1953: 116). Oakeshott contends that a belief "in a natural law to be gathered from human experience" is not entailed by "a disposition to be conservative in politics" (Oakeshott 1962c: 183).

Clearly there are genuine differences here among conservatives. But for the purposes of discussing political freedom, these differences can be resolved by noting the different senses in which conservatives can and cannot accept natural rights and natural law.

For example, Burke clearly rejected the claim that there are natural rights in the sense that the French Revolutionaries proclaimed them. Natural rights understood as the French did are independent of the society, its history, and character. They are also, quite frequently, presented as independent of any duties that an individual owes society. Such rights do not exist, Burke maintains (Burke 1973: 44). The problem is that those who defend natural rights (in this sense) and link them to freedom violate the above views concerning concrete studies. They violate conservative views since they hold that such rights are independent of particular political and historical orders. Further, anyone who claims that natural rights attach to humans simply *qua* human, not to this or that person who is a member of this or that class or nation which is owed various obligations, engages in abstraction at its zenith. Finally, exactly the same criticism is applicable to natural law. Thus, those like Mannheim who deny that conservatives can accept natural laws which are transcendent and universal would seem to be correct. Natural law is abstractly viewed if separated from the customs and traditions of each society.

Contrariwise, if one can speak of natural rights as those rights which citizens have in light of and because of the nature of the society in which they live, then Burke accepts natural rights. Similarly, if natural laws are viewed as embodied or immanent within each society, then the preceding criticism would not be appropriate.[28] But to defend natural rights or natural law in this sense is simply to defend the historic rights (and laws) of Englishmen (Hart 1967: 224). Thus, Kirk makes Burke seem opposed only to abstract natural rights, not natural rights themselves. Natural rights are abstract when they are *not* embedded in some custom and cannot be said to be in accord with God's law or will. Accordingly, conservatives think that natural law can only be known insofar as it is embodied in particular societies. We cannot simply appeal to the natural light of reason.

Secondly, conservatives also object that when natural rights are seen as independent of prescription, custom, and tradition, they become dangerous. Burke's argument is that no government is secure against such natural rights or rights of men:

> Against these [the rights of men] there can be no prescription; against these no agreement is binding; these admit no temperament, and no compromise . . . Against these their rights of men let no government look for security in the length of its continuance, or in the justice and lenity of its administration.

> (Burke 1973: 71)

His point is that the relations which define a human society require a general acceptance, an historical consensus. However, if one accepts the abstract doctrine of the rights of man and applies this to a society, such acceptance or historical consensus is worthless; it collapses to be replaced by a harmony between the forms of state and the abstract rights of man. But on this basis no state is secure.

For example, if natural laws are thought to take the form of deductive principles which are independent of each society and from which various conclusions concerning freedom can (supposedly) be deduced, then the most radical conclusions can be drawn. Such conclusions will not be restrained by the historical experience found in each society. Thus, conservatives must reject such a view of natural laws as dangerous to the security of a stable society. If, however, we recognize the role of prescription and convention in defining natural laws (Ibid.: 72) the security of the state may be protected.

Thus, conservatives must reject the view that there are natural rights in the common liberal sense, since for liberals natural rights exclude prescription, temperament, and consensus (Ibid.: 71). On the other hand, when these rights come embedded in customs, traditions, and social forms, conservatives can accept them. To do so, however, modifies not only the independence of these rights but also the liberal view that they attach simply to individuals.

VIII THE LIMITATIONS OF CONSERVATIVE FREEDOM

Can the conservative appeal to a natural moral order, to natural rights and natural law (as above understood), solve the problem of identifying the rights which constitute political freedom? It can, given two conditions. First, as we have seen, such natural rights and laws must be viewed as embedded in a society's customs and traditions. Secondly, we must be able to identify the natural rights or laws underlying these customs and traditions.

Now many conservatives contend that the natural rights which ultimately define political freedom are those willed by God. Conservatism and political freedom then have a theological basis. Burke held that first principles in the moral sphere come to us through revelation and intuition (Kirk 1986: 26). This is one of the reasons that conservatism and religion have been traditionally closely connected. We can know, then, which natural rights we have only by knowing God's will (Tocqueville 1969: 47). But how are we to know God's mind and will?

Conservatives answer: "Through the prejudices and traditions which millennia of human experience with divine means and judgments have implanted in the mind of the species" (Kirk 1986: 29). Indeed, unless conservatives simply relied on revelation or divine inspiration, they must pick out those natural rights and laws which come down to us through prescription. This is their realism, their practical nature. The importance of prescription, then, is unique and crucial to conservative views (Kirk 1986: 9).

On the other hand, since God's will comes embodied in our customs and inheritances, other conservatives may simply emphasize customs and traditions. In effect, they short-circuit the appeal to God. Thus, Oakeshott, for instance, though he is reluctant to speak about religion does speak of faith in one's tradition (Oakeshott 1962a: 54). It is in this sense that Burke claims that the rights Englishmen do have are founded on an (implicit) contract going back to the Glorious Revolution.[29] It is in this historical, customary sense that conservatives such as Oakeshott might accept natural rights. Thus, Kirk speaks of our rights being established through usage and custom (Kirk 1964: 23).

But then, quite obviously, we face a situation quite the same as we faced initially with customs and traditions. That is, if our only access to natural rights or natural law is through the customs and traditions of our society, we are back at the problem with which we began.

Consequently, conservative freedom faces a major problem. It takes the form of a vicious circle. To know which customs define political freedom we must look to natural rights or natural law (and possibly God's will). But to be able to identify these, we must look (at least ultimately) to customs and traditions. Since conservatives cannot appeal to "the light of reason", as liberals have, and seem to have no other outlets, there is an unavoidable tension or contradiction within conservatism.

Conservatives are aware of this criticism. Oakeshott, for example, simply maintains that there are no certain guides here (Oakeshott 1962b: 135–6). Instead, we must simply pursue the intimations of our societies. By this Oakeshott refers to the actual political activity in "hereditary, cooperative groups, many of them of ancient lineage, all of them aware of a past, a present, and a future, which we call 'states' " (Oakeshott 1962b: 133). Further, Oakeshott responds that to ask for general principles which definitely tell us what a society intimates, what we ought to do, is to ask for what is not possible. He denies that "in politics there is, what certainly exists nowhere else, a mistake-proof manner of deciding what should be done" (Ibid.: 136). As with other areas of life (science, cookery), we must use our judgment.

Similarly, Ortega y Gasset suggests that the problem is one of "invention" (Ortega y Gasset 1946: 47). Each nation must "invent" for itself its own political forms of freedom. His suggestion is interesting in that there are no rules for invention; what appears depends on the circumstances and the genius (the intuitions and feelings) of the inventor. Further, it allows that the various traditions, customs, and institutions of a society must be "recreated" in and by each individual in that society (Casey 1978: 98).

Nevertheless, these responses do not answer the problem.[30] They simply acknowledge it. In fact, there seem to be two closely related "resolutions" which conservatives adopt. On the one hand, the problem of political freedom is seen ultimately to be one of moral prudence and natural feeling (Kirk 1986: 9). But then what are these? It is far too abstract to say that prudence is "the means by which certain universal moral principles are translated into practical norms of conduct that allow men to deal with the circumstantial nature of their world" and thus choose which traditions to defend and which to modify (Harbour 1982: 93). To introduce abstract standards of prudence can hardly be a conservative solution. Instead, their solution appears to be that since prudence is gained only through experience, training, etc. we must turn to the wise person, the experienced statesman. Kirk mentions that, in the application of the general principles and institutions, we have inherited "the exercise of right reason by the leaders of . . . society" (Kirk 1964: 31). Burke's model of a statesman fits here.

But this is simply an appeal to authority. Further, how are we to know who are the wise statesmen? If they are the ones who defend the appropriate traditions, how do they know which is which? These questions are not simply an exercise in nitpicking. The danger is that this view easily leads to the imposition of class interests and the masquerading of private purposes under the guise of social concern. Of course, for conservatives, society is naturally class divided. For them, the imposition of class interests is not an objection. However, if any interest a class proclaims is one of its interests and those of society as well, then there seems ample room for oppression.

On the other hand, since there is no other standard than what some people or classes proclaim, conservatives lack objective justifiable grounds for their views. They point to the importance of personal ties, authority, tradition, and customs. But this is not enough. It may be granted that these have been treated inadequately both by liberals and radicals. But simply an appeal to them will not do. Thus, since the authorities themselves have no other standards by which to pick out political freedom, conservative political freedom ultimately simply collapses into a kind of natural conservatism, i.e. a psychological attitude which merely resists change.[31] We can, accordingly, understand the *ad hoc* nature of conservatism with its ever-present tendency to rely on authorities such as God or the wise statesman, or simply to defend the status quo.

Several observations are relevant. First, the preceding conservative views derive from (we have seen) a critique of theoretical reason as the sole basis of action and political knowledge. Conservatives hold that the narrow rationality, called "Understanding," is unable "of itself [to] satisfy human needs" (Kirk 1986: 8). Unbound by the past, prescription or authority, such reason is both innovative and dangerous. It also could not be the basis of morality or of the purposes and meaning we find in society (Ibid.: 30,31) – only divine providence will work here.[32] The ability of human reason to change and redirect the forms that the moral order has developed over the centuries is distinctly limited.

This is not to say that conservative freedom is opposed to reason, but that it believes individual reason to be distinctly limited. Thus, Burke claimed that "the individual is foolish, but the species is wise" (cf. Kirk 1964: 27; Burke 1973: 100f). Instead, reason must be found within the social forms which society has developed in cautious experiments over the centuries. Reason and knowledge are imbedded in instinct, custom, etc. (Kirk 1986: 38). These are forms of practical reason on which we can and must rely.

Now what seems to be correct here is that individuals do "naturally" view that which has been handed down as having some (rational) authority over them. Further, this may not be bad. Conservatives are right to remind us that our sense of identity and that of society as well are tied up with these practical and social forms of activity. Liberals and radicals have given far too little attention to these aspects of society. However, it is one thing to note this point, it is another to say that it can provide a basis for a legitimate and justified view of freedom. It cannot.

Of particular concern are the significant problems with this view in a quickly changing world. By its nature, the appeal to customs and traditions is an appeal to forms of behavior which (supposedly) have been suited to earlier times. Unless one assumes that such forms of behavior will always be appropriate there is no guarantee that they will be suited to the rapidly changing circumstances we face. Of course, conservatives allow that society must change. But their appeal to the importance of prudence, natural feeling, and the wisdom of the statesmen does not provide guidance for, so much as resistance to, change. They are calculated as a defense of the status quo.

The problem is that such views may be dinosaur-like in their abilities to react to importantly changed conditions in society. They may reach out with racism, authoritarianism, and blind defense of the status quo. And in their lack of responsiveness, they may allow exactly those pressures to build which undermine the very customs and traditions conservatives seek to defend. At best this approach recognizes important changes after they have occurred and then gives its blessings.

For example, Oakeshott's response to the question of the legal status of women is that

the only cogent reason to be advanced for the technical "enfran-
chisement" of women was that in all or most other important
respects they had already been enfranchised. Arguments drawn
from abstract natural right, from "justice", or from some general
concept of feminine personality, must be regarded as either
irrelevant, or as unfortunately disguised forms of the one valid
argument; namely, that there was an incoherence in the arrangements of the society which pressed convincingly for remedy.

(Oakeshott 1962b: 124)[33]

But this is, surely, a strange argument. It gives no reason or
justification for those, in the early days of the women's liberation
movement, who worked for securing women the right to vote or to
own property. All such efforts, on this conservative explanation, must
remain unjustified, not cogent, until there is a sufficient incoherence
(and what is this?) in the arrangements in society. In the end, such
incoherence would seem simply to be that sufficient powers are
arranged against the old order such that either it must change or
collapse. Indeed, this way of proceeding would seem to justify far
more than conservatives would ordinarily wish to allow. For what
are they to say about incoherences which develop in a society for
revolutionary or radical proposals? Conservatives must oppose these,
but would not seem to be able to do so on the reasoning Oakeshott
has given us.

It may be granted to the conservative that even "if technology is
marching ahead with seven-league boots . . . [the] basic institutions,
or . . . the primary social values, are [not] changing at the same rate"
(Wilson 1941: 43). Still, even in the twentieth century conservatives
have rejected alteration of the traditional roles of women in religion,
education and politics, and have "long opposed voting rights (and
economic too) for women on the ground that their presence on the
hustings would at once defeminize them and feminize the roles and
issues of politics" (Nisbet 1986: 50). Such a view of political freedom is
simply sadly out of touch with the changing conditions of society. The
"practical reason" which conservatives have trumpeted has failed them.

Finally, the preceding indicates how, for conservatives, political
freedom is derivative from a state of affairs which is appropriately
ordered, virtuous, and law-abiding. Freedom is not the precondi-
tion, but the consequence of an accepted social arrangement
(Scruton 1980: 19).

It is for this reason that Burke and other conservatives are not
ultimately interested in liberty *per se*, but in the order, harmony, the

peace and happiness of society. Conservatives are more concerned
with tranquillity as man's social goal (Hart 1967: 237–8). "To
the conservative mind . . . the object of understanding and policy
is again to reach social order and coherence" (Wilson 1941: 43).
This may be an important psychological and human need, but it
may also impose unacceptable moral and political costs. It manifests
itself in the conservative reluctance to confront, let alone admit,
various problems within society. Thus the conservative view may
require the forces of (personal and social) repression rather than
expression. As such, conservatives look not only to the past for
their view of freedom, but they also look past freedom to virtue,
order, and the law. This involves a legitimate and distinct concept of
freedom, but it is also one which, conjoined with other conservative
views, is unable to answer questions central to the nature of the
order which lies at the basis of the conservative view of political
freedom.[34]

IX CONCLUSION

Three points mark out conservative political freedom as unique.
First, it cannot be rendered by an abstract principle or definition
of freedom. Conservatives are severely critical of abstractionism and
exaggerated accounts of reason. Secondly, conservative freedom does
not hold universally in any substantive sense. As such, it is a formal
view, one which takes its content from the customs and tradition of
each particular society. Thirdly, conservative freedom does not center
on the individual, so much as the group (the community, society, or
nation). Even though all rights are the rights of individuals, only the
group has a sufficient historical continuity which can form the basis for
rights, duties and laws. The emphasis in such groups is on reciprocal
relations involving both duties and rights (Kirk 1951: 448). Only this
approach, conservatives claim, avoids disconnecting the generations
of men "into the dust and powder of individuality" (Babbitt 1924:
99).

One advantage of the present account is that it explains several
phenomena associated with conservative views on freedom. First,
individuals who identify themselves as conservatives give different,
though related, accounts of their views on freedom. Some emphasize
the connection of freedom to rights (Burke, Oakeshott), others
point to virtue (Montesquieu, Tocqueville, Adams), and yet others
responsible choice (Drucker). If conservative freedom is a formal
notion, equivalent to various rights distributing power and defined by

the customs and traditions of each particular society, one can imagine how it receives these different interpretations.

Secondly, this account explains why the primary proponents of conservative freedom have been politicians and practical individuals: Burke, Lord Cecil, Disraeli, Churchill, etc. Contrariwise, "recognized" philosophers seem to have played a fairly small role in the history and development of conservatism as an explicit view.

Thirdly, if conservatism ultimately collapses into a natural (conservative) attitude which distrusts change and what is new, then we can appreciate how difficult it would be to argue such a person out of his or her conservative views. This would be, however, a psychological explanation of the interminable debates noted in Chapter 1.

Finally, the preceding account implies that the dispute between those who have been called "traditional conservatives" and "libertarian conservatives" is actually much deeper than is often thought.[35] Both kinds of conservatives have quite generally been regarded as holding that freedom is simply the lack of constraint.[36] The difference between conservatives has then been said to be that traditional conservatives temper such freedom with virtue and order, while libertarian conservatives emphasize freedom, believing virtue and order to be secondarily important. This interpretation is wholly misleading if the argument of this chapter is correct. Traditional conservatives actually hold a rather different concept of freedom than the negative (or liberal) concept attributed to them. According to the view of conservative freedom identified here, a society, sensitive to its traditions, may not extend rights to people to engage in pornography, irresponsible publications, or homosexuality, without endangering freedom. Indeed, control of such behaviors may even enhance freedom. On the other hand, it also follows that libertarian conservatives are more libertarian or liberal than conservative. The theoretical gulf between them cannot be papered over by mutual agreement on particular concrete measures.

Nevertheless, the conservative model of freedom has significant limitations. It can not offer theoretical means for distinguishing among the customs and traditions which form the basis of political freedom. Conservative freedom presupposes a common and shared history, a community with known places in it, common views as to natural moral laws – items severely jeopardized by modern life. Its virtues are that it points to historical and experiential factors which liberals and radicals have forgotten or denied but which play an important role in many people's lives. Conservatives may overemphasize the importance of the past, but surely they are correct that the past cannot be avoided.

The idea of wiping the slate clean, the Lockean belief that we begin with a *tabula rasa*, is dangerously mistaken.

Thus, though conservatism remains a permanent and ineradicable part of the human condition, we can only see it as a reaction to, instead of part of an answer to, our problems. Conservatism is a counterbalance, a weight. It does not itself provide an acceptable view of political freedom. At most it usefully reminds us to step carefully.

3 Liberal freedom

Good fences make good neighbours.

(Frost 1955: 33)

I INTRODUCTION

The heart and the life blood of liberal freedom is the view that people are free only when they are not subject to constraint by others.[1] Everything else is elaboration, explanation, or justification. As Locke put it: "For liberty is to be free from restraint and violence from others" (Locke 1982: Sect. 57).[2]

Liberal freedom is the open road, the restrained hand of government, and the non-interference of others. Contrariwise, if people are stopped or diverted in what they are doing by someone else, if their efforts are made more difficult, if the range of their choices or alternatives is made less extensive, they are less free.

However, inasmuch as humans must live amongst others and the institutions they create, restraints on certain forms of behavior will be necessary. Thus, if people are to be politically free, we must secure for each individual a certain private area within which he or she will be exempt from political constraint. We must also reduce as much as possible the constraints, in other public areas, which must be imposed on individuals. Finally, since freedom is one value among others, the extent of freedom in a liberal society will depend upon what other values society also wishes to realize. For example, to achieve greater security or justice it may be necessary to reduce freedom by imposing greater constraints on individuals.

This view seems so simple and obvious that it is easy to forget that it arose during a particular historical period and is only one of a number of other meanings attributed to "freedom." Its familiarity makes it seem almost a truism. But it is far from that. In fact, liberal freedom is not only historically specific, it is also a very complicated view, loaded with political and metaphysical assumptions. It is not the simple, neutral, or ahistorical view which it is often taken to be.

The strengths of liberal freedom lie in its concern for the protection of the individual from the forces of government and society. This has involved identifying a social sphere of life separate from the political, opposing the constraining forces which other people and institutions may impose on individuals, and characterizing a private realm of freedom in which political power and coercion may not be legitimately used against individuals. In a world given to violence and domination, the historical importance of liberal freedom must not be underestimated.

However, liberalism's strengths are connected with important weaknesses. In seeking to identify the forces that constrain individuals, liberal freedom has painted a picture of society in which other people, as well as our social and political institutions, are constant sources of threat. It has fostered the separation and isolation of individuals rather than their union. By defining the realm of freedom as a realm of privacy, it has fostered a minimalist view of the individual self. By portraying political freedom as a neutral, non-political condition in which people are, in essence, free from politics, liberal freedom has left the determination of the political realm open to forms of government which need not acknowledge the political nature of humans.[3] These weaknesses are connected with what has been called the crisis of liberalism. At the center of this crisis is the following irony: the very view that seeks to protect individuals invokes other views which undercut and threaten them. As such, there is a fundamental tension or contradiction at the heart of liberal freedom. By exploring these contrasting features of liberal freedom, we can better understand not only liberal freedom but also why liberalism faces such a crisis. However, before we can do either, we must elaborate on the model of liberal freedom.[4] In doing so I will not follow the endless details with which liberals have occupied themselves in debating amongst themselves over freedom. Far more important are the shared views and assumptions which distinguish their (more or less) common views from those of others. The upshot of exploring this model of freedom is the need for some post-liberal view.

II FREEDOM AS THE LACK OF CONSTRAINT

There are two parts to the liberal model of freedom. The first focuses on the meaning of "freedom" as "lack of constraint." How is "lack of constraint" to be interpreted? Answers to this question tell us what "freedom" itself is, what a person who was "perfectly free" would enjoy. It is the core notion around which liberals circulate. As such, it sets the tone and direction of liberal accounts.

However, since humans cannot in fact live together without constraints being imposed on some individuals, the second part of liberal freedom asks when other individuals and/or the state may impose constraints. It is at this point that other values that liberals have come into play. Freedom then is weighed off against justice, security, happiness, etc.

Debate over these two parts of freedom has dominated liberal discussions of freedom. In various forms these discussions are found in Locke's *Second Treatise*, Mill's *On Liberty*, and Berlin's "Two Concepts of Liberty." Though they are often presented by liberals as "the" questions of political philosophy, they are, in fact, only "the" questions of *liberal* political philosophy.

To claim that freedom is lack of constraint is to say very little. It is a slogan roughly comparable to what one might find in a fortune cookie. It does not tell us what a constraint is or the manner in which it renders a person unfree. In fact, there is no simple or single answer which liberals have given to the question regarding the nature of constraints. This should not be surprising. There have been a number of stages in the liberal attempt to characterize the constraint whose presence results in unfreedom. We can, however, construct an account of constraint for our model of liberal freedom which captures its historical and philosophical development.

Inasmuch as freedom is highly valued by liberals, it is not surprising that some liberals would suggest that constraints, freedom, and morality are bound up together. Accordingly, Locke characterizes constraints and freedom in terms of doing what one wants within the law of nature:

> But freedom is . . . to dispose, and order, freely as he lists, his person, actions, possessions, and his whole property, within the allowance of those laws under which he is; and therein not to be subject to the arbitrary will of another, but freely follow his own.
>
> (Locke 1982: Sect. 57)

Constraints, then, will be those things which force a person to do something other than he or she desires, but will not include those preventions or impediments which accord with the law of nature.[5] For Locke held that "law, in its true notion, is not so much the limitation as the direction of a free and intelligent agent to his proper interest, and prescribes no farther than is for the general good of those under that law" (Locke 1982: Sect. 57).

However, proponents of this view have had difficulties identifying and interpreting the law of nature. Thus, many have thought it undesirable to link freedom to problematic doctrines of natural law. Further, liberals have come to hold that laws are themselves, however noble their ends, coercive or constraining; they are not simply rational signposts or directions. Even Locke speaks as if laws, both civil and natural, do (at times) restrain a person (Locke 1982: Sects 22, 66, 93, 129). Thirdly, Locke's view embodies an important distinction between freedom and license. When people do what is wrong, they do not act freely, but licentiously. However, liberals have also come to reject this, believing that one may freely do what is wrong. The criminal who robs a bank exercises his or her freedom in robbing the bank, even though robbing the bank is wrong. Similarly, Berlin comments that, though

> the freedom of parents or schoolmasters to determine the education of children, of employers to exploit or dismiss their workers, of slave-owners to dispose of their slaves, of the torturer to inflict pain on his victims – may, in many cases be whole undesirable, and should in any sane or decent society be curtailed or suppressed, [this] does not render them genuine freedoms any the less.
>
> (Berlin 1969: lvi–lvii)

Finally, it has been argued that paradoxical results follow from understanding "freedom" in terms of moral rules or laws. For example, if a person is not rendered unfree when he or she is punished for violating a basic moral law, then the person who is thrown in jail cannot be said to be unfree. This, however, has seemed the height of absurdity to liberals. Hence, they have abandoned moral accounts of the nature of "freedom" and "constraint."

Accordingly, liberals have generally sought to characterize freedom in a descriptive or factual manner, leaving value or moral judgments about its worth as separate questions. As such, liberals have sought to define constraints (and freedom) independently of morality. This means that freedom may be something valuable in many instances, but that in its very nature values and morality need not be mentioned. As such, liberals "demoralize" or "neutralize" freedom.

Some liberals (including Mill and Berlin) have thought that an account of constraint (and freedom) could be derived by simply dropping the moral dimension of Locke's view. Thus, they suggested that freedom simply consists in doing what one wants: "For liberty consists in doing what one desires" (Mill 1956: 117). Constraints, on this view, are obstacles to doing what one desires.

The advantage of this view is that people can agree on the nature of freedom, independently of their moral views or personal values. We would merely have to know what each person did, or did not, desire. The only question then would be how much freedom various people desired or how a certain amount of freedom was to be weighed against other values. Freedom might then be valued instrumentally for what people can do with it, as well as intrinsically for its own sake (Berlin 1969: 128).

But this view has also been shown to have significant problems. Berlin argues that it allows that a person might remove constraints and hence gain freedom simply by reducing one's wants (Ibid.: xxxviii). Surely this is not absurd in some instances. A person whose wants are extravagant will experience many greater obstacles and, thus, unfreedom. It might be important for him or her to have more modest wants. On the other hand, we are seeking here the nature of freedom. Liberals have thought that it would be absurd to be committed to a view that allowed that the person who succeeded in eliminating almost all his or her wants would be most free simply because he or she faced fewer obstacles.

Further, this proposal does not take account of the fact that one's wants may themselves be the result of constraint. J. S. Mill eloquently depicts how the desires of women have been shaped through forces in the societies of which they are members. This simple view of freedom and constraint cannot account for more subtle forms of constraint and unfreedom.

Thus, liberal freedom is not best characterized by either the moralized account of constraint – which is too narrow and problematic – or by some simple version of freedom and constraint defined in terms of people's wants.

Instead, liberal freedom is most plausibly defined by an account of constraint in terms of the options or alternatives which a person might choose. When obstacles are raised to choosing such alternatives, a person's freedom is constrained. This is the view to which Berlin has come: "the sense of freedom . . . entails not simply the absence of frustration . . . but the absence of obstacles to possible choices and activities" (Ibid.: xxxix:). My freedom is lessened when my actual and possible choices are constrained (xl).

Freedom as the lack of constraint is to be defined, then, by reference to options, not to actions (cf. Ibid.: 122), wants (Mill 1956: 117), or natural law (Locke 1982). As such, liberal freedom applies uniquely to humans. Thus, liberals have agreed with Locke and rejected the Hobbesian view that constraints are simply an impediment to motion. Though this is an intelligible sense of "freedom" – we do speak of animals being "born free" and "freely falling bodies" in space – this sense is much too broad for individual freedom. Though there are limits to the objects of possible choice (for example, walking on the sun), such objects of choice are logically restricted or restricted by the physical constitution of humans. They are not morally restricted as Locke held. Further, liberal freedom simply requires that objects of choice not be constrained; freedom does not require that opportunities and objects of choice be provided. As such, liberal freedom remains a negative freedom. It is this view of freedom which is appropriate for our model of liberal freedom.

III   RESPONSIBILITY, LAWS, AND VALUES

However minimal an account of constraint and freedom the preceding presents, it already embodies three other views that are noteworthy. To begin with, when freedom and constraint are so conceived, liberal freedom assumes that individuals have options, can make choices, and act. However, since those persons are free whose options are not constrained, liberal freedom is vastly different from courage, benevolence, honesty, or fidelity. It does not necessarily involve any character traits. Indeed, the person who merely sits still and vegetates may be equally as free as the person who actively participates in understanding and defending him or herself and others from violations of their rights and opportunities to act (cf. Berlin 1969: xlii). Thus, liberal freedom is not an achievement or success term. It is simply a question of the lack of constraints on one's options. Which moral or evaluative qualities characterize a person depends on what that person does with his or her freedom.

It follows that any traits or dispositions which people are urged to develop on behalf of freedom, e.g. "eternal vigilance" or personal responsibility for one's choices and actions, have only a purely instrumental and contingent relationship to their freedom. In short, freedom and responsibility are two very different things. This is one reason that freedom can be abused. Accordingly, responsibility must be imposed on people from outside freedom. This is not to say that individuals cannot impose responsibility on themselves. However, to the extent that they do so, they do not do so *qua* person who enjoys freedom as such.

Thus, in their search for a descriptive view of freedom, liberals have undone the knot which many still think connects freedom and responsibility, as well as freedom and character. It is not by accident that Robinson Crusoe is often mentioned by liberals as the ideally free person, one without responsibilities and any necessary connection with other individuals.

Secondly, there is also in liberal freedom a fundamental opposition between freedom and law (both legal and moral). As we have seen, whenever law is imposed there is a loss of freedom.[6] Locke's early view on the connection between law and freedom is said to be naive. At best it is part of Locke's conservatism. Further, since liberals highly value freedom any attempt to impose coercion, laws, or simply constraint on an individual requires justification for, by definition, they lessen freedom. Similarly, whenever the government regulates a business or a populace, that business or populace suffers unfreedom.

It is not surprising, then, that liberals have problems, *qua* advocates of freedom, with demands for "law and order," discipline, and regulations. Inasmuch as liberty is simply the lack of constraint and valued quite highly, they are less willing to use coercion or constraint than those, e.g. conservatives, whose views of freedom permit or require constraint. Further, inasmuch as rational justification has come, increasingly, to be viewed as ultimately subjective, liberals have been reluctant to impose what seem simply to be their own views on others (or, contrariwise, to have the views of others imposed on them).[7] Thus, they hesitate to impose discipline or restrictions on children as well as on other adults, even though they may need them to live harmoniously together. Since "all restraint, *qua* restraint is an evil" (Mill 1956: 116) there is always a prima-facie objection to constraint (Berlin 1969: 128).

It might be argued that such prima-facie objections can easily be handled by liberals. They merely need to argue that imposing certain constraints will minimize constraints overall, and hence maximize freedom. Though liberals do take this tack, this response does not solve the present problem.

First, we are considering here the liberal concept of freedom, not the balance of such freedom they are prepared to strike in relation to other values. Though they often do so, liberals cannot consistently use "freedom" to refer to that situation which minimizes constraints in a balance with other values. The reason is that this imports a different sense of "freedom" into the discussion, viz. freedom as "the minimum number of constraints compatible with an appropriate realisation of other values." Such a concept of freedom embodies values in the very definition of "freedom" and is a retreat from freedom simply as "the lack of constraint." It is because liberals value freedom simply as "the lack of constraint" that they are ever chary of imposing laws, controls, and rules – oftentimes in the face of a manifest need for such "constraints."

Secondly, since constraints are viewed as themselves undesirable, and, at best, necessary to accomplish other ends, they ever stand under the cloud of illegitimacy. As such, the liberal model of freedom creates an atmosphere within which laws, regulation, and rules are ever suspect. Even in the case of terrorists, murderers, and torturers we must take into account their loss of liberty when we decide whether to prevent them from attacking their victims. Berlin, for example, argues that preventing torturers from inflicting pain on their victims is causing them to suffer a loss of liberty (Berlin 1969: lvii).

But this also seems mistaken. Macfarlane claims that if a person stops another from "deliberately inflicting pain on a child, this interference is good in itself, quite apart from the compensating gain by the child" (Macfarlane 1966: 79). A somewhat better way to put the point would be to say that if we prevent a man from molesting a child, the constraint imposed need not be weighed against the protection afforded the child.

Berlin's view, on the contrary, assumes that torturers, murders, and molesters exercise their liberty when they torture, kill, and molest. However, "since the law or social conventions did not give [such liberty] to them, they could only have acquired it from nature" (Parekh 1983: 226). That is, his view presupposes that they have a natural liberty, one outside of society or government. Hence, society must justify its imposition of constraints on such people. But such a view is subject to serious problems. The reason is that people are not intelligible outside the social and moral relations that constitute their societies. They do not, first, enjoy a total lack of constraint, and then, secondly, have various social, moral, and legal norms imposed upon them. Surely the norms or constraints a society places upon its members should be justified. But we do not begin from some null situation in which people are not subject to any norms or constraints.

Living within constraints and being subject to limits is plausibly part of being a human. That is, various constraints, such as social norms, not only serve to define who we are but also may protect us from anomie (Arblaster 1984: 65). If this be granted, then liberal freedom is at war with the human condition. Any liberal ideal of complete freedom assumes a perfectionist, unlimited, as well as unrealistic view of humans (cf. Stephen 1967: 80f). Thus, the justification for imposing constraints on a murderer or molester need not refer to the loss of liberty that person will suffer. The option that is closed to the murderer was not open in the first place. Consequently, freedom as the lack of constraints leads liberals to many of the unwarranted problems they have with laws, discipline, and regulation.

Thirdly, if liberal freedom is, as we have seen, the non-restriction of various alternatives and options, then to be free is not simply not to have the course of action I am presently considering not blocked, but also to have other possible courses of action not blocked. These options or alternatives need not be ones of which the person wishes to avail himself. Freedom entails, Berlin holds, "the absence of obstacles to possible choices and activities" (Berlin 1969: xxxix). Thus, Feinberg urges us to imagine a situation involving two people, Roe and Doe, in which Doe could do 1,000 things including what he most wants to do, while Roe can only do what he most wants. He contends that in this situation Doe would be the freer of the two (Feinberg 1973: 7).

This argument assumes the sharp fact/value distinction that has been attributed above to liberal freedom. Accordingly we can enlarge freedom by expanding the alternatives, choices, or options that people have, without appealing to morality or values. In effect, this view portrays individual freedom as the situation sought by the ultimate consumer – the person who demands countless alternatives, even though he or she may never take them up and the alternatives are themselves minimally distinguishable.

The difficulty with this view becomes clear if one simply notes that, on the above argument, were Roe suddenly to have 2,000 things he could do including what he most wanted, we would now have to say that Doe was not the most free, but Roe was. But this is a silly exercise in empty numbers to the extent that we do not know the significance of these alternatives or options opened up to Roe. Perhaps all 1,000 "new" options consist of minimally distinguishable forms of the same product or ways of doing the same thing.

The only way that this contention can be made sensible is by invoking, explicitly or implicitly, some theory about which choices or options are valuable, rather than simply available. This means, then, that some form of value must be reintroduced into the very definition of freedom. This Locke understood, but subsequent liberals have resisted (cf. Taylor 1979; Norman 1987: 37-8).

Now it may seem that there is at least some recognition by liberals such as Berlin of this problem. For example, Berlin notes that not all doors are of equal importance (Berlin 1969: xlviii). He also says that the extent of my freedom seems to depend on . . . how important in my plan of life, given my character and circumstances, these possibilities are when compared with each other . . . [and] what value not merely the agent, but the general sentiment of the society in which he lives, puts on the various possibilities.

(Ibid.: 130 fn)

Hence, he allows that some value questions enter into determining the extent of one's liberty. However, this suggestion remains undeveloped by Berlin. More importantly, it does not answer the above problem.

As stated, Berlin's comments imply no more than a descriptive account of the values that oneself and others in society actually hold. It does not imply that the values which enter into judgments of freedom must be justified or rational. Nor does it say that the determination of the nature of free actions or constraints is bound up with "a principle of evaluating their worth or significance for human well-being" (J. Gray 1980: 515). It simply allows that if television watching is terribly important to John, something he and others value, then if the alternatives for television watching are not closed, John remains more free than otherwise. Similarly, supposing that child abuse were a prime value for John, he would be freer to the extent that his options to engage in child abuse were not constrained. It provides, at most, for a means of picking out alternatives which is relative to each person's values. But this will not solve the above problem, since though a person may hardly value a particular alternative, its loss to him may greatly reduce his freedom (cf. Ibid.: 516). Finally, if Berlin holds that what freedom is depends in part on "the general sentiment of the society" in which one lives, this would raise the possibility, which he attacks under the notion of positive freedom, of society proclaiming that a certain alternative was (or was not) terribly valuable and thereby forcing one to be free.

As such, Berlin's comments do not suggest a satisfactory connection between freedom and morality or values. If they did – indeed, if liberals pursued this normative or evaluative suggestion – their view of freedom could not simply remain descriptive and non-moral, but would invoke various value and moral premises at the outset. This would herald a new model of freedom, one which goes beyond the current liberal model. And yet it would seem that just this is needed to frame an acceptable view of freedom.

The question here, it must be emphasized, is not whether freedom should be valued more or less highly than other values. It is whether value or moral judgments must be part of the very nature of freedom.

Liberals reject this. Their rejection has led to the above problems. It is an area of problems which liberals have not resolved and which stand in conflict with their attempt to see freedom as a non-mo(ral, descriptive state of affairs.

What ties these problems together is the wholly individualistic bias of liberal freedom. Freedom as the absence of constraint to actual and possible choices focuses upon the individual, not as a social or political being, but as a choosing and acting being. The characterization of the concept of liberal freedom involves no reference to society at all. Reference to the public or political realm is not required. As such, the core notion of liberal freedom is private, non-political, and non-moral. Any necessary connections with other individuals are excluded. It is as if freedom were sought as a hedge against other individuals and society since they are viewed with suspicion. It is not surprising, then, that Feinberg defends this view of freedom because "we can rarely foresee with certainty the course of changes either in ourselves or in our circumstance, and so we feel much *safer* if there are genuine alternatives available, even though we have no present use for them" (Feinberg 1973: 6; emphasis added). Freedom is a hedge, on this view, against uncertainty and insecurity in society. Freedom protects what we may want or have to do at some other time. Liberal freedom thus assumes an individual at odds with, and threatened by, society.

IV IMPEDIMENTS, INTENTIONS, AND IMPERSONAL CONSTRAINTS

Once constraints and freedom are separated from moral and value considerations, and tied to possible options or alternatives rather than simply motions, wants, or even action, a number of other questions naturally arise which have led liberals to ever more refined and sensitive accounts of constraints, freedom, and human action. In short, liberals have come to see that those things which can close options and alternatives, and the ways and manners in which this can be done, are many and varied.

One question concerns whether constraints must block or prevent something from occurring, as some liberals have held, or whether a constraint may also "merely" hinder or impede the realization of an alternative. The former, narrower view seems overly restrictive for liberal freedom.[8] On this view, people are free even when threatened with injury because they may nevertheless do what they choose (although they will suffer the consequences). Thus, a newspaper editor threatened with imprisonment or execution remains free because he or she can in fact go ahead and print the story which has incensed the government. Workers who act out of fear of losing their job are also nevertheless free (Berlin 1969: 130).

Now of course, one may use "freedom" in this manner. Further, this use reminds us that alternative actions do remain even in the face of threats. We can refuse to take off our hat as the king parades by, even though we may be beaten. Still this use of "freedom" mocks those to whom it is applied since surely they would be freer if they were not subjected to threats or injury at all. Advocates of the narrower use seek to revise, not to express, the historical and philosophical nature of liberal freedom. They confuse at least one sense of voluntary action with liberal freedom (Ibid.: 130 fn). They transform freedom into an all or nothing affair: either the action is wholly prevented or it is not.

On the contrary, liberal freedom admits of degrees. Constraint (i.e. the non-interference with options) can be either entire or partial. Locke, Mill, and Berlin have pointed out that threats of death or torture, as well as other impediments which hinder or retard a person's activities, may also be constraints (Ibid.: 130).[9] Surely if someone threatens me or weighs me down with a burden and as a consequence I proceed more cautiously or with much greater effort, my freedom has been affected. Thus, liberal freedom holds that constraints need not simply block options or alternatives, but may also impede or hinder their realization. Clearly, this expands the number of constraints to which people may be subject.

The extent of constraints has also been expanded as a result of liberal debate over the question whether anything which constrains individual freedom must be intentionally imposed for it to interfere with one's options, or whether constraints may originate unintentionally.

For Locke the constraint which reduces freedom is primarily external, direct, and personal. Agents are constrained when they are subject to the arbitrary will of another, i.e. when they cannot freely follow their own will (Locke 1982: Sect. 57; Sect. 4). Constraint by another's will must be direct. This does not mean that a sovereign cannot have troops carry out his orders. But the constraint is directly imposed through individuals in such case as death and imprisonment. Since lack of freedom for Locke is due to one's subjection to the will of another, it would seem that such subjection or constraints must be intentional or deliberate. Similarly, since Locke thought that the state of nature was a state of "perfect freedom", even though there were surely various unintentional constraints on people in that condition, he must be said to view all freedom-reducing constraints as being intentional.

Mill's discussion of liberty focuses on when society may impose constraints on individuals, rather than on the nature of constraint. Accordingly, his discussion generally refers to intentional, rather than unintentional, constraints on individuals. Nevertheless, Mill believes that customs and traditions are constraining. To the extent that these are the unintentional results of human life, he is committed to the view that some constraint is unintentional.

Berlin has held that people lack freedom only if they are prevented from attaining their goals through the deliberate action of human beings. In short, he has identified constraint with coercion (Berlin 1969: 122). However, on reflection Berlin changed his view to hold that interference with one's goals or options need not be deliberate (Ibid.: xl). Thus, for example, if John is unintentionally locked in a room, he now argues, John's freedom is diminished just as if he had been intentionally locked in that room. The sole requirement is that such effects be alterable by human action (Ibid.: xl, xlviii). It is this broader view that constraints may be either intentional or unintentional that is part of the liberal model.

The stakes in this debate are enormous. If constraints may be unintentional, then freedom is not reduced only by coercion, since coercion implies deliberateness. This further implies that the number of constraints from which we may suffer is greatly enlarged. For example, the results of unintentional housing patterns, the design of voter districts, and the operation of the market which impoverishes certain classes but not others could all be said to be constraints which reduce the freedom of individuals. Accordingly, the defense of liberty might require that the effects of markets, housing patterns, and voting districts be modified.

Quite often the argument against unintentional constraints is carried on with these implications in mind. Some have resisted allowing that constraints may be unintentional since they feared that the actions of the market would then have to be controlled. However, this does not follow from the preceding arguments. Indeed, this risks confusing the characterization of the nature of a constraint with the question when a constraint ought or ought not to be imposed. Those who extend the notion of constraint to include unintentional constraints may still reject regulation of the market. The question they would face, however, is how to balance this constraint against other constraints. This is a question of the limits or extent of freedom, rather than the nature of freedom or constraint.

Thus, given the development of liberal views from Locke to Berlin, it seems most faithful to liberal freedom to allow that constraints may also be unintentional. Though this does not require that the actions of the market be controlled, this interpretation of constraints does bring the actions of the market, for example, within the realm of freedom-reducing or freedom-enhancing forces. The actions of the market are no longer portrayed as kinds of natural forces outside the social or political realm.

Finally, I have noted that early liberals took the paradigm case of constraint to have an external or physical nature. Thus, Locke sees constraint in the action of government as it makes "laws with penalties of death and consequently all less penalties" (Locke 1982: Sect. 2). As such, he does not view public opinion, custom, or tradition as forms of constraint. This is not to say that Locke was unaware of the existence of social forces outside the law and that the judgments of individuals in society may act to control people. He does speak, somewhat obscurely, of "the force of the community" (Ibid.: Sect. 3). Further, he acknowledges that "the law of opinion or reputation" may impose a punishment of censure and dislike which "no man escapes" (Wolin 1960: 343; cf. Locke 1959: Book II, Sect. 7–12). Nevertheless, he did not develop these ideas. For Locke individuals enjoy perfect freedom within the state of nature (a social sphere) in which we find other individuals and families, and, it must be assumed, customs, conventions, moral pressure, and traditions. This social realm was sharply distinguished from the realm of the government or state (i.e. the political) in which physical coercion and threats may be exercised by the government to restrain people and thus limit their freedom.

However, later liberals – such as Mill – have argued that the social tyranny of others which takes place in moral coercion, custom, and tradition is one of the most important constraints that people face today (Mill 1956: 7). For instance, if people express their views that homosexuality or polygamy ought to be allowed, but their neighbors and employers strongly disagree (even though the government does not), they may be constrained in their actions and lifestyles. Finding work may be more difficult; access to housing may be blocked. They may feel themselves compelled to move to other cities or countries to live (cf. ibid.: ch. 4). Thus, though early liberalism placed great emphasis on the limitation of freedom by physical constraint, it is false to maintain that it has only done this (cf. Parekh 1972: 84).

Some liberals have resisted this extension of constraint. For example, Hayek does not think that the moral opinion of the masses is coercive. He says, for instance, that "it *probably* makes for greater clarity not to represent as coercion the pressure that public approval or disapproval exerts to secure obedience to moral rules and conventions" (Hayek 1960: 146; emphasis added). But this is an extremely weak response to the Millian view. Hayek might be correct that public approval or disapproval is better not represented as coercion, if we assumed that coercion must be intentional and that public approval or disapproval was not intentionally directed at people. Still, this would not show that public approval or disapproval did not constrain people. On the other hand, any one who has experienced the constraining force of public opinion would have few doubts that it could be intentionally directed and, hence (on the above supposition), coercive.

Mill is simply much more sensitive than Hayek in recognizing that social pressure may be "more formidable than many kinds of political oppression, since, though not usually upheld by such extreme penalties, it leaves fewer means of escape, penetrating much more deeply into the details of life, and enslaving the soul itself" (Mill 1956: 7). Further, Mill's view has been dominant amongst liberals. Morality, custom, tradition, and the law are viewed as constraints on people's freedom. One is less free to the extent that he or she is constrained by any of these institutions.

The implication of the preceding expanded concept of constraint is that any narrow or restricted model of liberal freedom can no longer be defended. Once the Pandora's box of constraints is opened, the thrust and momentum of this view is not to be detoured. The burden will always be placed on the person who claims not to see an obstacle by those who claim to see the obstacle and claim that their activity is hindered, retarded, or impeded by that obstacle. Some liberals have tried to stem this tide, but they fight an overwhelming flood. The thrust of liberalism is such that if an obstacle can be humanly removed, then it will be seen as inhibiting someone's freedom if it is not removed. The upshot is an enormous extension in the number and kinds of constraints to which people are thought to be subject. The implications of this are of the first importance.

V ISOLATION, COMMUNITY, AND DEPOLITICIZATION

As the list of freedom-limiting constraints expands, people find themselves literally surrounded by constraints. Constraints may be total or partial. The customs, laws, and traditions by which people live, and by which their society is defined, are constraints. Constraints may be intentionally as well as unintentionally imposed. It is sufficient that humans can remove them. Indeed, if what is crucial is that humans may remove such constraints, then some liberals have gone even further to argue that there are natural constraints such as blindness and lameness which are also constraints on one's freedom (cf. Crocker 1980). Though this cannot presently be said to be part of the liberal model of freedom, it is arguably a plausible extension of this model.

Accordingly, the liberal concern to identify what constrains people and sets them free leads to the view that we are enveloped by constraints. It is not simply the policeman, but also a multitude of other aspects of our daily lives which constrain us. People's options or alternatives may be hindered or restricted in the most untoward ways. Thus, if freedom is very important, the world has become a terribly threatening place, ever seeking to impose itself upon us.

Consequently, to the extent that people seek to be free, this heightened sensitivity means that people are increasingly distanced from each other if they do not want to interfere or be constrained. One must be careful not to impose one's values or conceptions on others (Sandel 1982: 5). A person dare not comment on another's life, actions, or views except insofar as he or she knows that what is to be said will be agreeable, not an invasion of privacy or not too intrusive, to the other. Similarly, given this sensitivity, one must be careful to have the correct emotional reactions, e.g. we may dislike but not have anger towards others who are imprudent (Mill 1956: 96–7). However, since the difference in the effect of such reactions on others may be slight, and since people may feel interfered with in either case, the upshot of this view is that freedom implies, for the liberal, the increasing separation of one individual from another. One dare not meddle in someone else's business. I must be careful not to say certain things about the way you raise your children, about your political views, your religious views, or even your aesthetic views. Thus, we remain distant, speaking in platitudes and generalities.

Accordingly, as the kinds of coercion and constraint expand, the area within which one can be "perfectly" free shrinks. Only within a diminishing private realm, behind a fence that must be constantly enlarged, can one enjoy perfect freedom. Thus, on the liberal model of freedom, people are separated from each other more than ever before. Their isolation and alienation from each other are promoted. As a consequence the continuation or formation of many forms of community is inhibited.

In this sense, it is not only those who appeal to a positive concept of freedom, but also liberals who are involved in a retreat to an inner citadel (cf. Berlin 1969: 135). Quite ironically, liberals such as Mill have wanted people to have spirited discussions and interchanges. But the reality of their views is that the discussion is actually quite muted so as to preserve freedom. Only in this way do people escape "the tyranny of the prevailing opinion and feeling . . . the tendency of society to impose . . . its own ideas and practices . . . [and] to fetter the development and, if possible, prevent the formation of any individuality not in harmony with its ways" (Mill 1956: 7).[10]

One of the basic problems with liberal freedom is, then, not so much the attempt to define a private realm of self-regarding public actions. There are, assuredly, problems with this attempt, as we shall see below. But a more serious problem is the attempt to flee from constraint, as constraint comes to be increasingly broadly interpreted. It is an attempt, we have seen, that separates and isolates people one from another.

Two other characteristics of liberal freedom deserve mention. Freedom as the lack of constraint is defined in a manner which is indifferent to whether it is realized in modern society, ancient society, Western, or Eastern society. Similarly, liberal freedom is compatible with an aristocratic, democratic, or oligarchic society. Berlin explicitly notes that "liberty . . . is not incompatible with some kinds of autocracy . . . Freedom in this sense is not, at any rate logically, connected with democracy or self-government" (Berlin 1969: 129–30). It is false, then, to suggest that liberal thinking about freedom is primarily political (Arblaster 1984: 58, 66). It is does not require any particular society or political system.

It might be objected that those liberals who invoke rights to define freedom (a right not to be constrained) at least unwittingly link freedom to Western society. But it is one thing to develop a concept of freedom which could only be developed in Western society; it is another for that concept to be logically or conceptually linked to various primary political features of Western society. Liberal freedom does not do the latter. At most, liberal freedom presupposes a moral basis (individual rights) which has, historically, been typical of Western society. But this hardly makes liberal freedom at its heart a political view.

Accordingly, liberals assume that freedom is something which individuals can and do possess outside of society. Society and politics simply are institutions which may (or may not) foster such freedom. However, the attempt to define individual freedom prior to characterizing social or political freedom is an exercise in the myth of natural, pre-social man (cf. Parekh 1983: 225). It assumes that people may be free within a wholly "natural" setting, rather than that they derive their liberty from society. The contrary is, however, more plausibly the case: individuals are not natural but social beings. They derive their liberties from society. The question we should be asking is not what "portion" of people's pre-existing and pre-social liberty they should be asked to give up, but rather what liberties they should enjoy (Ibid.).

Secondly, surely freedom as liberals characterize it is a condition which is rarely, if ever, met. That is, if freedom is the lack of constraint, then human life is not free. Human life is lived within various constraints. This means that freedom in effect slips through the fingers of liberals as they have tried to refine it. It has gone from something which is specific and real (someone else not coercing one) to a general, abstract, and unreal situation, which might exist only in the vacuum of space. Berlin implies as much when he claims that freedom is the "conception of a field (ideally) without obstacles, a vacuum in which nothing obstructs me" (Berlin 1969: 144).

But it is nonsensical to attempt to guide our lives by such a concept. As soon as there are other people, there will be interferences and constraints imposed on one by others. Liberal freedom ensures our frustration with other people. The point here is not, as Berlin suggests, that the attempt to live according to complete lack of constraint (an unlimited liberal freedom) would bring "social chaos or . . . the liberties of the weak would be suppressed by the strong" (Ibid.: 123), but rather that the idea at the core of liberal freedom is wholly unrealistic. Berlin gropes towards some analogy between freedom and the vacuum of interstellar space. However, this ideal of freedom is not merely never realized, as space is not simply empty, but impossible.

This suggests that liberal freedom generates a permanent tension. Those who seek it as a basic value face a self-induced frustration. They must always chafe at their constraints. They can never be satisfied but must always seek more alternatives simply to have more alternatives. "Even if there is no chance that our desires will ever change, it is reassuring to know that there are always alternatives, just in case" (Feinberg 1973: 6). Such people live according to a dangerous, negative ideology, opposed to part of the human condition. There is, or should be, no a priori reason why being subject to one more constraint, than some other situation without that constraint, is less desirable, even from the standpoint of freedom. Instead, we must know what is the nature of such a constraint, what role it plays in our lives, and what ends it fosters.

Then we can begin to assess the relation of such a constraint and freedom.

The upshot, then, of the preceding sections is that there are serious problems with the notion of liberal freedom as the absence of constraints to possible choices and activities. The next several sections take a different tack. Assuming that freedom is the absence of constraint, liberals must say which constraints will be excluded and which permitted in a society. This means that they must say what forms such freedom will take. This is not to look to the nature of constraint, but to the justified limits on the lack of constraint. Hence, we must ask liberals on which occasions may constraints (unfreedom) be justified. This shift of perspective requires that we consider the values according to which liberals impose or remove constraints so that there will be as much freedom as possible in a society.

VI POLITICAL FREEDOM AND FENCES

If there is an image which liberals share with regard to political freedom, it is one of a fence. Locke introduced this image in his *Second Treatise* where he spoke of freedom as a fence for our preservation (Locke 1982: Sect. 17). Political freedom serves as a fence to protect the individual from the constraint of others. Thus, for liberals freedom implies not simply the lack of constraint by other individuals and/or by the state, but also the necessary existence of boundaries, frontiers, barriers, or fences between individuals which ensure this lack of constraint. In short, their supposed realism leads them to claim that without fences there will not be fields of freedom. Hence, "good fences make good neighbours."

Accordingly, for freedom to be a reality, constraints have to be imposed on some so that others may be free. This requires the creation of a political state which, through its own system of constraints and coercion, will maintain order (i.e. control the constraints that some people might otherwise impose on others) and dispense justice. Thus, the political realm is an artificial construction whereby individual freedom may be protected and preserved – at least to the extent that it is compatible with other important values. Political freedom is that system of constraints which promotes individual freedom more so than some other set of constraints. It is the best of a bad situation.

It is not surprising, then, that liberals affirm that constraints are an important and desirable part of social and political life. Mill put it this way: "All that makes existence valuable to anyone depends on the enforcement of restraints upon the actions of other people"

(Mill 1956: 8). Thus, paradoxically perhaps, liberals can not be wholly opposed to constraints. Though constraints reduce freedom they are important and needed to protect freedom. Indeed, such restraints are more than necessary evils for Mill – they can play a positive role in individual development (Gildin 1964: 289).[11]

Several questions arise: first, what are the limits of individual freedom? That is, when should we place constraints on a person's freedom and when may we not? Secondly, what is the nature of the boundaries or fences beyond which we ought not to impose constraints? How high or dense should they be? Finally, how are these limits, boundaries and fences to be determined? These are matters of some disagreement among liberals.

The standard liberal answer to the first question is that individuals can only be restrained when they harm others.[12] Locke appeals to a law of nature which says that "no one ought to harm another in his life, health, liberty or possessions" (Locke 1982: Sect. 6). This law consists of various rights which describe an area within which the government and others may not come.

Mill appeals to his self-protection (or harm) principle which holds that "the sole end for which mankind are warranted, individually or collectively, in interfering with the liberty of action of any of their number is self-protection" (Mill 1956: 13). Sounding like Locke, he continues: "the only purpose for which power can be rightfully exercised over any member of a civilized community, against his will, is to prevent harm to others" (Ibid.). Unlike Locke, he tells us that this principle is founded upon utilitarianism. Nevertheless, Mill also speaks about liberty in terms of rights. Conduct may be prevented coercively that injures "the interests of one another, or rather certain interests which, either by express legal provision or by tacit understanding, ought to be considered as rights" (Ibid.: 91; cf. 95; ch. 4). Further, the area circumscribed is prohibited not simply to forcible entry by the government and other individual, but also to their entry through coercive measures of personal opinion, custom, and tradition.

Finally, Berlin speaks more simply and vaguely of "frontiers being defined in terms of rules so long and widely accepted that their observance has entered into the very conception of what it is to be a normal human being" (Berlin 1969: 165). These frontiers or rules would seem to be of the nature of various rights that individuals have. Violation of them raises "a qualm of revulsion" in people (Ibid.: 166). Such invasions attack "fundamental needs of men as men" (Ibid.: 169).

Thus, for most liberals the boundaries or fences of liberty are constituted by a number of rights, whether grounded in utility or natural rights (McCloskey 1974: 17). Among the most important are the rights to freedom of expression, property, security of person, assembly, and one's own religious views. Behind these "fences" is the individual, something precious, which must be protected from the constraints that others would impose. In effect, the free individual is seen as something of great, though delicate, value, lodged within a fortress with liberties which serve as its windows and portals, and a protective moat of rights built around it to protect it from others.

The reason these boundaries exist is to protect individuals from harm. But what is the nature of the harm for which people may be restrained? Surely it must include not simply physical but also psychological harm which one person does another. People ought to be stopped not only from breaking other people's arms, but also from using manipulative techniques to destroy their sanity. How is such harm to be characterized?

The answer cannot be simply that a person experiences pain at the hands of another, since the person inflicting the pain may be a physician who is seeking to heal a patient with the patient's agreement. Constraints ought not to be imposed in such cases. The reason is not simply that the pain is minor, since considerable pain might be caused by a physician. On the other hand, at least in certain circumstances, even if the pain is minor, its infliction should be stopped – for instance, a man who pinches a woman in an elevator. Finally, surely a person's freedom can be violated and the person experience no pain or suffering at all. The banning of a book some people are not interested in reading still violates their freedom. It reduces their freedom by imposing constraints on possible alternative choices.

Such considerations make it difficult to accept that the harm can be explicated simply in terms of a person's existing interests. Nor can liberals appeal to those interests or rights that an individual might simply claim to have. This could lead to any number of improbable accounts of harm. Instead, an account of harm must be developed in terms of one's basic interests or rights which might be violated in various ways. Mill says that people may remain free to the extent that their conduct does not injure "the interests of one another, or rather certain interests which, either by express legal provision or by tacit understanding, ought to be considered as rights" (Mill 1956: 91). Berlin suggests this view when he speaks of "fundamental needs of men as men" and frontiers whose observance has entered into "the very conception of what it is to be a normal human being." That is, liberals must appeal to an ideal (or justified) set of basic interests or rights.[13] Accordingly, if James pinches Mary it is not so much a question of physical pain, but that her right to privacy has been violated. If Jane is offended by an interracial couple, her offense is not a reason to interfere with such couples, since Jane does not have an ideal right against such offense.

Resolution of these questions requires a theory of interests and rights, and consequently a theory of the nature of human beings. "Conceptions of freedom," Berlin reminds us, "directly derive from views of what constitutes a self, a person, a man" (Berlin 1969: 134). Harm occurs when these various ideal interests and/or rights are violated.

This answer is, by no means, a complete statement of the liberal view. There are several difficulties with it over which liberals have struggled. First, harm is clearly not a sufficient condition for restraining a person. As Mill points out, certain actions of a person may harm another, but this does not imply that we should restrain him. For example, in competitive situations, one person's actions may harm another's chances, but that does not mean that we should restrain the first person. Thus, there may be overriding considerations why we do not impose restraints even though one person is harmed by another (cf. Mill 1956: ch. 5).[14] An additional set of conditions is required for the harm principle to be sufficient.

Secondly, some have argued that harm done to another individual is not even necessary for imposing restraints on others. People need not be harmed, but simply offended, in order for society to be justified in restraining certain activities. For example, if a male exposes himself to a woman walking past a doorway, it is unlikely that he has harmed her. More likely he has engaged in an act offensive to her. Other similar instances include sexual intercourse in a public park and public defecation. These do not seem to cause harm so much as offense to people.

Most liberals have argued, plausibly, that these kinds of acts should be restrained. But if they may be regulated because of their offensiveness, what about the offense some take at interracial couples, sexually explicit literature, homosexual couples, or nudity. To avoid prohibiting such items, must the liberal show that offense to some (or most of the public) is caused by them in a way that is significantly different from the offense caused by public intercourse or defecation? This would seem difficult to show if we focused simply on the feelings of disgust or annoyance that people might experience in such situations.

Nevertheless, at least some liberals want to supplement the harm principle by appeal to an offense principle which is limited to exclude prohibition of inter-racial couples due to offense, but to allow prohibition of sexual intercourse in public. How, then, might an offense principle be circumscribed? It has been suggested that (a) the reaction of offense must be one that "could be expected from almost any person chosen at random from the nation as a whole, regardless of sect, faction, race, age or sex" and that (b) it could only be effectively avoided with unreasonable effort or inconvenience (Feinberg 1973: 44). However, these conditions are so strong, that one suspects anything that would fulfill them would not simply provoke universal offense, but create significant harm to the members of society. On the other hand, anything less strong might well permit restrictions that Mill and other liberals would reject. A satisfactory theory of justified restraint must answer these problems.

The two additional conditions that Mill believes supplement the harm principle speak to some of these questions. Mill argues that the behavior of any individual may be subject to the authority of society under circumstances that seem to go beyond simply harm. Specifically, an individual may be required to bear "his share . . . of the labors and sacrifices incurred for defending the society or its members from injury and molestation." Thus, a person might be "compelled . . . to give evidence in a court of justice, to bear his fair share in the common defense or in any other joint work necessary to the interest of the society of which he enjoys protection" (Mill 1956: 15). Further,

> the acts of an individual may be hurtful to others or wanting in due consideration for their welfare, without going to the length of violating any of their constituted rights. The offender may then be justly punished by opinion, though not by law.
>
> (Ibid.: 91)

The addition of the latter condition is not surprising given the liberal sensitivity to constraints that individuals may suffer. If people are to remain free, they have grounds upon which to object when another person hurts or injures them, even if such injury violates none of their rights. It might seem that Mill's claim that a person may be the object of constraint when his or her acts are wanting in due consideration for the welfare of others, would speak to the difficult case of offense. Mill does not, however, develop this condition in such a direction. In fact, he explicitly seeks to reject the restriction of an other's behavior based upon the offense some people (even the majority) take in it.

Thirdly, supposing that some form of harm (or appropriately circumscribed offense) must be involved for liberals to advocate constraining an individual, must the injury one person causes another be intentional in order for one's actions to be constrained?[15] Locke's and Mill's principles are stated such that if the injury is done to a person by another, whether the latter intended it or not, constraint may be appropriate. However, Mill is not always clear on this; sometimes he says that the conduct "must be calculated to produce evil to someone else" (Ibid.: 13); at other times he simply says that we may intervene "to prevent harm to others" (Ibid.)

Berlin also has spoken of the injury which one person intentionally causes another. But Berlin realized, as Mill ought to have, that the actions of those who in fact harm others may be controlled even if they are not intentional. It seems more in keeping with the spirit of liberal freedom to say that such injuries may be intentionally *or* unintentionally caused. If a person will be injured, then we are prima facie justified in restraining the person who causes such injury.

Thus, the liberal model of freedom is that injuries, whether intentionally or unintentionally imposed upon another or an institution by the actions of a person, are the grounds upon which that person's actions may be constrained. Except in special circumstances, a person's opinions may not be constrained. People may be harmed (or offended in a manner justifying restraint) when their welfare is not duly considered, when others do not bear their share in defending society from injury or molestation, or when their ideal interests or rights are damaged or injured. What these interests or rights are is drawn from a theory of humankind. Liberals are committed to expanding on the nature of harm and individual interests according to which individuals are to enjoy freedom. It is this we find in *On Liberty*, the *Second Treatise*, and "Two Concepts of Liberty."

Quite clearly liberals are drawn in two different directions here. On the one hand, their views on the concept of freedom and constraints lead them to see threats to freedom in almost every quarter. Thus, they should seek to reduce, eliminate, or escape these threats. On the other hand, they can do this only by imposing constraints on others. This they are extremely reluctant to do, given their opposition to constraints. Thus, the liberals find themselves on the edge of a constant tension between fighting to eliminate constraints and urging their imposition.

VII FREEDOM, PRIVACY, AND THE SELF

There remains one essential aspect of the liberal determination of when constraints may be imposed on other individuals. How directly or indirectly may individuals impose injuries on themselves or others without being legitimately subject to restraint in the name of freedom? To decide this issue is part and parcel of the liberal attempt to define a sphere of privacy as opposed to publicity – a private realm of freedom, in which people may act, think, and relate to consenting others without constraints imposed by others. In this private realm, and only in this private realm, may that ideal of complete freedom discussed in the first half of this chapter be most fully realized. Mill refers to such a sphere of personal, private life, where society may not legitimately interfere as "the appropriate region of human liberty" (Mill 1956: 16). In this realm, Mill says, "in the part which merely concerns himself, his independence is, of right, absolute. Over himself, over his body and mind, the individual is sovereign" (Ibid.: 13). We can further appreciate the difficulties liberals face in defining an injury principle by looking to their views on how the private realm is to be distinguished from the public realm.

Unfortunately, Locke has little to say directly on these matters beyond his discussion of natural law and rights. In *A Letter Concerning Toleration*, Locke speaks generally and vaguely of one's "private domestic affairs" by which he includes the management of estates and the conservation of bodily health (Locke 1955: 28). In this realm one may do as one wishes. However, Locke is unhelpful in drawing the boundaries of the private realm more exactly. For example, he holds that the jurisdiction of the magistrate reaches to the following civil interests: "life, liberty, health, and indolency of body; and the possession of outward things, such as money, lands, houses, furniture, and the like" (Ibid.: 17; cf. 29). Stated so broadly, it is little wonder that a Lockean magistrate might intervene in affairs that other liberals have held are private. Thus, Locke maintains that the state must prohibit not only the sacrifice of infants but also the pollution of oneself by promiscuous uncleanliness (39). Further, it may prohibit: "opinions contrary to human society," or to those moral rules which are necessary to the preservation of civil society" (50). Thus, "those are not at all to be tolerated who deny the being of a God. Promises, convenants, and oaths, which are the bonds of human society, can have no hold upon an atheist" (Locke 1955: 52). In short, the two realms (the public or civil realm and the private or religious realm) are not wholly separate. What their boundaries ought to be remains obscure.

Mill's attempt to distinguish the private from the public is notorious. He claims that "all that portion of a person's life and conduct which affects only himself or, if it also affects others, only with their free, voluntary, and undeceived consent and participation" falls within the private realm (Mill 1956: 16, 92). This realm is "a sphere of action in which society . . . has, if any, only an indirect interest" (Ibid.: 15–16). However, this distinction has proven to be rather tenuous, one which Mill and and other liberals have had great difficulty drawing (cf. Ibid.: 92). Surely many activities, even riding a motorcycle without a helmet which may affect hospital costs, can affect others. The present problems of AIDS and cocaine make this all the more clear. If the above public/private distinction were adopted, the private domain would seem very limited. Mill realizes this difficulty. Hence, he suggests that we differentiate between the consequences of one's actions which affect others primarily and directly and those which do not. Only the former fall within the public realm and may be restricted by society when they cause, without their consent, harm to others. Accordingly, he argues that

> with regard to the merely contingent or . . . constructive injury which a person causes to society by conduct which neither violates any specific duty to the public, nor occasions perceptible hurt to any assignable individual except himself, the inconvenience is one which society can afford to bear, for the sake of the greater good of human freedom.
>
> (Ibid.: 100)

However, on this view the breadth or narrowness of the private realm will depend upon the nature and number of duties which individuals have to others. As we shall see, we cannot appraise the private realm without looking to the duties that define individuals within liberal society. Further, to the extent that Mill permits interference with individuals on grounds of the insufficient consideration for the welfare of others, his views hardly suggest any rigorous definition of a private realm. Indeed, they may allow that the liberal fence of freedom may be breached in a host of ways. Berlin also explicitly invokes a private/public distinction (Berlin 1969: 124). However, he claims that Mill's effort to mark the distinction between private and social spheres breaks down (Ibid.: 155). How, then, are we to determine the location and nature of those frontiers which no one can cross (Ibid.: 164)? Berlin responds by linking the rules specifying the frontiers to what it means to be a normal human being (Ibid.: 165–6). He explains this concept as follows:

> When I speak of a man as being normal, a part of what I mean is that he could not break these rules easily, without a qualm of revulsion. It is such rules as these that are broken when a man is declared guilty without trail, or punished under a retroactive law; when children are ordered to denounce their parents, friends to betray one another, soldiers to use methods of barbarism; when men are tortured or murdered, or minorities are massacred because they irritate a majority or a tyrant. Such acts . . . cause horror even in these days, and this springs from the recognition of the moral validity . . . of some absolute barriers to the imposition of one man's will on another.
>
> (Ibid.: 165–6)

But this does not so much resolve the problem of the distinction between the private and the public realm as identify it as a moral question without indicating what relevant moral principles, rules, or considerations would answer it. Even though Mill's views on freedom would leave individuals open to interference, Berlin's moral appeal remains terribly indeterminate.

Thus, the attempts of liberals to define a private, as opposed to public, realm remain problematic. Neither Mill's distinction between what primarily affects us as opposed to what indirectly affects others, nor Berlin's appeal to our conception of the normal human being has achieved widespread support. The liberal model of freedom suffers a serious weakness at this strategic point. A number of reasons for this difficulty are discussed in the remainder of this chapter.

Liberals are quite correct that individuals require privacy, some refuge from the public. This is not in question, even if, on some occasions, a person's privacy simply amounts to the averted eyes of others. Thus, this is a problem that any model of freedom must face. What is in question here are the manner and assumptions which liberals adopt in their design of a sphere of private freedom.

What is important for our present purposes is to note the "privatizing" of individual life and the implications for the self which this view carries with it. Berlin is quite correct when he maintains that "conceptions of freedom directly derive from views of what constitutes a self, a person, a man" (Ibid.: 134) The question here is *not* one concerning the nature of constraints, as it was in sections

above, but of the way(s) in which liberals separate the private from
the public, or the realm of perfect freedom from that of a diminished
political freedom. There are two aspects to this claim. First, liberal
characterizations of private freedom have been criticised for adopting
views of the self and its private realm which are atomistic as well
as materialistic. For example, some object that liberalism sees
individuals simply as particular, isolated entities. Others object that
they define the self in terms of the limits of the body (Parekh 1972).
There is some truth to these objections. But liberals need not defend
these views. Berlin, for example, is willing to admit the interpersonal
nature of individual selves (Berlin 1969: 155). Thus, the problem of
privacy, freedom and the self would best not arise on this ontological
level, since liberals are not necessarily wedded to it.

The question is whether liberals can use a broader, more social
view of individuals and be true to their negative concept of freedom.
On the contrary, I suggest, in spite of allowing that individuals may
be intelligible only in terms of a social network, liberal freedom
nevertheless ends up seeking to define a space for the (private) self,
rather than a private space for the (social) self.

The problem is that liberal views about the social interrelations that
define a self do not translate into a social self, or an understanding of
ourselves as social beings (except in intellectual ways). The reason is
that the social relations to which liberals appeal define us as private
beings. That is, though the liberal self may be defined in terms of a
social network, the social realm is itself a privatizing system.

Primary here are the social relations which define private property,
monogamous male/female relations, the nuclear family, and the
pursuit of self-interest. It is these relations that which define the
liberal self as a private self, and liberal freedom as a private freedom.
Through these relations, liberals hold, the least constraint will be
imposed on individuals.

Since constraint is defined in terms of the individual's interests or
rights, requirements on individuals within these relations would not
be impingements if the individual explicitly agreed to them. The
only relations which are condoned then between these private selves
are ones that are conscious, rational, and voluntary. The relations
between individuals then become negotiated settlements. Only when
people interact voluntarily do they interact in ways such that their
freedom is not diminished. From this follows the importance for
liberals of reciprocity between individuals and voluntary associations.

However, it is doubtful whether any transcending sense of oneself
can be founded on this basis. Membership is always to fit my ends;

when this ceases, so too will my membership. Thus, the liberal does not give him or herself to the association so much as adopt the association as a means to his or her own ends. Accordingly, it is doubtful whether liberal freedom can be compatible with or foster any sense of community. Communities are not simply intellectual and voluntary associations. Indeed, since constraint is so broadly viewed, even voluntary arrangements may not be enough. Liberals as sovereign over their minds and bodies engage in diplomatic exchanges as do foreign countries. Thus, in a similar manner they too remain foreign to each other.

It is in this situation, when individuals are separated from each other, when the world seems constituted by constraints, and the community seems rent, that concerns understandably arise with society's use of power over the individual. Liberalism is then primarily concerned with the use of such powers to control individual actions. Liberalism assumes that the average individual does not have such power, since it has become separated from him or her and then may be imposed upon them. More than this, liberalism embodies a profound skepticism against the use of power by other individuals. Thus, it is "the nature and limits of the power which can be legitimately exercised by society over the individual" (Mill 1956: 3) which Mill identifies as the subject of his essay on liberty. And it is "political power" which Locke notes at the outset of his *Second Treatise* which he undertakes to discuss (Locke 1982: Sect. 2). Power, political power, remains a problem for liberals. They attempt to limit the exercise of power over individuals, rather than to construct a system in which individuals are empowered. This problem arose, in part, because of the liberal view of individuals as private beings separated from one another. Secondly, when liberals seek to define a private realm of freedom distinct from the public realm they seek to define this private world so as legitimately to keep others out and to eliminate constraints. Still, this private freedom can only exist – to the extent it can exist at all – due to constraints (laws, moral rules, etc.) which are imposed on other people. Nevertheless, to the extent that people seek more and more freedom, they must seek to reduce such constraints to their minimal level. Liberal freedom ever drives us to remove this or that restraint. Now the temptation in this situation will always be to place the burdens of constraint on other people. This means that there will be a tendency toward imposing both external and internal constraints on other people, all the while reducing constraints on oneself. If ideology cannot persuade others to adopt internal constraints, then laws will impose external ones. Since this is the effort of all private individuals seeking to enlarge their own private realms, the burden of constraint will fall on external means. In practical terms this means, for example, that the inner constraints on people which restrain them from walking across the lawn, will be increasingly replaced by external constraints (chains and laws) that stop everyone from walking across the lawn. Liberal organizations, e.g. free-market businesses, will seek to remove their own constraints by placing them on others, e.g. they may pollute the surrounding areas. Still, this very attempt to project the evil of constraint onto others inevitably results in the imposition of constraints on themselves as well as other people. Further, these constraints are perceived as constraints, not inner characteristics or essentials of people which serve (as Locke said) as guides to rational action. This is yet another aspect of the contradictory situation liberal freedom faces.

The success of liberal freedom has, in part, flowed from its un-acknowledged (even unrecognized) dependence on the constraints of more conservative times: customs, traditions, religious injunctions, etc. To this extent, conservatives are right that freedom also involves commitment, identification, and responsibility. Liberal freedom was able to flourish, early on, because it relied on the various restraints which people took to be part of themselves, and hence not constraining. The reduction of social and political restraints liberals advocated could successfully proceed because people had internalized many other restraints.

Thus, earlier liberals could leave off the chains along the grass so long as people did not walk on the grass. This fits quite nicely with Locke who asks: "What gave him a free disposing of his property, according to his will, within the compass of that law?" and then proceeds to answer: "I answer; State of maturity wherein he might be supposed capable to know that law, that so he might keep his actions within the bounds of it" (Locke 1982: Sect.59). That is, Locke sees the importance of people following a law of nature so that there may be freedom in society. We see this even portrayed in Locke's view of the state of nature or "perfect freedom." It is a social state. But by the time of Mill the realm of freedom is no longer a social state, but has withered into a private condition. In seeking ever greater expanses of freedom for themselves, and to avoid more and more constraints which impinge on them, liberals have eliminated from themselves social determinations that bind them to society and a state. Only their own private selves are left.

Nevertheless, for a society of such individuals (i.e. people who seek to reduce their own restraints, both external and internal) practically to exist, external constraints will have to be imposed on them. Bars will have to be installed on windows, chains erected along the grass, and hidden cameras placed in stores and at intersections. Homes will have doors that take on the fortified appearance of medieval castles and businesses will be designed to be commercial bunkers. These are the outer manifestation of the liberal search for freedom. The upshot is that the search for liberal freedom has led to its undoing.

VIII THEORY, PRACTICE, AND ABSTRACT REASON

Crucial to the liberal attempt to define a private realm and to formulate a principle of injury is the assumption that this requires an appeal to some form of rational principle arrived at on the basis of reflection. Mill states that

> an opinion on a point of conduct, not supported by reasons, can only count as one person's preference; and if the reasons, when given, are a mere appeal to a similar preference felt by other people, it is still only many people's liking instead of one.
>
> (Mill 1956: 8–9)

It is worth remembering that this liberal appeal to reason is the other side of the liberal view that liberty is opposed to customs or traditions. Liberals have consistently questioned the authority of custom and tradition. Thus, Locke contrasted those who let themselves be guided by customs with those who use their liberty to think for themselves (Parry, 1982: 399). Mill, as we have seen, was even harder on custom and tradition. He maintains that the love of liberty is antagonistic to custom (Ibid.:85–90). China was an example, he thought, of a country dominated by custom and stagnant as a result. Mill's objection to customs and tradition, then, is not merely that they are coercive, but also that they stifle the development of human faculties and (more particularly) human reasoning abilities:

> The human faculties of perception, judgment, discriminative feeling, mental activity, and even moral preference are exercised only in making a choice. He who does anything because it is the custom makes no choice. . . . He who chooses his plan for himself employs all his faculties. He must use observation to see, reasoning and judgment to foresee, activity to gather materials for decision, discrimination to decide, and when he has decided, firmness and self-control to hold to his deliberate decision.
>
> (Ibid.: 71)

We must appeal to our reason and other critical faculties, not the customs or traditions of society, to determine the bounds of freedom.

In general, liberals tend to view reason as individual and calculative in nature, concerned primarily with the means to ends, rather than the determination of ends (cf. Arblaster 1984: 79–84). However, some liberals have held that reason is also applicable to ends. Mill held that we can reason concerning the *summum bonum* (Mill 1957: 3). Locke even thought that reason was capable of certainty in areas such as ethics. Thus, he held that "morality is capable of demonstration, as well as mathematics" (Locke 1959; II: 156). But this says as much about his views on ethics as on reason.

In contrast, most liberals have rejected Locke's rationalistic views. Mill attributed much more modest powers to reason. When it comes to the basic principles of morality, he believes that "questions of ultimate ends are not amenable to direct proof." Instead, he claims that:

> there is a larger meaning of the word "proof," in which this question is as amenable to it as any other of the disputed questions of philosophy. The subject is within the cognizance of the rational faculty; and neither does that faculty deal with it solely in the way of intuition. Considerations may be presented capable of determining the intellect either to give or withhold its assent to the doctrine; and this is equivalent to proof.
>
> (Mill 1957: 7)

However, this view applies only to questions of the ultimate end to be attained, which is, for Mill, the happiness of all sentient beings. Other questions, concerning how this end is to be promoted, are matters of science (Mill 1851, II: 518). How much freedom ought to be granted each individual would seem to fall under this latter heading. Still, though this view of things falls far short of the certainty Locke thought possible, Mill thinks that reasonable individuals will come to a similar conclusion.

Berlin is even more hesitant about the powers of reason: no single solution is possible to conflicts concerning the ends of life. In the end, he appeals to long-lasting views on humans, etc. (Berlin 1959: 165f, 171f). Thus, as others have pointed out, one must be careful not to overemphasize the powers which liberals attribute to reason (Wolin 1960: 294–9). The modest powers that liberals have come to attribute to reason (due to the influence of both Hume and Freud) manifest themselves in the increasingly subjectivist view which they attribute to values and morals. Some have argued that the subjectivist influence on morals arises from an abandonment of a teleological nature of humans (MacIntyre 1981). But it is also true that subjectivism has risen because of a view of the declining powers of reason. Contemporary liberals lack the confidence earlier liberals possessed that reason could also establish the ends by which we should live. Thus, Berlin says that "in the end, men must choose between ultimate values" (Berlin 1969: 171). Further, he is willing to appeal, as we have seen, to "rules so long and widely accepted that their observance has entered into the very conception of what it is to be a normal human being" (Ibid.: 165). This allows an historical, though not necessarily customary, dimension to the determination of the frontiers and fences that other liberals have not allowed. In general, however, the liberal model has held that it is reason which must establish, and determine the nature of, the fences, barriers, and frontiers that separate people and ensure political freedom. It is reason that must determine the nature of the injury that will justify intervention in a person's affairs by other people and the state, as well as the balance to be sought among freedom, justice, and fraternity in a society.

Accordingly, liberal freedom, which has given itself over to the determination of reason and thereby burned any bridges (of custom, tradition, or convention) to other sources of the objective limitation of freedom, finds itself increasingly with a guide of dubious power and authority. As Sheldon Wolin comments, "while the liberals often proclaimed the need for rational political policies and objective public judgments, they actually produced a theory which made objective social and political judgments impossible" (Wolin 1960:332). Where to draw the lines and what the nature of the fences or frontiers must be increasingly become a matter of dispute, contention, and litigation.

Since reason's powers and authority are dubious, liberals must ask to whose reason they are to appeal. And, what is to be done with those who find other policies and paths to be the rational ones? Berlin is led to say, at one point, that "where [the frontier between private life and public authority] is to be drawn is a matter of argument, indeed of haggling" (Berlin 1969: 124). Similarly, what amounts of freedom are to be fostered at the expense of justice, security, or fraternity, will also be a matter of debate, negotiation, and "horse-trading." It is ironic that at the very time contemporary liberals' confidence in reason has decreased, they have tried to impose increased government intervention in society, something which presupposes great powers of reason. In this sense, liberals have acted, once again, in opposition to themselves.

The implications of the preceding are significant, for they imply that the determinations of the limits of freedom will ultimately be political ones made within the social and political order.

Interestingly, Locke recognized this explicitly. Were the law of nature itself sufficient, and not terribly vague, humankind might remain in the state of nature which Locke describes. But in the state of nature the more precise specifications of this law of nature are underdetermined; further there are no impartial judges to settle disputes. Thus, simply a rational principle or natural law is not sufficient for the determination of the limits of freedom, let alone its protection. A governing body, a state, must be formed which will specify the further aspects of this law.[16]

Similarly, though Mill does not accept Locke's views on a state of nature, he recognizes that the particular determinations of freedom must come about "either by express legal provision or by tacit understanding" (Mill 1956: 91). Though what such "tacit under-standing" amounts to is cloudy, what is clear is that legislators (or benevolent despots) and judges will have to decide these matters on two bases: first, through such theoretical insights as Locke, Mill and other liberals can give them; and, secondly, on the haggling and the "common sense" application of liberal principles and views to particular cases.

Accordingly, if the determination of the limits of freedom must ultimately be made by legal provision, it is obvious that it is terribly important what the nature of the legal and political process is, as well as who holds the positions through which such legal provisions are to be made. However, since liberal freedom is compatible with a variety of political orders, we can imagine that important differences may result. Locke, for example, limited participation in such determinations to males. Mill attempts to restrict participation in these determinations to the upper classes. Thus, he advocates limiting those who can vote by intellectual tests. Further he would give the votes of the educated greater weight (cf. Mill 1962). Finally, Mill also limits such determinations to those who have achieved the age of reason and are capable of being influenced by reason – a condition which, in Mill's views, eliminated most of the non-Western world (Mill 1956: 14). Berlin leaves the matter quite wide open. Thus, one can appreciate why liberals come to rather different views on the limits of individual freedom.

The point here is that liberal freedom does not require democracy let alone an egalitarian society. It does not require any particular distribution of power or constraints in a society. It only requires that the government of a society minimize the constraint on the (adult) individuals under its authority (Berlin 1969: lvii, 129, 165). Within this broad qualification, liberals allow that the determination of freedom is ultimately defined by those who control the public and political institutions. And since liberal freedom allows that those with wealth and social position in society are those who will obtain such posts, as well as implicitly requires that they apply (their own) value judgments in determining what counts as constraints, it is not surprising that liberal freedom has been compatible with class and even aristocratic society. This is the practical basis of the unequal freedom which persists in liberal society.

In a sense, then, liberals such as Mill are subject to Mill's own complaint that these matters are decided simply on the basis of individual preference, rather than on the basis of principle (Mill 1956: 12). The liberal injury principle requires interpretation in practical situations by concrete individuals. If liberal freedom is silent on the nature of the government which must decide these issues, then, realistically, they will be decided on the basis of various interests and pressures within the political body. Liberal freedom is, in this sense, cunningly naive. For it turns out that the defenders of liberal freedom have been those who are members of the dominant classes and parties in society.

This consequence flows from the non-political nature of liberal freedom. It is, at the same time, in opposition to the historical direction in which liberals have generally striven, viz., to reduce the level of constraint for all people. What this suggests (once again) is that liberal freedom, even along the lines that liberals have pursued it, is too simple. It requires a more adequate account of the relation of reason and the principles determining the limits of freedom, as well as the political structures within which the determination of the extent of freedom will take place.

IX CONCLUSION

What the preceding discussion reveals is a view of freedom which has been widely persuasive and just as widely the source of a number of profound problems and difficulties in modern society. It rests on a set of interlocking assumptions. Though liberal freedom has played an important and positive role in the development of modern society, there are a number of underlying tensions and conflicts which characterize it.

First, liberal freedom holds an abiding suspicion of politics and power. To its profound credit it has done much to protect individuals from the power of the developing modern state. Still, the liberal view of political freedom seeks to escape from politics as much as it seeks political freedom. To define a private realm, to enjoy complete or absolute freedom in such a realm, is what drives liberal freedom. Government and politics are simply necessary means to this end. The ends of life are, as it were, all individual and personal. But this undercuts the very society and community which are essential to humans. In isolating individuals from each other, it robs them of a great deal that is important in life.

Secondly, by identifying freedom with the lack of constraint and then attempting to give a purely descriptive account of freedom, liberals have been driven from one account of constraint to another unable to call a halt at any particular point. As a consequence, the world appears as a place of constraint and threat; it is an hostile environment. Liberal freedom leads us to an alienation from others as well as ourselves.

Finally, liberals have given the determination of the extent of freedom over to various political orders. Their antipathy towards power and politics, however, impedes if not stymies any positive characterisation of politics and the political order. Consequently, liberal theory has not developed an adequate theory of *political* freedom.

It is remarkable how enduring these views and implications have been. But it would also appear that they are historically unique: the product of a particular historical and material situation, one in which prospects of abundance remained alive and the conflicts between individuals not so massive that they proved detrimental to those individuals as well as society as a whole. It is doubtful, however, that such a view of individuals, society and political freedom can be maintained.

4 Radical freedom

> While the state exists there is no freedom. When freedom exists there will be no state.
>
> (Lenin[1] 1966a: 343)

I INTRODUCTION

Some truisms are significant. That radical freedom is radical is one of them. Its significance is that it reminds us that radical freedom is not taken seriously if it is viewed simply as an extension of liberal freedom. Radicals themselves are explicit about this. Marx and Engels contend that the communist revolution "involves the most radical rupture with traditional [religious, moral and juridical] ideas" (Marx and Engels 1976b: 504). Lenin comments that

> general talk about freedom, equality and democracy is in fact but a blind repetition of concepts shaped by the relations of commodity production. To attempt to solve the concrete problems of the dictatorship of the proletariat by such generalities is tantamount to accepting the theories and principles of the bourgeoisie in their entirety.
>
> (Lenin 1971b: 505)

Finally, Marcuse claims that "the transition from servitude to freedom requires a total transvaluation of values" (Marcuse 1972: 214).[1]

These claims are not mere exercises in hyperbole.[2] Unlike conservative or even liberal freedom, radicals see an extensive, almost unbounded, system of unfreedom in the forms and structures of modern social and political life. Admittedly, liberals and conservatives may seriously question particular aspects of their social and political systems. However, the challenge which radicals pose is significantly greater. Whereas conservatives and liberals may disagree about what the political system should do to protect or enhance individual freedom, radicals reject such political frameworks.[3] Though liberals have come to identify ever greater numbers and kinds of constraints that render people unfree, these are believed, most usually, to be capable of remedy within the broad framework of present political society. Radicals deny this. Whereas conservatives seek political freedom within political society, and liberals seek it through an escape from political society though *within* civil society. Radicals seek to escape from both politics *and* civil society. Consequently, radical freedom rejects political freedom, the state, and civil society.[4] They must be replaced by a communal system which allows for a human, not simply a political, freedom (Marcuse 1969a: 6).[5] The freedom radicals advocate demands not simply a new social order but a new individual as well. It is for these reasons that radicals tend to speak of liberation or emancipation rather than liberty or freedom. Even their terminology reflects the dramatically different view they take.[6]

The model of radical freedom which underlies such claims requires both relief from constraints and participation of individuals in the determination and rational direction of their lives. The concept of radical freedom which lies at the heart of this model is rational self-determination. This is a contentious and paradoxical claim. It is contentious inasmuch as many argue that radicals such as Marx adhere to a negative concept of freedom.[7] I think that they are mistaken. For example, Marx identifies freedom with "complete and no longer restricted self-activity, which consists in the [rational] appropriation of a totality of productive forces and in the development of a totality of capacities entailed by this" (Marx and Engels, 1976a: 87). Lenin equates the liberty of all oppressed peoples with "their right to self-determination" (Lenin 1971a: 165). Marcuse explicitly links freedom with "man's ability to determine his own life without depriving others of this ability" and then calls this "real self-determination" (Marcuse 1972: 213). These remarks require interpretation, but should be taken as serious indications that radicals understand freedom to be rational self-determination.

My claim is paradoxical in that rational self-determination seems to be a familiar notion, one that might even be said to have an ancient Greek lineage. Further, different interpretations of this notion can be found in the writings of liberals as well as conservatives.[8] Nevertheless, it is radicals who have been particularly drawn to this concept and best exemplify its nature and power. Others, radicals hold, can give only a cramped and limited interpretation to rational self-determination due to their limited understanding of the self and rational determination.

They leave unfreedom – the domination and other-determination of individuals – in place. They cannot capture the freedom radicals defend in which humans as communal beings create themselves and their world, while exercising rational direction and control over their creations. This radical interpretation of rational self-determination offers a powerful understanding of freedom, one providing insights into the narrowness of liberal freedom and the unfreedom of the private life. It has found a strong response from many who seek to determine and control their own lives.

However, the radical view also suffers from important difficulties concerning the subject of freedom, the nature and role of rights in society, the non-political nature of freedom, and the relation of rationality and freedom. Though non-radical accounts of freedom as rational self-determination may be naive and insensitive to forms of unfreedom from which people suffer, radical efforts to eliminate domination run the risk of reintroducing it in new forms (Berlin 1969: 131–72; Crocker 1980; Walicki 1984; Heilbroner 1980: ch. 5). This is not a new criticism of radical freedom; but it is an important criticism. I hope to develop this point in a rather different way.

Particularly problematic are the hyperbolical views of reason and the self which radicals have used in defending freedom as rational self-determination. Their efforts to formulate more sophisticated views of the self and rationality tend not only to extend these notions beyond plausibility but also, as a result, to undercut the very rational self-determination or freedom they seek. This is the fundamental tension or contradiction that lies at the heart of radical freedom.

II RADICAL FREEDOM, CONSTRAINTS, AND UNFREEDOM

Freedom as rational self-determination may not seem to be, initially, particularly radical. If people are able – as they often seem to be – to decide for themselves what to do and do so rationally, are they not thereby rationally self-determining and consequently free? Further, would not only workers and capitalists but also murderers and hermits exemplify such rational self-determination, at least when they carefully and rationally carry out their plans? However, such examples are hardly instances of radical freedom.

Further, even on this naive interpretation, the lack of education, information and welfare might be said to undermine a person's rational self-determination. Hence, freedom would require their provision. This would, surely, have significant implications for most societies today. The point, however, is that such proposals have often been made *within* capitalist society. It is not surprising, then, that rational self-determination has often been identified with autonomy and said to be possible without a radical revolution.

Still, surely there is some important difference between the radical and the ordinary interpretation of freedom as rational self-determination. This is suggested simply by the various things which, radicals claim, dominate people or render them unfree. This list includes (but is not limited to): laws, the class struggle, the police, the army, the judiciary, the state, economic necessity, private property, violence, coercion, rights, duties, ideology, religion, morality, the market system, the law of supply and demand, money, the division of labor, the mental/physical division of labor, the town/country division, the separation of private and public, and aggressive desires. All of these (and more) have been mentioned by radicals as part of the unfreedom which daily and concretely afflicts people. Individuals are subject to an extensive system of unfreedom in present society. Those who claim that rational self-determination is possible within present society are, radicals claim, simply mistaken.

What explains this incredible sensitivity of radicals – a sensitivity that somehow implicates almost every recognizable feature of contemporary (and past) society in the unfreedom of humans? Why is it that on radical views people may be rendered unfree in so many ways beyond the ordinary understanding of rational self-determination?

The underlying problem, radicals would say, is that our ordinary understanding is both methodologically and substantively naive. It assumes that the self is essentially unrelated to others. It accepts a view of reason as an individual capacity, fully realizable outside of the social contexts within which people live. It presupposes a set of epistemological and metaphysical assumptions which are characteristic of liberals rather than radicals. Only by exploring these points can we understand the nature of radical freedom.

At the outset, we may consider three characteristics of radical freedom which partially explain why radicals see unfreedom so widely. They will lead us to the fundamental views underlying radical freedom.

First, it is natural to think, on the ordinary (liberal) understanding, that if people are not rationally self-determining, something or someone must be blocking, confining, or constraining their self-determination, if not their rationality. All that is required is to relieve people from these constraints for them to be rationally self-determining. As a result, accounts of freedom as rational self-determination become focused on a theory of constraints. Nevertheless, though radicals may agree that a theory of constraints is part of an account of freedom, they cannot agree that an account of rational self-determination can be reduced to a liberal constraint model.

There is, of course, nothing that prevents a liberal account from picking out constraints that are internal as well as external, negative as well as positive, and unintentional as well as intentional. In this way, even a liberal account of unfreedom can be much more extensive than most such accounts are. Still, radical unfreedom is not limited simply to various obstacles or constraints upon the actions of individuals. It is not linked simply to the prevention of the purposes which people presently have. Radicals see unfreedom arising also from *fulfilled* purposes and aims, when they are perverted, corrupted, or degraded. In short, radicals understand unfreedom not simply as a number of different kinds of constraints, but ultimately in terms of a set of positive ways of acting and relating to others which people do not fulfill (Marcuse 1972).

It is for this reason that one of Marx's objections to human rights is that they are the rights "of man separated from other men and from the community" (Marx 1975c: 162). His point is not that such rights create obstacles, so much as that the protection such rights supposedly afford people does not integrate them into a community of rationally self-determining individuals. It is for this reason that Marx identifies the freedom (or emancipation) he seeks with a "human emancipation" rather than a "political emancipation."

Accordingly, radicals reject the separate identification of negative and positive freedom.[9] Instead, the two come bound up together. As such, the radical concept of freedom is a unique concept of freedom. It is neither simply an extended version of negative freedom, nor a form of positive freedom unconcerned about constraints. This is one reason that radicals see unfreedom as much more extensive than does the ordinary (liberal) understanding of rational self-determination.

Secondly, those same liberal accounts suggest (though they do not entail) that constraints are individual and independent of each other. Though semantically connected they may be otherwise quite unconnected. The relation of constraints is a separate question to be settled by empirical study. Thus, if I am constrained by the actions of the police, by my employer, as well as by various duties others impose upon me due to their (property) rights, then these three constraints are joined only by the common meaning. Otherwise they are three (logically) separate constraints. They may or may not be empirically connected.[10]

On the contrary, radicals hold that we cannot understand what a constraint is independently of understanding the system within which it plays a role. In this sense, we can only understand freedom systematically, not individually or merely semantically. In short, the nature of a constraint consists of various real relations in the world. When we look simply to the meanings of such concepts we indulge in a form of semantic idealism. Like the German philosophers Marx criticized, "it has not occurred to [those who so proceed] . . . to inquire into . . . the relation of their criticism with their own material surroundings" (Marx and Engels 1976a: 30). If they did, they would find that constraints are joined within the system of which they are part. They are not necessarily, logically or conceptually, linked on their own individual level. It is the identity of the system which unites them.

Underlying this view is the radical claim that the features of the real world, in terms of which we understand what constrains us, are themselves interconnected in various systems of relations. Radical views on dialectics play a significant role here, particularly as they relate to the complexity and interrelatedness of the world. This is, it should be noted, to pin a particular kind of theory of meaning and metaphysics on radicals. But so radicals have seen themselves. They are not simply exaggerated versions of empiricists.[11] Liberals tend to hold other theories so that they can keep things separate. Dialectics views the world as complex and interconnected in ways in which the empiricist does not. This is not to say that radicals cannot engage in empirical examinations of constraints. Surely Marx and Lenin were interested in such. What they are not open to is allowing that these constraints do not have a unity beyond the semantic one captured in the meaning of "constraint."

In this way, the different attempts to answer the problem of political freedom are bound up not simply with different concepts but also different ways of viewing the world. Thus part of the radical model must be understood in terms of its distinctive epistemological and metaphysical views. It is not surprising on this account that empiricists tend to make poor radicals.

There are two important implications. First, this means that though some constraints could be removed or changed, doing so might not essentially change or alter the system within which they are found. It might remain virtually intact. Thus, though a strict conceptual or logical connection does not necessarily exist between constraints, that which joins them is more than an empirical connection. People might remain unfree or constrained by what replaces other constraints to the extent the system itself remains unfree.

Secondly, this explains why radicals tend to focus on systems of unfreedom rather than on the particular individuals who experience unfreedom. It is not that radicals are unconcerned about the latter, but that their concern for freedom requires that their primary attention be given to the systems within which individuals live. Further, if what causes unfreedom is bound up with other aspects of a social system, then it is natural for radicals to see each of these aspects of the system as linked with a greater unfreedom. Thus, the sources of unfreedom tend to spread on radical views.

The upshot of the preceding is that if we are to understand unfreedom we must examine the systems of constraints within which people live. However, since unfreedom does not consist simply of a number of unrelated individual constraints, since the systematic nature of human unfreedom is also found in the various ways in which people fail to be rationally self-determining, we must also look to various positive forms of behavior that constitute radical freedom. Radical freedom cannot be identified by means of a (liberal) constraint view of freedom; at the least, we must look to some positive form of "human freedom." Thus, Marx says, "if you . . . want to be emancipated politically without emancipating yourselves humanly, the half-hearted approach and contradiction is not in you alone, it is inherent in the *nature* and *category* of political emancipation" (Marx 1975c: 160). Human emancipation, unlike political emancipation, requires a positive form of rational self-determination, not simply the release from political constraints.

Both these characteristics explain (at least in part) why radicals see unfreedom as so pervasive. There is, however, yet a third reason. Inasmuch as unfreedom or constraints are parts of systems, we must ask about the nature of the systems which involve the constraints and unfreedom from which we suffer. This will help us further specify the nature of radical freedom and unfreedom.

III UNFREEDOM AND DEEP STRUCTURE

When radicals look to the unfreedom which engulfs people they see an unfreedom which is not only systematically interconnected but also structured. The constraints, for instance, which afflict self-determination are not simply connected with one another, but arise from, and are anchored in, fundamental contradictions which constitute the nature of pre-radical societies. This view is crucial to understanding radical freedom.

By "fundamental contradictions" I mean basic oppositions of interests, held by different members and classes of that society, which are both constitutive and ultimately destructive of the structure of society (Heilbroner 1980: 39; Marcuse 1967: 351). Thus, for instance, when the basic institutions of a society divide the members of society into various classes, such as capitalists and proletarians, or feudal lords and serfs, we have a fundamental contradiction, since each class has its own interests which are opposed by others and the working out of these conflicts undermines the structure of their society.

The implication of this view is that, since the constraints we daily face spring from such fundamental contradictions, it is not possible to eliminate them within present, capitalist society. They are inherent to it. Radical freedom, however, is incompatible with societies whose very nature or structure consists of underlying basic conflicts. Consequently, radical freedom as rational self-determination can only hold for individuals living in a particular kind of society, viz. communal society (Marcuse 1969a). This is in marked contrast with liberal and conservative views. It is one further step in understanding the dialectical complexity of unfreedom. It is also part of the explanation of the sensitivity and nature of radical freedom.

Radicals have tended to identify private property as the most basic underlying contradiction in modern (bourgeois) society. When understood within a system of free competition this contradiction is said to constitute the economic or material basis of society. Within such a system, the ownership of the means of production tends increasingly to fall into the hands of one class, while all other classes are excluded from such ownership. Such private and exclusive ownership of property with its self-interested ends is assumed to breed conflict and domination of the weaker by the stronger. "In this sense," Marx and Engels say, "the theory of the Communists may be summed up in the single sentence: Abolition of private property" (Marx and Engels 1976b: 498).

There are two crucial aspects to this view. First, out of this division of ownership, with the different and opposed interests, arise class struggles and various forms of domination and oppression from which people suffer. Secondly, beyond this primary level of conflict and domination, radicals claim that all forms of domination, oppression, and conflict ultimately arise out of private property and its division of interests. Even such problems of daily life as crime and suicide ultimately stem from the basic economic conflicts in society. Thus, Engels claims that when "we eliminate the contradiction between the individual man and all others, . . . we put the axe to the root of crime . . ." (Engels 1975: 248). Accordingly, radicals have held with Marx that "the whole of human servitude is involved in the relation of the worker to production, and all relations of servitude are but modifications and consequences of this relation" (Marx 1975e: 280). It is this view which finally accounts for the multiplicity and extent of forms of unfreedom which radicals perceive. In short, radicals hold that if the mode of production is antagonistic then the accompanying forms of life which derive (directly and indirectly from it) will similarly be infected with unfreedom.

This second claim is surely the least plausible of the two. It is hardly credible that all forms of domination and conflict stem (even ultimately) simply from the nature of the economic base. Why radicals have held this view can only be explained below (sections VI and VII).

The first claim is certainly more plausible. It has several dimensions. First, consider the situation when there are conflicting basic economic interests in society. Within the private property system, solutions emerge (within various constraints) from individual transactions. The details of these transactions and the kinds of conflict are less important and might vary from society to society. But, in general, in the economic realm of private property (in the market) social mechanisms do not control the system. At most they prescribe broad limits, i.e. no fraud, violence, etc. As such economic matters are left up to the market, i.e. to chance. There is no overarching rationality imposed by society on social activities.

This means that one's self-determination is directly conditioned upon the determination of those who have opposed interests. Sometimes this will work to the mutual advantage of both. However, more generally, a person's rational self-determination is contingent upon the antagonistic actions and hostile interests of other people. Radicals contend that people cannot rationally determine their lives when their fate, income, security, family life, etc. are dependent on the vagaries of the market (Marcuse 1969a: 13–15); when one day they might have sufficient funds to live and another day not; when their source of income might flourish one day, but be destroyed the next day by fire, storm, crowds, or the market; when they might be fired for no reason at all from their jobs or injured on the job with little or no compensation. In all these cases, which arise out of societies with fundamental economic conflicts, radicals claim that people cannot be rationally self-determining. At best, they try to rationally figure out how to make the best of a bad situation. They are not free, so much as forced to cope; they do well (perhaps) at coping; they do less well at freedom. In contrast, Marx claims that, with regard to the realm of production, "freedom in this field can only consist in socialised man, the associated producers, rationally regulating their interchange with Nature" (Marx 1967b: 441).

Secondly, under such a system the products of human activities come to dominate their producers. People suffer from a fetishism of commodities. That which they have produced dominates them. Their products are viewed as having their own independent powers over humans. Further, various private economic powers develop which can then assert their interests over others. Liberals and conservatives accept this determination of people's behavior as "natural" and unavoidable. Thus, liberals tend to hold that "if my actions must be limited, let it be by an impersonal and invisible force rather than by another 'autonomous' man" (Pennock 1972: 11). This liberal willingness to be "coerced" by impersonal systems stands in stark contrast to the radical view. For radicals, on the other hand, people under these circumstances are not free.

Marx and Engels' comment is appropriate:

> Or how does it happen that trade, which after all is nothing more than the exchange of products of various individuals and countries, rules the whole world through the relation of supply and demand – a relation which, as an English economist says, hovers over the earth like the fate of the ancients, and with invisible hand allots fortune and misfortune to men, sets up empires and wrecks empires, causes nations to rise and to disappear – whereas with the abolition of the basis of private property, with the communistic regulation of production . . . the power of the relation of supply and demand is dissolved into nothing, and men once more gain control of exchange, production and the way they behave to one another?
>
> (Marx and Engels 1976a: 162)

People must recognize that the powers exercised over them by products they have produced are their own powers. They can be, radicals contend, rationally controlled and directed. Only when this is done will people be able individually and collectively to be rationally self-determining and hence free.

Thirdly, political institutions and disputes derive from the contradictions and conflicts within the material or economic basis of society. For example, Marx and Engels claim that the social structure and the state are continually evolving out of the life-process of definite individuals, however, of these individuals, not as they may appear in their own or other people's imagination, but as they *actually* are; i.e., as they act, produce materially, and hence as they work under definite material limits, presuppositions and conditions independent of their will.

(Marx and Engels 1976a: 35–6)

Because of conflicts and problems of maintaining order within the material realm various political mechanisms associated with the state have emerged. Such mechanisms include the police, courts, army, the bureaucracy, as well as laws, rights, and procedures such as elections.

Political institutions and mechanisms – both substantive and procedural – keep order by imposing constraints (both positive and negative, as well as external and internal) on members of the society, by controlling their behavior and thoughts through ideology, and by excluding various groups from basic social decisions. These instruments of control are institutionalized forms of coercion, force, and power. They are part of the superstructure of a society – a response to conflicts, tensions and contradictions within the base of society. Thus, these institutions do not arise due to particular disputes among individuals and their independent need for production. Rather, they arise from the fundamentally conflictual structure of society. As such, politics is society's attempt to control the basic struggles arising from the mode of production.

Now such an account would be compatible with liberal views if the state and the police, etc. were neutral mechanisms which used their forces and violence to control conflicts engendered on the material level. However, radicals reject this view.

On the contrary, political institutions in the superstructure reflect that which gives rise to them, not simply in the sense that they must fulfill certain functions of control, but also in the sense that they partake of the nature of that from which they arise. Accordingly, given that the systematic and structural conflicts within society are ones in which one class is dominated by another class, the state is itself one more item in the class struggle. Specifically, it represents the interests of the ruling classes and works to dominate the subordinate classes. That is, these superstructural institutions are not simply neutral instruments that referee disputes in society. They are the institutionalized force of one class against another (or other) class(es). They are the expression of the productive (economic) forces and antagonisms in society. Thus, Lenin comments that "the state is a special organization of force; it is the organization of violence for the suppression of some class" (Lenin 1966a: 287). Similarly, Marx and Engels say that "the state is the form in which the individuals of a ruling class assert their common interests" (Marx and Engels 1976b: 90). Both social and political institutions, the family, private property, the government, police, army, and the courts are expressions of the conflicting interests in society, partisans within those conflicting interests (Marcuse 1964; 1969c). They do not, ultimately, rise above them. Accordingly, questions of economics and politics are much more closely interconnected for radicals than they are for liberals or conservatives.

This does not mean that these institutions are not beneficial in specific cases or do not help people, on occasion, out of benevolent motives. This is, again, to view them too superficially – on the particular level. Nor must radicals deny that on occasion such institutions may exercise a degree of autonomy. But fundamentally (both systematically and structurally) their role in society is to maintain the given, class-bound, order. The state (and with it the police, army, courts, etc.) imposes its will on society for the benefit of the ruling class.[12]

This means that "freedom" within the political realm is bound up with unfreedom; it requires domination, coercion, and force; hence it really requires unfreedom. More than this, political freedom presupposes a contradiction in the basic interests of the major classes of society.

These comments also hold for rights, laws and general elections. Thus, Lenin claims that even universal suffrage in the hands of the bourgeois is an instrument of domination – it does not express the will of the majority of toilers (Lenin 1966a: 279). Marx is more optimistic about elections. However, when it comes to rights Marx holds that rights are themselves a reflection of the onesidedness and antagonisms of preradical society. "There is here, therefore, an antinomy, right against right, both equally bearing the seal of the law of exchanges. Between equal rights force decides" (Marx 1967a: 235). Rights speak only to the individual as the limited and partial being which capitalism, for example, requires.

Paradoxically, however, this is not to say that rights take account of the individuality of people. They do not. Marx argues that

right by its very nature can consist only in the application of an equal standard; but unequal individuals . . . are measurable only by an equal standard in so far as they are brought under an equal point of view, are taken from one *definite* side only, for instance,

. . . are regarded *only as workers* and nothing more is seen in them, everything else being ignored.

(Marx 1978b: 530)

Rights presuppose the individual who is characteristic of bourgeois society, namely, the abstract individual.

Accordingly, societies in which rights play an important role are societies that presuppose underlying basic conflicts in which people will be dominated, coerced, and have little or no say in the determination of the direction their lives take. Though political freedom is ballyhooed in such a society, this in itself reveals the kind of unfreedom to which people are subjected. It is the freedom of a "civilised" jungle. In short, such societies cannot be free societies and the people in them cannot be free. Though the institution of rights has sought to moderate these conflicts by guaranteeing to individuals certain protections while imposing obligations on others, the intensity of the conflict has been (in some cases only) moderated. When workers or people get out of line, the full force of the state can be brought to bear against them. The irony is that the rights people claim presuppose in their very nature that there is conflict, that it cannot be avoided, and that those outside the ruling class will be least protected.

In contrast, radicals argue that we can be free only when our interests (and activities) are harmonious. The presence of conflicts and fundamental contradictions implies that there is a lack of rational direction of harmonious interests. Instead, conflict, force, coercion, and domination hold sway. Thus, people can be radically free only in a society in which all basic conflicts have been overcome.

In this sense, one cannot be free or rationally self-determining simply as an individual. Unlike liberal freedom, radical rational self-determination does not, and cannot, pertain simply to oneself. Radical freedom cannot be limited to one's narrowly circumscribed world, to a private realm one carves out, or to one's rose garden in which one seeks to remove oneself from the world and its irrational forces. This approach is blind to the positive, systematic, and structured aspects of freedom. It attempts to shrink the self to enlarge one's freedom. This does not gain freedom, since it does not gain but the most narrow, cramped, and limited self-determination. The forces of oppression are not driven from one's garden gate by concentrating on the roses. The most that is accomplished is a fantasy of self-determination.

Instead, human freedom requires a particular communal context. Unlike conservatives and liberals, one cannot be free within a variety of political forms of government. In this sense, the nature of society within which one lives is much more crucial for radicals. It must be a society whose activities and structures are rationally self-determined by its members. There must be a system-wide rationality for individuals to be free. Freedom calls for more than indifference between the lives of individuals and the rationality of the system within which they live. Only within this context can individuals themselves be radically free. These views further explain the radical nature of rational self-determination and why radicals are so sensitive to forms of unfreedom.

However, radicals are of two minds here. On the one hand, some claim that there are degrees of rational self-determination. A partial freedom can be realized now, but only full freedom in some future radical society. Others claim, on the other hand, that radical freedom can only be realized in some future society. We are not able, at the present, to experience even some lesser degree of such freedom. In either case, radicals are convinced that freedom can be fully realized only in a revolutionized society.[13]

What, then, would a free society without underlying contradictions look like? Since rational designs do not just happen, there must be rational designers. Who will they be and what criteria will they use? Are those who simply follow these rational designs, perhaps even begrudgingly, also free? Would radically free people never, in fact, disagree? How can people remain rationally self-determining when this requires one's cooperation, participation, and coordination with others? If I must redirect my plans to fit those of others or the group, aren't I less self-determining then and more other-determined? These are problems that radicals must confront in answering what it means to be rationally self-determining.

IV RADICAL FREEDOM POSITIVELY VIEWED

There are two interpretations of a free society – one without basic contradictions – which can be rejected at the outset. The first claims that a free society is one in which love prevails. People are fully in tune with each other's needs and simply give them what they need (Ollman 1977). Apart from its utter unreality, this view also suffers from the fact that Marx and other radicals have strongly condemned its romanticism. Radical freedom does not require that utterly all conflicts be overcome.

The other view is that free individuals will be mutually and collectively self-determining only when all individuals actually participate in all decisions. Though some have claimed that Marx was committed to some such direct form of democracy (Lukes 1985b), this view seems hopelessly impractical and theoretically undesirable. Further, Marx's "Contribution to the Critique of Hegel's Philosophy of Law" and his comments on the Paris Commune in which there were elected representatives indicates that Marx's views were less extreme (Easton 1981: 200-1).

Instead, a radically free society is much more complicated. It is also more difficult, prior to its realization, to describe. In fact, radicals have generally refused to describe such a society in any detail.[14] Still, they do say a number of general things that may form the basis for further exploring radical freedom.

To begin with, though a free society is not a political society, i.e. it does not include a state, laws, police, courts, rights or duties, this does not mean that a free society will not have different kinds and levels of institutions. Radical freedom is *not* envisioned as some utterly harmonious state of nature, without any formal institutions. A radically free society will include various hierarchies of groups, from the local to the national or international level. There is not simply one general association of all people. These multiple associations and subsocieties voluntarily relate to each other and the central administration of society. They serve as administrative bodies for the areas of their competence and authority.

Such administrative bodies are not, however, bureaucracies or states. This is to say that they do not include judiciaries and do not coercively impose their views on people. Apparently, legislative and executive functions in a free society are exercised by the same working body.[15] Nevertheless, such groups would apparently formulate various goals, guidelines, directives, and recommendations by which society as a whole is to act. This is not incompatible with freedom since the object of such institutions and their activities is rationally to direct society such that it and its members are fully free.

This appears, however, to concede that such bodies will have authority over people. How else can society be rationally organized and coordinated? Over this question of authority there has been a great deal of dispute amongst radicals. Bakunin sees in the principle of authority nothing but the idealised expression of brute force (Bakunin 1950: 18). Consequently, he rejects the authority of the state and hence the state itself. Similarly, Agnes Heller argues that for Marx "the individual is free if there is absolutely no external authority for him and beyond him" (Heller 1981: 347).

On the contrary, I suggest, the main current of radical thought has defended views incorporating central authority, planning, and direction within a society. It is not opposed to authority. Thus, though Marx and Engels reject the authority of the state, they allow for other forms of authority, both central and subordinate. For example, Engels speaks of the importance of authority in the instances of the cotton spinning mill and the railway (Engels 1978: 731). Again, he emphasizes the importance of authority when he points to the example of the director of an orchestra. Lenin explicitly agrees with Engels:

> Take a factory, a railway, a ship on the high seas . . . is it not clear that no one of these complex technical units, based on the employment of machinery and the ordered co-operation of many people, could function without a certain amount of subordination and, consequently, without some authority or power.
>
> (Lenin 1966a: 316)

Similarly, Marcuse speaks of collective ownership, planning and control (Marcuse 1969a: 87). Indeed, the central direction they assume is crucial in order to coordinate the various parts of society. In short, Marx, Lenin and Marcuse are all centralists (cf. Lenin 1966a: 325; 310).

Now the obvious question is how such rational planning by administrators, and the authority they are said to have, is compatible with the rational self-determination of others, indeed, with individual rational self-determination. What does such centralism reveal about radical freedom? What problems does it raise? How extensive must the authority within a free society be? An answer to these questions is absolutely necessary if we are to understand radical freedom.

The standard radical response is to propose practical measures which will make authority compatible with freedom, or at least not a threat to freedom. This involves, first, simply eliminating organizations or institutions which have dominated people in the past: the army, police, the state, judiciary, etc. Society will not have a paid or professional army at its command; there would, instead, be a people's army (Lenin 1934: 18,46,49).

Secondly, the institutions through which society is rationally determined must be radically transformed. Thus, to prevent the office holders of such administrative bodies from forming groups with interests separate from those of others, Marx and Lenin advocate that those in the administration (those who have authority) do not have this as a lifetime sinecure, that they are elected through universal suffrage and subject to recall, that they are paid workers' wages and that measures are taken to prevent them from acquiring honors not available to others (cf. Lenin 1966a: 355; Marx 1968: 57-9). In this sense, the administration of such a society is an open administration. Though such a representative body may seem to be a "sort of parliament" it is importantly different from a bourgeois parliament (Lenin 1966a: 355). Lenin says, following Marx and Engels, that it will be a working body. In this sense, radicals have rejected parliamentary views. Parliaments, Lenin holds, are simply "talking shops" where "the actual work of the 'state' . . . is done behind the scenes" (Ibid.: 304-5). Apparently, the alternative is for working, representative bodies to openly and jointly plan the productive activities of the society.

Thirdly, radical freedom requires genuine universal suffrage for, and participation by, members of society. The control of society is to be exercised such that all people (not simply the elite, the wealthy, or the lucky) participate in a system which seeks its ends rationally and equally, and whose ends are human ends (e.g. people are able to develop themselves). This is possible, Lenin holds, once we "abandon the prejudiced bourgeois-intellectualist view that only special officials, who by their very social position are entirely dependent upon capital, can administer the state" (Lenin 1966c: 56). A crucial role in this will be played by the abolition of private property: "Ever since private property in land and factories has been abolished and the power of the landowners and capitalists overthrown, the tasks of politics have become simple, clear and comprehensible to the working people as a whole" (Ibid.: 1966c: 70).

The importance of participation is suggested in Lenin's complaint that "in the ordinary peaceful course of events the majority of the population [in bourgeois society] is debarred from participating in social and political life" (Lenin 1966a: 336; cf. 337). Contrariwise, radical freedom consists in their mutual rational self-determination. Each will have a voice. This is not to say that each person must directly participate in all decisions. Marx and Lenin indicate that some representative system is compatible with rational self-determination.

Thus, the claim seems to be that if the administrators, those in authority, do not constitute a separate class (they are subject to election, recall, worker's wages), if ordinary people may serve as administrators (all are literate, the tasks are simple), and if the role of such administrators is to "watch" over people's interests, then the directives of such an administration are not incompatible with freedom as self-determination.

There are, however, significant problems not only with these particular suggestions, but the entire direction of these answers.

To begin with, radicals tend to assume that the matters of running a free society will be primarily a matter of technical determination (Heilbroner 1980; Lenin 1966a). Marx himself speaks about the administration of things (cf. Engels 1939: 307). But more than this, radicals speak as if the free society, a society relieved of domination and antagonisms, would be relatively simple to manage. Lenin claims, on the basis of the large-scale production, factories, railways, the postal service, telephones, etc. which capitalist culture has created, that

> the great majority of functions of the old "state power" have become so simplified and can be reduced to such simple operations of regulation, filing and checking that they can be easily performed by every literate person, and it will be possible to perform them for "workmen's wages," which circumstances can (and must) strip those functions of every shadow of privilege, of every semblance of "official grandeur."
>
> (Lenin 1966a: 302)

The point is, as Lenin remarks, that all have become enabled (this is one of the results of capitalism) to take part in the administration of the state (Ibid. 347). Due to universal literacy, and the training and disciplining of workers, Lenin thinks it is possible simply to assume "immediately, overnight" the control of production and distribution (Ibid. 348). This ability to keep accounts and exercise control over social functions, social production, eliminates the need for the state or government (Ibid. 348-9). Thus, an authority would not be one who possesses powers or information of a kind which others could not possess.

Similarly, Engels notes that the public functions of the state will "be transformed into the simple administrative functions of watching over the true interests of society" (Engels 1978: 732). Even more strikingly, Engels says,

> in communist society it will be easy to be informed about both production and consumption. Since we know how much, on the average, a person needs, it is easy to calculate how much is needed by a given number of individuals, and since production is no longer in the hands of private producers but in those of the community and its administrative bodies, it is a trifling matter *to regulate production according to needs*.
>
> (Engels 1975: 246)

The point here is twofold. To begin with, if jobs can be passed around, if special knowledge is not involved, and if private possessions are not allowed to become sources of power over others, then it is possible to avoid the formation of an elite, dominant class. Job holding need not be the basis of a class or segment of society which is oppressed by others. Society can avoid the creation of a class of bureaucrats who are independent of and powerful over the ordinary member of society (Lenin 1966a: 355). In addition, if such matters are terribly simple, then the likelihood that people would disagree over what is to be done, once the underlying conflicting interests were overcome, would be relatively remote. Hence, people would come to agree on the necessary courses of action. The use of force or coercion would not be needed.

These views, however, are extremely dubious. Even the examples radicals use suggest something different. An orchestra conductor is not simply a passive administrator. Lenin suggests that the administrators "watch" over real social interests. Though this could be interpreted passively, it need not be. Similarly, Lenin claims that methods of commanding and subordination are to be replaced by bookkeepers, accountants and the like (cf. ibid.: 306f). However, this belies the fact that the representatives and rational planners of society will have to determine what the interests of people are, mobilize action to protect and organize efforts to fill them. It is true that many think that various administrative tools for decision making such as cost/benefit analyses are normatively neutral. But this is simply false, as others have shown (MacIntyre 1977). Further, Marcuse points out that self-determination is not simply *Selbstverwaltung* (self-government), but a different form of administration, in which what is decisive is the kind of life to be produced and "what priorities are set and translated into reality" (Marcuse 1969b: 25). Thus the suggestion that in place of a political authority we can have passive, merely watchful administrators is mistaken. The problem of authority cannot be resolved in this simple manner. We will need administrators, they will be authorities, and they will have to play active roles.

Secondly, as I have indicated above, radicals have been extremely unclear as to the principles involved in such participation. Do they require that all people participate? Or must people simply have the opportunity presented to them? What if they do not choose to participate? The decisions of those who participate, at least as suggested by Marx's comments on the Paris Commune, would be reached on the basis either of consensus or some voting procedure. But if a vote is less than unanimous, can people adhere to the result and still be rationally self-determining?

It might be objected that part of the problem, which participation is intended to address, is due to the different interests that people have in pre-radical society. That is, participation is a vehicle whereby those of differing interests can protect their different interests. But if, ex hypothesis, people's interests are not fundamentally different or antagonistic (hence, people are fundamentally changed), if the administrative work is extremely simple and technical, then the problem which participation seeks to solve has been reduced, if not eliminated. Why would participation be needed in such a society?

Radicals can respond that participation does not simply serve instrumental values. It may also serve the purposes of rational self-determination by enhancing people's awareness of their communal system, by reinforcing the similar interests that people already have, as well as by strengthening in people their abilities and skills to determine their behavior mutually with other people. Thus, even when people's basic interests agree it is important for people to participate.

On the other hand, it is true that the processes radicals envision by which participation occurs remain obscure. Would individual guarantees such as are associated with liberal freedom of speech, assembly, religion, and press be instituted? If rights are to wither away along with other aspects of pre-radical society, would any form of guarantee be required by individuals against majority decisions? However, since guarantees usually connote some force or coercion available to enforce what is guaranteed, it is not obvious that radicals can give an affirmative answer. Further, what institutions or individuals would make these determinations? In short, what radical freedom positively implies or requires remains obscure.

Thirdly, radicals cannot escape these problems by saying that such administration is limited to work; that the true realm of freedom arises outside. For example, Engels allows that authority does, at times anyway, depend upon the subordination of individuals. He speaks of the despotism of the machinery in a factory which he seems to link with authority (Engels 1978: 731). On this interpretation, one can understand why Marx in his later writings held that the realm of work remained one of necessity, while the realm of freedom only began beyond it – a view which contrasted with his earlier views in which he speaks of labor as a prime need and freedom being possible within the realm of labor (Marcuse 1969b). But to take this line is to concede the impossibility of a full-fledged freedom, which was the basis upon which prior society was criticized. Clearly work plays a crucial role in people's lives. Of course, radicals postulate the reduction of work time, but this seems only to try to escape this important issue.

Marcuse, it is true, has defended talk of utopian possibilities of a new mode of life in which the freedom people enjoy transcends any distinction between a realm of necessity and one of freedom (Marcuse 1969a; 1969b; 1970). However, even if there are grounds within the radical movement to return to Marx's broader views of freedom, this move does not resolve the problem of authority and the administration of such a society.

Finally, and most importantly, the preceding answers given by radicals do not answer the initial, theoretical question as to the compatibility of such authoritative bodies and freedom. Even if participation is simply the means whereby people occasionally are administrators and authorities, this does not show us why they are not thereby reducing the freedom of those over whom they have authority. Further, this question cannot simply be put off to the future, as the nature of the administration might plausibly be put off. The latter question is technical and practical; the former is theoretical and fundamental. Though radicals seek to unite theory and praxis, we must have some reason, in the case of administration and freedom, that the two can be united.

There are two aspects to this theoretical problem. On the one hand, we need to know how self-determination and authority are compatible in a radically free society. In short, what kinds of authority can radicals (Marx, Lenin, and Marcuse) consistently allow? For example, if a person or institution simply provides information which is already available to everyone, then we can hardly speak of an authority. For there to be a free society it would not be sufficient that authorities merely undertook "the simple administrative functions of watching over the true interests of society" (Engels 1978: 732). Much more is involved. Contrariwise, a person who does exercise authority by requiring or commanding people to do various things would seem to conflict with the self-determination and hence freedom of individuals. As we shall see, radicals meet the problem of authority not only by modifying the nature of the authority but also by a different view of the nature of individuals within a radically free society. These views also, partially, explain the extensive nature of radical freedom.

On the other hand, crucial to radical freedom and the problem of authority is the nature of rationality which a free society must embody. Thus, we must also look to the claim that radical freedom requires that our self-determination be rational. This rationality, we have seen, requires central direction. Only in this way can we overcome the irrationality and arbitrariness of the productive base which, in the form of the market, has played such an influential role in society. This is an additional feature of radical freedom which explains the extensive and pervasive nature of unfreedom which radicals perceive in present society. But, first, we must look to the relations between authority, freedom and the self.

V   FREEDOM, THE SELF, AND THE COMMUNAL INDIVIDUAL

Radical society, we have seen, will have institutions which rationally plan the activities of society. These institutions will have authority over individuals. Further, there will be a central authority in society. This authority will not be a state which coercively imposes its demands on society. The activities of such an authority will be (supposedly) rather simple. This character of radical authority will reduce, at least partially, the tension between authority and freedom. But the relation between rational self-determination and such rational institutional authorities is still unclear. How is such authority, albeit rational, compatible with radical freedom?

It seems clear that radical authority could not be a command authority, i.e. an authority to which obedience was due simply because the authority dictates or orders people to act in certain ways. Command authority is incompatible with radical freedom since it need not be rational and usually connotes that those who disobey may be forced by the authority to obey. Lenin comments that "the specific 'commanding' methods of the state officials can and must begin to be replaced" (Lenin 1968: 117).

On the other hand, radical freedom might be compatible with a different kind of authority, such as respect authority. To say that someone has respect authority is

> to assert that his words on the subject in which he has expertise should be sought out and listened to carefully. This is the characteristic way in which one shows respect for someone who is an authority on a subject.
>
> (Ladenson 1972: 339)

But if Lenin and Marx are correct, those who are in authority do not have any special expertise. As we have seen, one of the striking features of radical views on the administration of a radical society is that it will be relatively simple involving activities that almost anyone could perform. Indeed, it is to eliminate such expertise in running a country that they are concerned. Thus, this form of respect authority does not capture the relation between radical freedom and radical authority.

Perhaps we could, however, speak of a respect authority which attaches to positions, rather than special knowledge. Thus, I respect a person's directions not as commands, or as revelations of a special knowledge I lack, but as indications of what must be done by all of us if we are to achieve what we mutually believe important. The idea would be that this position is a focal point for the unified values we share, a point through which these mutual values are expressed, organized, and directed. Thus, for instance, the leader of an athletic team might be respected and followed not out of a command authority – or even out of any special knowledge (or talent) – he or she has, but out of respect for the position he or she occupies. Someone must call the signals; this is the person who is presently doing it. In short, this person in this position organizes and directs us in the realization of our mutually held values and interests.

In this sense, radical authority could not be characterized as command authority, since people do not follow what is directed *simply* because it is directed and would not be subject to punishment by the authority if they disobeyed (cf. Wolff 1970: 9). Nor is it respect authority. Instead, it is what we may call a position or focal authority. Its authority lies in the designation of those holding certain positions to direct the activities of society. Though the knowledge and skills required for such a job may be simple, it may not be the knowledge, information or skills that everyone presently has. Thus, we follow this person simply because he or she is the one who coordinates the rational self-direction of our society. As such, it is a genuine form of authority.

However, simply to identify such an authority hardly solves the radical's problem. Though problems of disagreement over information, facts, etc. are supposedly solved by the simplicity of the tasks, radicals must still assume that we share basic interests and values. Only then can an harmonious or communal order (i.e. one without conflicting basic interests), which radical freedom requires, be realized. Only then will the directives of a (focal) authority not violate people's freedom.

Though some have sought to solve this problem by a social contract in which all people agree to certain procedures, rules, etc., radicals have not, by and large, taken this route. They have sought something more fundamental than an agreement among people who may, nevertheless, have different and conflicting values and interests. They have looked to the development in people of harmonious values and interests. Engels, for example, holds that it is an obvious, self-evident truth that the interest, the well-being, the happiness of every individual is inseparably bound up with that of his fellow-men. We must all acknowledge that we cannot do without our fellow-men, that our interests, if nothing else, bind us all to one another.

(Engels 1975: 246)

But though this may be "an obvious, self-evident truth" its realization requires a revolution and the development of a new individual (Marcuse 1969a: 19f).

It is not surprising that we arrive at this point. Marx indicates that "to be radical is to grasp the root of the matter. But for man the root is man himself" (Marx 1975a: 182). Thus, if radicalism is to rest upon what is fundamental, we unsurprisingly end with man. Indeed, however we twist and turn the nature of authority and the rational direction of society, a different kind of participant in this process is needed. This should not a priori be rejected – unless one holds that people have for all time been the same – which seems false. Radicals themselves not only recognize this point but proclaim it. Marx and Engels comment that for the success of the cause which strives for freedom "the alteration of men on a mass scale is necessary" (Marx and Engels 1976a: 53). Forces within the modern period are generating a new society and, consequently, a new self, one which will be a communal self. Similarly, Lenin speaks of a "person unlike the present man" (Lenin 1966a: 345). The necessity of this alteration is that only in this way can society "succeed in ridding itself of all the muck of ages and become fitted to found society anew" (Marx and Engels 1976a: 53).

The question is: what kind of person does radical freedom required such that radicals can speak of a person being rationally self-determining while, at the same time, a member of a community in which institutions rationally plan the activities of society?

The answer demands the development of a self which is united in its interests and values with others: "In communist society . . . the interests of individuals are not opposed to one another but, on the contrary, are united" (Engels 1975: 246).[16] Though Engels' comment above suggests that individuals presently have such shared interests, but are simply not aware of it, this is false. These unified interests, and values must be developed. They do not presently exist because of the basic structural contradictions in society. But which values and interests must be developed and how close must be their connection? What must be the nature of the individuals involved?

To begin with, radical individuals must be persons who find accomplishment in cooperating, rather than competing with or conquering others (Marcuse 1969a: 4–5). However, how far does this extend? Does this include not only production but also sports? Surely the radical self must be one which is not defined by class or particular interests, but by general or universal interests. Further, not simply any unified or universal interests will do. Only those which are cooperative, harmonious, and productive of collective self-determination will do. Both Marx and Marcuse are quite clear that a new kind of sensitivity not only to others but to one's surroundings would also be part of the unified interests and values radically free people shared (Marcuse 1969b: 24; Marx 1975c: 322–6).

At times Marx makes the connection of interests seem very close indeed. For instance, he claims that

> in your enjoyment or use of my product I would have the *direct* enjoyment both of being conscious of having satisfied a *human* need by my work . . . and of having thus created an object corresponding to the need of another *man's* essential nature.
>
> (Marx 1975d: 227–8)

This is stated in a rather romantic way. One is emotionally bonded with others on a rather particular level. This is, however, closer than radicals need or usually claim. Indeed, such a unity of (all) interests seems excessively romantic. Even those truly in love may disagree, dispute and differ. What is clearly required is a unity of basic interests as well as (it would seem) agreement on priorities and weightings of those basic interests and willingness to agree on means to realize them.

However, what is additionally important in such suggestions is that the very structure of one's self and its interests will incorporate others. Within pre-radical societies, individuals have existed as abstractions in the sense that they are identified with their physical selves, or with their labor-power. With radical society, individuals are seen as sets of physically anchored social or communal relations. This can be comprehended and its positive implications realized only in a radical society. Accordingly, one can appreciate why Marx says that "the essence of man is no abstraction inherent in each single individual. In its reality it is the ensemble of the social relations" (Marx 1976: 4). Usually philosophers speak of people realizing in themselves their (human) essence. A person is thought to be a rational or sensitive being. These qualities are believed, in some sense, to be "embedded" in each individual. To realize one's humanity is to fully develop these characteristics within oneself.

In contrast, Marx is obviously not saying that each person is (or can realize) in him or herself the ensemble of social relations. However, what he might mean is terribly unclear. Further, there are problems if the ensemble of social relations includes all social relations – good as well as bad. Surely radical freedom does not include realizing bad social relations as well. In addition, it makes little sense to think that people could (individually) realize in themselves all social relations. How could they take part in all of them? And if the human essence were the ensemble of social relations, then what is it that is related? Since no individual can realise the ensemble of social relations by him or herself, the conclusion follows that no individual can be (by himself or herself) fully human. But this may not be shocking. It may indicate that humanity and rationality are similar in that just as people cannot be fully rational by themselves, so too they cannot be fully human by themselves. Similarly, I can only be a self through my interrelations with others. As such, I can only be free or rationally self-determining through my relations with others.

In the end, radical freedom is only possible when people are rationally self-determining *qua* human being, that is, *qua* communal being. Only in this manner will the plethora of forms of unfreedom be avoided and the possibility of self-direction be realized. In short, people can only be free as human beings, as beings who have control over their activities, when they choose as members of a radically free society. That is, they choose on the basis of mutual, harmonious, and universal interests. Accordingly, Marx says:

> Only when the real, individual man re-absorbs in himself the abstract citizen, and as an individual human being has become a *species-being* in his everyday life, in his particular work, and in his particular situation, only when man has recognised and organised his "*forces propres*" as *social* forces, and consequently no longer separates social power from himself in the shape of *political* power, only then will human emancipation have been accomplished.
>
> (Marx 1975c: 168)

Under capitalism, one chooses as a member of a capitalist society, hence, as a self-interested individualist (as an egoist), as a class member. However, this leads to unfreedom. Under radical freedom, one chooses as a member of a radically restructured society. In the process, one is oneself not only radically restructured but also, for the first time, free. Thus, it is not just any person who can be rationally self-determining.

There are several additional problems with this view. The reason that radicals believe that such a person is possible is because of an environmental view of the self they share. Radicals hold that the nature of people is effectively determined by the nature of the society, or the context within which they live and work. Marx and Engels, for example, comment that "as individuals express their life, so they are. What they are, therefore, coincides with their production, both with *what* they produce and *how* they produce. Hence what individuals are depends on the material conditions of their production" (Marx and Engels 1976a: 31–2). In short, radicals have held an environmental view of humans, one focused on production. Private individuals predominate in capitalist society. Social or communal individuals will predominate in radical society. To view the relation of individuals to society as that of the collection of separate and separable individuals is simply to accept the liberal contract view of society. Instead, radicals see individuals and society complexly interwoven, such that to speak of an individual is to speak of a social or communal being.

This view is, however, highly dubious. Two objections are relevant. On the one hand, it embraces a nineteenth-century exaggerated optimism in the malleability of individuals. In fact, it is in this area that some radicals have sought changes. Thus, Marcuse has suggested that various biological desires must be recognized as basic among all humans (Marcuse 1969a). If this were the case, then the changeability of humans through modifications in their productive systems would be dramatically reduced. Unless these basic biological needs or desires are harmonious, the project of radical freedom would be seriously threatened. The problem that then faces radicals is what modifications must be made in the environmental view of the self which their model has traditionally held.

On the other hand, it has been objected that this view of the self effectively disintegrates the individual self. For example, G. W. Smith objects that

> if social relations remain in communism and the exercise of true freedom and individuality consists basically in choosing those relationships then we have to make some sense of the idea of an individual who creates his own identity by acts of social choice. Yet . . . the individual seems necessarily to disappear, for how can he intelligibly be said to endure through a series of changing relationships which constitute him as an individual person?
>
> (Smith 1982: 241; cf. Heilbroner 1980: 163)[17]

That is, since the freedom of such a self lies in choosing its relations and since there is nothing which can be continuous through this alteration of interrelations, the self simply disappears on radical views. Thus, radicals cannot give an adequate account of the self or individual freedom (Smith 1982: 238–42).

This, however, seems to be a problem to which radicals might be able to respond. Surely radicals need not say that all social relations under communism need always to be changing. The continuity of relations could provide for the continuity of social selves. Further, people do have particular memories and perspectives from which their social relations are viewed. Since these also come attached to particular physical bodies, radicals could plausibly argue that this would be enough to guarantee a sense of individual selfhood.

There are other problems however. Free individuals, radicals claim, will not require coercive agencies to make them follow these fundamental forms of behavior. However, when they break such "rules", they will punish themselves (Marx 1975f: 179) – or others (neighbors, friends, etc.) will discipline them. Lenin appeals to the armed majority (Lenin 1966a). In any case, there will be greater self-monitoring and other-monitoring under human freedom. Thus, formal coercive agencies will not be needed.

However, this raises at least two very worrisome problems. On the one hand, self-punishment can be even more restrictive than the punishment of oneself by others. If people have so modified themselves through identifying with others and becoming self-disciplined that they do not need external disciplining forces, then the self may suffer under the weight of this introjection of authority more than if some command authority and punishment were left external. Perhaps it is not surprising that this view of the self seems to emerge in the nineteenth century prior to Freud.

On the other hand, if disciplining in society is at the hands of the armed majority (and this is not simply during the dictatorship of the proletariat) one must be fearful of what discipline such armed groups of people would seek to "impose" on other people. Strong-armed tactics are, of course, an immediate concern. However, since radical freedom emphasizes rational self-determination, one can well imagine that such groups might also "encourage" self-confession and self-accusation as more compatible with radical freedom. The historical instances of this approach are well known.

Nevertheless, if the preceding does capture the nature of radically free individuals, then it is clear, I think, that radical freedom suffers from significant problems related to the nature of the self. Indeed, it may be that the central problem of radical freedom lies with its notion of the self.

Radicals presuppose a self which must be not limited for it to be free. This follows from their environmental view of the self and the demand that distinctions and dichotomies in productive and social life be overcome. As a free being, the self must not be limited or bounded by almost any distinction, force, restraint, etc. that one could think of. Its reasons, grounds of action, interests, and values must be universal, rational, non-particularistic. They must also relate to concrete features of people and objects, not abstract features. These two aspects of the self must be synthesized. If they are not, the self is limited and cannot be rationally self-determining. This is manifested in the extended list of "things" which radicals see as impinging on individual freedom. Thus, radicals complain that liberals fail to see how far domination or more subtle forms of power extend. Because of their naïveté, liberals tend to view the self as some unimpregnable fortress. Radicals argue that they are mistaken.

The failure of radicals, however, is to see that the self *qua* self does (and must) have limitations. They too have been naive. The truth would seem to be that to be a self is for one to be limited in various ways. These limitations define one's self. Whenever we work with others, we must give up certain things. It might be objected, however, that this should not be perceived as a "giving up" rather than a "going beyond" our own limited horizons. We see it as a "giving up" because of the implicit assumptions we make about ourselves, our individualism. It is conceivable, it is true, that such accommodations could be viewed as a "going beyond" our narrow selves, as coming into touch with something more general and important. Something of this sort might be the case in scientific studies where one's research is modified, corrected, or extended by colleagues such that the results exceed what one began with. To the extent, that is, that people view themselves as engaged in a common and mutual project this could be the case. However, for this to occur, there cannot be underlying and basic conflicts of interest. Others must not be threatening, but supportive sources. Still, even if this objection be granted, the self that results, though more expansive than before, will (necessarily) still be a limited one.

In contrast, any unlimited self might be a mystical self, one which identifies with all of nature. However, it is only in religious experiences, if there, that we may talk about such a self. There is a sense, then, in which the radical view of self obliterates the very self which it seeks to defend and develop – and hence loses grasp of freedom. The failure to appreciate this is at the heart of the problems of radical freedom.

On the other hand, it is clear that criticisms of radical freedom which claim that it involves distinguishing between a higher and lower self, the former of which is imposed on the latter, are mistaken (cf. Berlin 1969). There is little indication here that radical freedom demands any division of individuals into higher and lower selves. Such a division is not to be found in Marx, Lenin, or Marcuse. This is not where the problem of radical freedom lies. Indeed, as just noted, it is the divisions of individuals, within individuals, that radicals seek to overcome. Thus, the division of the person into a personal and a class self is exactly what Marx finds unacceptable; it is part of the unfreedom such a person experiences. Radicals seek a unification of the self, a whole self. But it is exactly here that their real problems begin.

The upshot is that if to be human is to engage in making various compromises and associations, if it is to be limited in various ways, not contingently, but in the nature of what it is to be a person, then politics may be unavoidable. As such, both liberalism and radicalism, though in different ways, may represent forms of alienation from politics and not acceptable accounts of political freedom. Exploration of the radical view of reason casts further light on these problems and on the nature of radical freedom.

VI   REASON, CENTRAL AUTHORITY, AND RADICAL FREEDOM

There are several striking characteristics of the radical view of rationality and hence *rational* self-determination. First, radicals assume that free activities are rationally self-determined only when they are chosen with full consciousness in light of broad knowledge. In short, the radical view of reason requires the conscious direction or determination of a course of action by an individual or individuals. It is this that is captured in Marx's comment that

> the religious reflex of the real world can, in any case, only then finally vanish, when the practical relations of every-day life offer to man none but perfectly intelligible and reasonable relations with regard to his fellowmen and to Nature.

(Marx 1967a: 79)

Contrariwise, that which simply happens or is unclear is not (necessarily) rational; it may be arbitrary, a mere quirk of fate. Thus, Marx and Engels object that the "right to the undisturbed enjoyment, within certain conditions, of fortuity and chance has up till now been called personal freedom" (Marx and Engels 1976a: 80-1).

For them this is not freedom. It is for this reason that they go on to say "thus, in imagination, individuals seem freer under the dominance of the bourgeoisie than before, because their conditions of life seem accidental; in reality of course, they are less free" (Ibid.: 78–9).

On this view, a person is not rational simply because his or her behavior, for example, accords with certain standards or has certain results. Nor is a person free simply when not coerced or dominated by other people or institutions. Rather, the manner in which a person's behavior comes about is crucial. And for it to be free, or an instance of rational self-determination – rather than luck, happenstance, or other-determination – the person must know what he or she is doing and be the one who determines that behavior. When this occurs, a person is acting freely. These claims are also true for society. It can be free only to the extent that the activities of society are rationally monitored and directed by some central agency. These views constitute the positive aspect of radical freedom.

Secondly, radical reason is non-historical in the sense that it does not include any appeal to particular forms of custom or tradition to justify present patterns of behavior. Radicals believe that the results of reason are historically conditioned. Further, they believe that there are historical laws underlying the development of society. Nevertheless, history, custom, and tradition play virtually no role in the radical concept of rationality. Rationality is embedded in the historical development of society only in the sense that the development of society allows us to forge on and form a rational society. The conservative trust of historical experience, custom, and tradition is anathema to radicals (as well as liberals). Such historical experience has only resulted in narrow limits of self-determination. Radicals are out to create a new self-determination which is as complete and full as possible. In doing this, rationality is not something which is enshrouded in the darkness of the past. It is not intuitive, nor unclear; it is conscious, purposive, intentional, fully informed, and without mystification.

This does not mean, however, that radicals are wholly opposed to everything that is past. Far from it. Horkheimer notes that "if social progress is really to live up to its name, it must preserve what was good in the past" (Horkheimer 1974: 138). And indeed, radical views on social change maintain that in social development what is good from the past is to be maintained while transformed in being raised to a higher level; what is bad destroyed (Marcuse 1969a: 87). This is part of the dialectical notion of transcendence (*Aufhebung*). Still, the appeal here is not simply to past forms of behavior or customs as with conservative reason. Conservative reason seems embedded and inextricable from such past forms, while radical reason is extricable. The former implies that change of such past forms of behavior may eliminate what is rational in them, whereas the latter does not. Herein lies their basic difference.

Thirdly, radical reason requires, we have seen, the overcoming of dichotomies, disunities, and arbitrary distinctions. Thus, Marx and Engels call for the abolition of the distinction between town and country (Marx and Engels 1976b: 505). They, as well as other radicals, demand the overcoming of the division of labor into mental and physical labor, the elimination of the distinction between owning and non-owning classes, the supersession of national literatures, and even the transcending of races (Marx and Engels 1976a: 425). Similarly, on the international level, Lenin claims that the aim of socialism is to end the division of mankind into tiny states and the isolation of nations in any form (Lenin 1971a: 160). Marx and Engels speak of liberation requiring that individuals overcome "national and local barriers" (Marx and Engels 1976b: 51).

In short, there is a pervasive universalism to radical reason. This has direct implications for the extensiveness of central direction under radical freedom. Radicals have held that such freedom must extend to the entire world; it cannot be simply partial or abstractly realized. Rational self-determination must be universal in nature (Marcuse 1967).

Thus, the elimination of conflicting interests and the search for a harmony of interests derive not simply from the radical notions of constraint and self, but also from their view of reason. Likewise, radical concern with productive forces derives not simply from the desire to reassert human control over these forces but also the need to render them rational. This helps us to understand what they mean by, and how far they would go, in achieving an harmony of interests. It is not mistaken to see radical objections to the distinction between the public and private as derivative from these views.

Quite obviously, then, the radical view of rationality is not simply a technical or instrumental form of rationality. Radical reason is different from the reason which liberals have defended. It is conceivable that a person could be technically rational within a setting in which there were conflicts and contradictions. In fact, this is what happens in capitalist society, or (more generally) within pre-radical society.

On the contrary, radical reason (and freedom) is a global concept involving the coherence and conscious directedness of the various parts of this whole. Hence, radicals have looked to an international culture, language, literature, etc. What is bounded is not rational; only what is unbounded, universal, and open to all is rational. It is not by chance that the song of the communist movement is the "Internationale."

This universality of radical reason is both its strength and weakness. What is contingent, arbitrary and local is opposed to reason. Only when there is a reason for our behavior and we act upon it can we be rationally self-determining. By contrast, conservatives deny that there is a reason for everything. Liberals allow that such reasons may be individual. Radicals reject both views. This is a basic dividing line between radicals and others.

The problem the radical view raises is that what is important in human life may not be, after all, universal; rather it may be particular and local. Radical views imply that we are freer when, in the process of procreation, we can choose the sex of our children – and perhaps beyond that, the color of their eyes and hair, their height, and skin complexion. But this is not obvious. The human race can ill afford genetic manipulations which deplete the gene pool or which skew it in certain ways due simply to particular fashions (e.g. brown hair rather than blonde hair, tall persons rather than short persons, etc.). Accordingly, a rational society would have to monitor the results of such sex determinations. This means that other people will have an important role in various basic life decisions. Radicals such as Marx object that they are not out to submerge everything into a bland sameness or a constraining environment. But the views they defend raise these distinct possibilities.

Secondly, one reason that radicals seem to hold that there must be a central, rational direction of a society is that they begin with examples such as those above which involve factories, orchestras, and the like. Each of these obviously involves some form of central authority or direction. Similarly, radicals hold that there will also be a central authority in any country. Just as an orchestra or factory need a strong central director, so too, they have held that society requires some strong central direction.

Another reason is that they follow the implications of freedom as being a rational self-direction. If to be free involves rational *self-*direction, and one views the self as a central controlling "entity" or force, then analogously a society which is free will have a central controlling force. This is a particularly likely extrapolation if society itself is viewed, in some sense, as an organism, rather than simply a collection of individual persons. Since radicals have tended to hold such an organic view, they have naturally extended the rational self analogy to society itself.

Now this leaves considerable room for disagreement with the radical model by those who do not accept these analogies. Radicals do not compare society to string quartets without conductors, but to orchestras with conductors. On their behalf this exhibits a measure of realism inasmuch as large groups of people who seek to work together for some purpose do require some central direction. But it may be questioned whether societies have (or should be) viewed as having the unity and coherence that specialized groups (such as factories and orchestras) have in their efforts to work for some single purpose. Further, even with a person, it may be best not for his or her self always to seek to exercise a dominating and controlling function in everything that the person seeks to do. Some things are simply better if they happen spontaneously or unreflectively. Of course, a person might decide to let this happen. And amongst radicals there have been those who advocated a kind of spontaneity. However, they have been less historically influential than those who have held a view of the self as a dominating self. In addition, this view of large enterprises as involving a strong central, rational direction is rather outmoded. We see this in recent accounts describing the management of large international corporations – descriptions which emphasize decentralization and relative autonomy of various parts of the corporation (Peters and Waterman 1982).

Finally, radical rationality tends to be result-oriented, rather than procedural. That is, something that is rational must itself be designated by rational considerations. It cannot be an unchosen consequence of other subordinate rational and voluntary decisions. Hence, radicals reject as rational the order, which others claim to see, in market exchanges. Instead, they see booms and busts, waste and inefficiency. Here we see a genuine tension in our views of what is rational.

To be rationally self-determining is not to remain victim to the market. A free society is not one in which a natural disaster may reduce one person to poverty and permit another person, consequently, to sell his or her goods at inflated values. Such a society, trumpeted by some libertarians as a free society, is better viewed simply as a gambling casino. Radicals reject this view. Instead, they hold that one's freedom is connected indissolubly with others. Only in a community can people be free, because only in such a society can the production of life and the powers of nature be rationally controlled. To remain a pawn of the market is to give up self-determination; it is to define freedom in terms of the lack of individual coercion, but remain

subject then to institutional domination and the restrictions of nature
(Waliki 1984: 220f). The decisions of thousands of individuals which
result in a person's impoverishment, though not intended by them
still impoverishes that person. This is not a natural result; it could be
changed by conscious and planned decisions by society. In this way,
such a person is oppressed and rendered unfree. He or she is not
rationally self-determining.

What we see here is a distinctly radical sense of "rational." The
radical view cannot be measured by the conceptual point of whether
or not this is what "rational" means. Rather, it should be weighed
against the implications of adopting this view of rationality. And it
is here that it faces serious difficulties. The centralist view of
reason is simply fraught with dangers to individuals as well as
deficiencies in the information available to it so that it can make
the rational decisions it is supposed to make. Others have persuasively argued that the information requisite for rational central
direction of the kind which radicals have advocated is impossible
(cf. J. Gray 1986b).

The problem is that radicals have adopted a mistaken model of
rationality as it supposedly appears within individuals and applied it
to society. If, on the contrary, what is rational is an outgrowth of the
exchanges and dialogue of many people (as I contended in Chapter
1), then not only may the individual model of reason have to be given
up, but also we should reject the centralist view and hence the radical
interpretation of freedom as rational self-determination.

In short, if liberals have been optimists about the goodness of human
nature, radicals have been optimists about the powers of reason. For
radicals the powers of reason seem virtually unlimited. If there are any
limits, they are considerably far removed. Liberals and conservatives,
on the other hand, tend to emphasize their proximity.

In an important sense radical reason is the upshot of the rational
dream Descartes had – the dream of a world fully subject to universal
reason. To the extent that our increasingly technological world is the
result of such rationalism, and rationality is captured by some form
of central calculation, radical reason and freedom are outgrowths
of the development of modern society. But this understanding of
reason is outdated. It poses practical problems in society's tendency
to try to control everything through the use of computers, cameras,
polygraphs, observers, etc., etc. It also raises theoretical problems
inasmuch as it appears impossible to gain the knowledge required
for such rational control. Rationality is something different than
the calculations of some central (or internal) source. In this way,

radical freedom forms another part of the modern problems we must overcome.

Though some radicals (such as Marcuse) have worked towards modifications in this view, the central, universal character of radical freedom as it has developed out of the writings of Marx, Engels, and Lenin have been crucial to the radical model. It is this hyperbolical view of reason which carries important problems for freedom.

VII CONCLUSION

The world of unfreedom which radicals see is one in which humans actively create themselves and their world, and yet at the same time are bound and subdued by it. They are caught in a kind of double bind. Forced to produce they are forced by their products to act in ways other than they would collectively and rationally choose. Like sorcerer's apprentices their creations control them; they do not control their creations. In contrast, radicals propose a world in which humans are masters of their destinies, rationally controlling that which they have produced. It is this view that I have called freedom as rational self-determination. It is an important and intuitively appealing view.

We have seen how this view of freedom naturally leads to radical views. Beginning with the idea of self-determination, radicals extend this to society. Inasmuch as individuals are members of society, their self-determination depends upon the nature of society and, hence, the extent to which individuals collectively are self-determining. However, to say that society must itself be self-determining suggests that the determination must come from some "self" of society, that is from some "center." Thus, we get the radical view that the rational organization of society can only come from some central administration. Similarly, rationality seemingly connotes a central organizing, coordinating and harmonizing center – as it does with an individual. Rationality as a process which culminates from a number of different individuals is not part of this classical radical view.

It is clear that radical freedom is quite different from liberal or conservative views. It is also clear that it leads to dramatic consequences and implications, some of which are extremely insightful in thinking about freedom, while others are quite simply dangerous. The problems of the radical view surrounding these central concepts drive us on to seek some other solution.

Though there is no necessity which connects radical views to freedom as rational self-determination, there is a particular affinity between the two. Berlin makes a similar point with regard to negative freedom and liberalism – liberals tend to be drawn to negative freedom, rather than positive freedom. The particular affinity between radicalism and rational self-determination is the connection people make between freedom and having some kind of rational say and control over what happens to them. On this basis radicals criticize and condemn major forms of contemporary life without appeal to the subjective wishes or desires of individuals. This affinity also encourages the relentlessness with which radicals develop rational self-determination, as opposed to liberal freedom. In these affinities lies both the danger and the strength of the radical view. It is the danger because the subjective desires of individuals may be overridden by radicals. It is the strength inasmuch as the radical critique of complacent and manipulated desires may awaken us to forms of unfreedom to which we have been blind.

Part II

5 Political freedom as empowerment

A man has no more and no less freedom than he has power.

(E. Martin 1930: 239)

I INTRODUCTION

Political freedom, I shall argue, is a form of empowerment. It is the effective ability of individuals to exercise their right to political self-determination. Since individuals are necessarily and inherently social beings, their self-determination is a social self-determination.[1] Thus, political freedom is a form of conjoint empowerment. We should take seriously the claim that the loss of freedom by some is a loss of freedom for all.

This concept provides the basis for a model of freedom which is adequate for our time. It responds to changes in our society as well as overcomes the defects we have seen in the preceding concepts and models of freedom.

There are three interconnected aspects to political freedom as empowerment.

Entitlement. Political freedom is an entitlement inasmuch as it involves a right to self-determination. Not only must individuals and their actions not be coerced or restrained by others (including institutions and governments), individuals must also be in a position to demand protection from these forms of interference. Thus, rights to freedom of expression, conscience, and assembly play a significant role in political freedom. However, these rights are only partly constitutive of a more basic right of self-determination. In short, to be free is for one's self-determination to be protected and guaranteed. The simple lack of constraint is insufficient.

Involvement. Political freedom is a form of involvement in that individuals may (and significantly do) effectively participate in the determination, by institutions of which they are members, of policies and activities which affect the major features of their lives. When mutual courses of action are required, freedom implies that individuals jointly determine the course of action to be taken. Thus, they are self-determining. Self-determination would be a pallid notion if it only applied in the privacy of one's garden. Accordingly, freedom is closely connected with democratic views of society. It is not a neutral commodity which (theoretically) may be equally promoted by aristocratic or oligarchic societies as well as by democratic societies.

Enablement. Political freedom is an enablement in that individuals have available to them various opportunities and means required to carry out activities essential to their lives as political beings. Thus, one is free only when one is *enabled* both to exercise one's right of self-determination and to participate in determining matters of substantial importance for oneself. Included among the features here at stake are cognitive conditions and material means. These do not guarantee that the empowerment is necessarily rational or successful in its pursuits, but they do set various minimal standards.

Enablement is not simply an external set of conditions. It also refers to the abilities of individuals to make use of these external conditions. Still, these abilities can be acquired only through society and its institutions – which is *not* to say that they can simply grant them. Consequently, one *cannot* be politically free, or even personally free, simply by oneself. One cannot gain freedom by escaping to some desert island. We have labored too long under the delusion that freedom is simply the open road or the unobstructed path. We forget that others have built the road and maintain the path.[2]

Such a view of political freedom is complex. One of the great mistakes people make in thinking about political freedom is to assume that it is something simple.[3] Thus, it stands in contrast to the spartan view of liberal freedom as lack of constraint, as well as classical views of freedom as autonomy. It also contrasts in other ways with conservative and radical freedom. Still, the view defended here draws, in varying degrees, on the models of freedom we have discussed in Part 1.

More importantly, freedom as empowerment is suggested by various recent social, political, and philosophical developments. For example, demands for participation in the workplace and greater worker rights, concern for social welfare minima, increased emphasis on the importance of the social nature of humans, their interdependencies and need for protection are often tied to current concern for a broader and more complex view of freedom. These developments are important, I believe, in justifying this as the concept and model of freedom we should explicitly adopt. Philosophical views must be in touch with social and historical developments, which is *not* to say that they must simply ape all of them.

Nevertheless, it has often been held that a view such as freedom as empowerment is both mistaken and dangerous. It is dangerous because its reference to self-determination aligns it with a positive view of freedom, one which Berlin has warned us has historically led to coercion and totalitarianism. It is thought to be mistaken because it conflates a number of concepts that should be kept separate. Both these charges are, I think, false.

To justify adopting freedom as empowerment I will consider the entitlement aspect of political freedom in this chapter, and the remaining aspects in the following chapters. The aim of the present chapter is to argue that freedom involves a right to self-determination. Political freedom cannot simply be characterized as the absence of coercion or obstacles. Though individuals cannot be politically free who are harassed or coerced by governments or other citizens, the equation of this truth with political freedom is too simplistic. Part of the contemporary (liberal) problem with political freedom is that liberals take the part for the whole – they assume that the mere lack of coercion or constraint is the whole of freedom. Though this is important, it is only part of freedom.

One implication of the present view is that, though we must look to individual freedom as a basis for political freedom, individual freedom is much more closely bound up with political freedom than liberal accounts usually recognize. However, my main focus is not to discuss liberal freedom once again. Rather it is to develop an account of freedom which is not subject to the problems of the three models we have just discussed and is responsive to the problems contemporary society faces.

II NATURAL FREEDOM VERSUS HUMAN FREEDOM

At the outset I concede that the words "free" and "freedom" may be used to speak of a simple lack of physical interference.[4] People speak of streams flowing freely, an animal freeing itself from a trap, as well as objects in "free fall" in space. On this view, the physical interference or prevention of any motion, movement, effort, or action on the part of anything is a restriction of its freedom. We might call this "natural freedom."[5]

This concept could, of course, be applied to humans – after all they are also natural objects. Nevertheless, such a concept of freedom is inadequate for any discussion of the ideal of freedom which applies to humans as beings which are something more than physical objects. As such, natural freedom cannot be used to define either individual or political freedom. It may be an interesting concept from the standpoint of lay physics, but not from that of human society or politics.

The argument here does not appeal to the meaning of our words. Our use of the words "free" and "freedom" is systematically ambiguous.[6] It is impossible simply on semantic grounds to arrive at a single meaning of freedom. Further, ordinary language is itself molded (at least in part) by past theories of freedom. Simply to appeal to ordinary language is to beg the question. Instead, we must argue about the ideal to which these words refer. The argument must be normative and substantive rather than semantic or formal.

There are at least three reasons why natural freedom is inadequate for individual or political freedom – at least as these concepts have been historically important. First, humans are not simply natural things in the manner of rivers, boulders, geraniums, lions, or viruses. In contrast, humans perform actions, are conscious and self-conscious, and can be self-determining. Humans have purposes and goals; they exist within various social relations and not simply natural physical relations. Indeed, humans cannot be understood outside of these relations. Natural freedom, however, gives no consideration to these crucial differentiating aspects of humans. Insofar as it applies equally to humans and non-human things it neglects the subtle ways in which humans, but not plants, animals, or boulders, may be limited. Thus, humans – but not streams, boulders, or plants – can have their freedom reduced by threats and various forms of intimidation. An employer who threatens to fire an employee for speaking out on public affairs has reduced that person's freedom of expression. Similarly, brainwashing, intimidation, and censorship limit the freedom of individuals. Natural freedom cannot account for such unfreedoms. Indeed, according to natural freedom none of these ways of "working on" humans counts as making them unfree. However, since humans can be dealt with in ways other than non-humans, their freedom may also be limited in different ways.

Secondly, to interpret the cry for individual or political freedom in terms of natural freedom raises the problem of balancing the freedom of humans against the freedom of other non-human beings or things in the world. Simply based on freedom itself, the freedom of a boulder, lion, or human would all be comparable. Any distinctions could only be made on grounds external to freedom. Our treatment of freedom then might be like our treatment of water in a drought. Gardens and plants would have to forgo water so that humans could have it. Both have demonstrable needs for water, only since we humans think we are more important, we get the water. Freedom (the absence of physical interference) would be one of many natural goods.

But this means that what does the work in our search for freedom is not really freedom, but some other good (related to our importance) according to which some interferences are to be rejected, while others are permitted.[7] One does not so much seek freedom on this view as that balance of some interferences over others which most promotes some other good. To call this resulting balance "freedom" is to change meanings, since it involves interferences – only more of the benign sort than not. Thus "natural freedom" implicitly recognizes the need for another sense of "freedom." At the same time, it effectively excludes, by definition, those significant historical movements which seek freedom rather than some other good that freedom promotes. As such, "natural freedom" is neither historically nor philosophically neutral. We cannot simply accept it as *the* meaning of "freedom."[8]

Thirdly, according to natural freedom, the very structure and features of our world are a mixture of freedom and unfreedom. The planets, having been trapped by the sun, could be said to be not free in their motion since they are restricted by the sun's gravity. Any force (such as the gravity of another body) which caused a planet's path to deviate (and from what course would that be?) would restrict its freedom. Even the stream which supposedly flows freely to the ocean is trapped in its course by gravity and restrained by its banks. However, if there were no banks and if gravity were to disappear, there simply would be no stream. Similar claims might be made about the possibility of human life – it too would be based on unfreedom, perhaps as much as (if not more than) it is based on freedom. The ways in which we walk, run, and interact are all based on various forces which physically constrain us in a multitude of ways. On this view, it is conceivable that what we should seek is unfreedom (at least certain kinds), rather than freedom. These implications are at odds with a serviceable notion of freedom.

Why, then, have people tended to slip into talk of natural freedom when they speak about humans and human society? One of the main reasons is due to a misplaced scientific bias which has characterized modern thought from the time of Bacon and Hobbes.[9] In order to understand anything, it has been thought, we must reduce it to the simplest level of nature and its interactions; we must get down to "the facts" and abstract from value; we must use concepts appropriate to inanimate matter and thus not speak of purpose or intentions but the motions of particles and bodies. On this level, we can speak meaningfully of one thing or body not physically impeding or constraining the movement of something else. However, to identify this as freedom and then anoint it as the single sense of "freedom" to be used on all other occasions is misguided, for when it is invoked in discussions of political freedom, the latter become confused and unproductive.

In short, there is a set of metaphysical and epistemological assumptions about the explicability of humans and human society through a reductive science which lies behind talk of natural freedom. These assumptions continue to influence our thought on freedom long after they have themselves been rejected or sharply questioned. We must move not only beyond these past views but also their associated notion of natural freedom. We need a more adequate view of freedom. Accordingly, we must seek a sense of "freedom" which is particularly relevant to humans as beings who perform actions and live within relations which constitute a political society. Our view of political freedom must not assume that humans can be treated passively and indifferently as mere physical objects.

III FREE ACTIONS AND FREE AGENTS

It is often thought that the problems of natural freedom can be overcome by linking freedom to the lack of coercion or constraint of human actions. On this standard liberal view, people are unfree because their *actions* are blocked or impeded.[10] Inasmuch as trees, boulders, or rabbits do not perform actions, this sense of freedom applies uniquely to humans. Since freedom applies to actions, it is primarily a local concept. Only derivatively does it apply to the person behind the action and then it does so as a summary concept – it sums up one's status based on the freedom of one's actions. If an action is blocked then the person may be said to be unfree. Hence, on this view, an account of free action is basic.

This view of freedom has already been discussed in Chapter 3 where difficulties central to it have been explored. Now I wish to look at another aspect of this view – one that leads to a different view of freedom, indeed, to the first aspect of freedom as empowerment.

It is clear, at the outset, that to speak of free actions is not to speak of dumb movements or motions which are not (somehow) coerced or constrained. Rather it is to speak of something which involves, at least, consciousness and purposiveness. In short, any account of free action presupposes an account of action. Quite clearly such an account will contrast actions with mere movements, twitches, or spasms. These need not be (and especially the last two are not) conscious or purposive. They simply happen or occur. Freedom applies to actions, not mere movements, twitches, or spasms.

Accordingly, were a delirious patient thrashing about in bed, a nurse or physician who strapped the patient down would not restrict or limit the patient's freedom. Such crazed movements do not constitute actions. The patient is not aware of these movements, could not have controlled them, and did not know that he was endangering others and himself as well.[11] As such, the patient has not been coerced into staying in bed. Likewise, to stop a sleepwalking person from jumping off a bridge is not to restrict or hinder that person's freedom – though it does to impede the "natural freedom" of the person's body. The necessary consciousness and purposiveness are absent.

Hence, to speak of freedom as lack of interference of actions is to speak of the lack of prevention or hindrance of something that cannot be viewed simply externally or physically. Freedom – even when linked to actions – cannot be understood without reference to the inner nature of what is constrained. This distinguishes, at least in part, this view from natural freedom.

However, talk about freedom as the lack of constraint implies not simply that we speak about actions, rather than movements, but that those actions are brought about by agents whose actions they are. Too often discussions of free actions sound as if actions float around unattached to persons or agents. Obviously this is false. For freedom to be in question and constraint to have its bite there must be a person who acts. Freedom as the lack of constraint presupposes agency.

Further, the consciousness and purposiveness that particular actions presuppose must be those of persons or agents with some temporal unity. It is conceivable, I suppose, that we could identify an action which someone does with a person who only exists intermittently. This action could then be coerced, at least while the person existed. When that person was non-existent, only dumb movements by the person's body would occur; in this latter case, no coercion or restraint of freedom could be imposed. Still, this kind of example exhibits the limits of our concepts of freedom, coercion and action. Actions must be understood as part of ongoing agencies. They are something a person does. They are tied to the ongoing purposes, plans, values, and expectations of the person. In short, actions do not simply happen to people; they are what people do. Contrariwise, to the extent such agency breaks down, e.g. the person becomes seriously psychotic, we can no longer speak of his or her actions.

The unfreedom, then, which arises from constraining an action does not simply remain unattached to the person who sought to act in some other way. It is an unfreedom of this person who was prevented from acting otherwise. It is an instance in which the person could not be self-determining, but was other-determined. The unfreedom arises from the restraint or prevention of the purposive agency of a person, or what I shall call a lack of self-determination.

Thus, even the unfreedom of an act must be determined by reference to the situation of the agent. This occurs most simply and obviously when what the person sought to do was blocked or prevented. On the other hand, the mere fact that one arrives at a goal or accomplishes what one set out to do – that is, is successful in his or her action – does not mean that one's freedom has not been violated or reduced during the journey. Suppose, for example, that a person has determined that he will take a particular course of action, in spite of a threat. She will give a speech for the present governor even though she has been threatened with physical harm. It is sometimes objected in such a case, supposing the person to go ahead and give her speech, that she must still be considered free. After all, she did give the speech. But surely this would be a peculiar sense of "freedom."

Admittedly, to have determined one's own course cannot require that one does so in the complete absence of other people and their influences. People can and do follow their own course of action in the midst of others. However, to follow one's own course must surely mean that those other people and influences do not impose forces upon one which only an heroic action or some extraordinary amount of courage could overcome. Freedom would be a joke if people could be said to be free even though their lives and courses of action required amazing feats of effort at each step. Thus, the freedom or unfreedom of this particular action must be judged in light of the person and the circumstances within which he or she seeks to act. If the threats that must be overcome demand a prodigious effort, the act and the person are unfree. If they do not, if the threat is more of a tease, then the person and his or her actions remain free. In between these extremes, we may say that a person's freedom is diminished or increased depending upon the situation.

As such, the notion of the self-determining person is conceptually more basic than that of a free or unconstrained action.[12] We must look behind the action to the person who seeks to bring it about to learn about the freedom we seek. We constrain an action only through the person who does the acting. Thus, to understand free actions, we must look to the self-determining agent or person. The self-determination spoken of here is that of an ongoing agency which brings about those actions. It is basic to our understanding of freedom.

Further, what is basic to freedom concerning this self-determining agency is not simply that it is not constrained, but rather the positive ability to determine one's own actions and life. It is this, rather than the lack of interference, which is the focus of freedom. We can imagine, for example, a person wholly without interferences or obstacles who is, nevertheless, not free because of her inability (due to various reasons) to determine what she should do at the moment or even with her life. She may feel trapped, boxed in, even though no one or even no institution is restricting her. She may simply feel inadequate to the situations she faces. She is unfree.

It is true that some have attempted to account for this situation through the notion of "internal negative constraints" and, thereby, to identify freedom even in such cases with the lack of constraint. However, as I argued in Chapter 3, this attempt is unacceptably problematic. To characterize an ability as the lack of a lack of ability is to engage in Newspeak in order to save negative freedom. In such a world, hiring a person is the lack of leaving a person unemployed, executing a political opponent promotes the lack of negative support, while the ability to vote is the lack of exclusion from the political process. Though we could speak in these ways, it is much more clear and correct simply to speak of the positive actions or abilities involved. Further, classical liberals surely did not recognize such forms of negative constraint which are proposed to eliminate talk of positive freedom. For a contemporary liberal to attempt to accommodate constraints of this kind reveals how far liberals have traveled from their original basis.

Accordingly, it is false to think that freedom is simply a local concept.[13] Freedom does not pertain simply to this or that action. Instead, it is a more global concept. Freedom is tied to our ability to be self-determining, not as a lack of restriction on it, but as the exercise of it.[14] Of course, one may suffer unfreedom when subject to constraints, but a person may also suffer unfreedom in other ways. If some insist on speaking of the exercise of such an ability as the exercise of the lack of a lack of ability or power to do something, I suppose there is little that can stop them. On the other hand, it is a circuitous way of speaking of a positive ability and an attempt to preserve a wholly negative account of freedom. In any case, it seems fully compatible with the positive view of freedom.

The point here is *not* that "freedom from" implies "freedom to." Often it is argued that when people claim they are free from something it must be in order to do something else. Thus, to say I am free from Jones chaining me to the floor implies I am free to go fishing. To this argument Berlin plausibly replies that we can think of being free from something without having anything else in mind which we wish to do.

The problem with such discussions of freedom is that they remain on the level of particular actions. They dispute whether freedom from chains here and now implies freedom to go fishing at Lake Liberty. But it is clear that we may understand a person determining his or her own actions without referring to some (specific) thing from which they are free. In this way, "freedom from" and "freedom to" are intelligible independently of each other. I can intelligibly determine to walk down a mountain path without attempting to list all the possible things from which I am free: bears, snakes, marauding gypsies, alien invaders, and screaming infants.[15] I am free in the direct and immediate sense that *I* am determining what I am doing.

Thus, to understand "freedom from" we need not already understand "freedom to" but that to which "freedom from" applies, e.g. the agency which brings about actions. Accordingly, the level with which we are concerned is, more generally, that of the determination of those actions. To speak of freedom (whether "from" or "to") is to speak about a person's self-determination. That is, talk of freedom is not limited to the *lack of interference* with self-determination. The freedom of individuals and their actions lies in the ability to exercise one's self-determination, not simply in the lack of interference with that determination. A free person is one who is able to determine his or her own course. Thus, people whose ability to determine their own course has been effectively destroyed through years of slavery and domination would not be free persons even if suddenly released. Though they were no longer dominated or enslaved, they could not determine what to do for themselves. They would have to turn to someone else to tell them what to do. They would lack the ability of self-determination. They would not be free. To insist to them that they were free would ring hollow since they could not "get on with their lives." To render them free would be to aid them to recover this ability to determine their own lives and not be wholly dependent on others.

The perfect form of unfreedom, then, is not one in which guards stand watch over people. At least some freedom remains even in this situation, so long as prisoners or slaves are still able to seek ways to overcome the guards and escape their confinement. Nor is it even where people actively impose restraints on themselves, i.e. they seek to control other determinations they would make. Then the guards are internalized, though since resistance remains some sense of self-determination has not been eliminated. Rather the perfect unfreedom is where people's own sense of themselves as self-determining agents has been undone. Only passive instruments of someone else's determinations remain. Then freedom is dead.

Thus, freedom implies an ability to determine oneself to do various things. When a person is unfree it is this ability to determine one's own actions which is impeded. To understand this ability, I shall claim in the next part, we must also understand a set of criteria, values, etc. which the person performing the action understands. In short, we must understand the person or agent who makes the determination of these actions, according to certain beliefs and values.

IV FREEDOM AND SELF-DETERMINATION

Self-determination, we have seen, requires an enduring agency that underlies free action. We need to look yet more closely at such self-determination and its relation to freedom since there are a number of different forms of self-determination that can be distinguished. Freedom is most plausibly connected with only one of them. In short, it is mistaken to equate freedom simply with self-determination.

We can start by noting a view of self-determination which some have mistakenly linked with freedom. It is a view of freedom we have already rejected. For example, Epictetus held that "he is free who lives as he wishes to live . . . whose desires attain their purpose."[16] A person who lives in this manner has been called self-determining. After all, that which leads the person to do certain things – the "moving force" as it were – comes from "within" the person.

However, there is nothing in such "self-determination" that would require that the person whose desires attained their purposes was a rational or coherent being. Self-determination in this sense is compatible with a person being insane or irrational. I might have contradictory desires which, successively, "attain their purpose" but, as a consequence, virtually destroy me. If that is the case, then this is a dubious account of self-determination as well as freedom, since such a person might be at the mercy of his or her desires which tug and pull in contradictory directions.

Suppose, however, that such a person's desires were at least minimally coherent and rational. Even this modified view, we have seen in Chapter 3, cannot be equated with being free. For example, such a view of self-determination is compatible with shrinking one's desires to ensure their fulfillment; it is compatible with complete withdrawal from social and political life, and, indeed, with being a prisoner or slave.[17] That is, one can restrict one's self-determination to a very narrow area by shrinking the self and its determinations. The person in chains who proclaims her freedom because she no longer desires to walk about may "feel free" but is a paradigm case of a person who is not free.[18] In short, sour grapes don't make people free.

Thus, though Epictetus, Hobhouse, and Mill (among others) have called this (or something like it) "freedom," this form of self-determination is a weak version of self-determination and an inadequate view of freedom. With regard to freedom, the problem is that it confuses contentment or a lack of conflict with freedom (cf. Smith 1977: 236). It confuses "feeling free" with "being free" and "acting freely." It trades the gilded cage for free flight. It is a poor trade.

On the contrary, freedom is not simply some internal state of an individual as stoics have sometimes maintained. Were freedom simply some "inner state" the historical struggle for women's liberation, the battles to eliminate slavery on the grounds of freedom and the efforts of millions to change their political systems would be unintelligible. Women, slaves, and others could have saved a great deal of trouble and bloodshed simply by striking a different attitude.

Still, since we do not want simply to quibble about words, we might call the present view *subjective self-determination*. People who live in this manner might even be said to have "subjective freedom." But this is not the form of freedom we must seek. "Subjective freedom" lacks significant elements of freedom.

There is another sense of self-determination that retains the idea that the determination of one's acts must come from the agent or person whose acts they are. The person's actions must occur at his behest or her direction. However, this self-direction assumes, we shall see, a self with some relatively "normal" complement of values, ideals, desires, and aims. In short, it precludes a self that has shrunk itself to a point.

This sense differs from the preceding one in that it is not simply the direction of an act by one's wants. Wants are only part of a person's self-determination. Rather such actions manifest one's self-determinations, hence a unique set of values, beliefs, aims, as well as desires which may be hierarchically arranged. When one is free, one's actions and life activities are directed or determined by this self. This is to refer to the "positive power or capacity of doing or enjoying something" that T. H. Green refers to in his account of freedom (Green 1889: 371).[19] When I so act, I am my own instrument. I am a subject, not an object in my activities. My actions and activities can be explained by reference to my ideas and purposes, not those of others.[20] This is the positive side of freedom. Charles Taylor captures this view when he says that "on this view, one is free only to the extent that one has effectively determined oneself and the shape of one's life" (Taylor 1979: 177). Berlin's description of this form of self-determination is often cited:

> I wish to be an instrument of my own, not other men's acts of will. I wish to be a subject, not an object . . . deciding, not being decided for, self-directed and not acted upon by external nature or by other men as if I were a thing, or an animal, or a slave incapable of playing a human role, that is, of conceiving goals and policies of my own and realising them.
>
> (Berlin 1969: 131)

There are several features to this self-determination. In identifying them, we may also distinguish yet other forms of self-determination. To begin with, crucial to such self-determination is not simply that a person have various desires, values, and ideals, but also that a person have second order reflections or determinations whereby present desires and alternatives may be effectively weighed and selected. A person who is self-determining does not simply act on her present first order desires or values. Rather, she can reflect on these and thereby decide to pursue them, or to block their fulfillment. She may seek to structure her environment and life plan so that this or that desire stands a greater or lesser chance of being satisfied. Thus, in reflecting on and modifying various first order desires and wants, the self-determining person may respond to various changes in his or her conditions and is thereby able to take different courses of action. In short, the person's behavior is not rigid.

It is impossible to specify exactly the extent to which this must be possible. Quite clearly those who are completely rigid in following their first order desires are not self-determining in the manner of someone else who can respond to changes in the environment. Thus, the compulsive hand washer, kleptomaniacs, and psychopaths do not fulfill this criterion of self-determination.[21] On the other hand, one must not reflect on each particular desire on each specific occasion. A person can be self-determining in this sense and exhibit a broad range of ability to engage in second order determinations of his behavior. Finally, those actions in which a person does engage as a result of second order reflections will tend to be viewed as "his" or "hers," though this need not always be the case. People may be self-determining in the present sense and be alienated.

Nevertheless, what is crucial for this sense of self-determination is that the individual is able, through second order determinations, to alter behavior and select between courses of actions. A person who acts in this sense is *reflectively self-determining*. Further, in making these determinations our notion of self-determination becomes embedded in normative and evaluative judgments. We must judge that certain individuals are so far from the range of self-determination that "normal" individuals are capable of, that they are not self-determining. Obviously we do this in the case of people whose behavior is wholly rigid and unresponsive to changes in their circumstances.

We can, therefore, make two additional distinctions. A person who is self-determining must be able to undertake various courses of action. However, the importance of these alternative courses to the individual, as well as understanding their nature, must also play a role. This involves weighing the significance of the alternatives and being able to comprehend various aspects of the situations within which they appear. But the nature of this determination may be rationally based or arbitrary and subjective. For example, if the person does something he believes is important only because of abnormal or irrational desires – desires which if "corrected" would lead him to believe and act differently – then he is, at most, subjectively self-determining. He may not, subjectively, suffer unfreedom, but rationally he is unfree, since he cannot do what he would want to do if his desires or beliefs had been "corrected." Similarly, if the person chooses to act due to a deranged view of the situation he faces, the person is at best subjectively self-determining.

In such cases, we clearly may presuppose a view of what either (in some rough sense) the normal reflective person or the rational person would want to do. A person is *reflectively self-determining* when his or her second order preferences effectively direct first order desires within an understanding of the world that is open to public investigation and correction (cf. Benn 1976: 144). A person is *rationally self-determining* to the extent that he or she only acts on rational beliefs and desires. Thus neither rational self-determination nor normal reflective self-determination is dependent simply upon a person's present wants and values. Still, they are not unrelated to them to the extent that they play a role in determining (are related to) what the rational or reflective person chooses to do.

A second aspect of a person who is self-determining can be identified by looking to one way in which such self-determination might be constrained. Suppose a person had determined to do exactly what a coercer sought to make him do. For example, I decide to vote in the next election and set myself to do so. However, someone calls me up and threatens me with great physical harm if I do not vote. Since the would-be coercer will not exercise any force on me if I vote, and this is what I have determined that I will do, how can I still be coerced in such a case?[22] How can my self-determination be reduced if this is where I am headed anyway?

The answer is surely that I can be coerced in such a situation and that both my self-determination and my freedom are reduced. The coercion takes the form of a threat that, if I do *not* vote, I (or someone or thing I value) will be harmed. Thus, when I vote, the lack of self-determination lies in the fact that my range of choices or alternative courses of action has been reduced to one, albeit the one I myself had decided upon. But for a person to be self-determining *qua* free it must be that the person could do not only what he has chosen or wants to do, but could also, if he so chose, do something else. This suggests that self-determination requires that there be a range of options or courses of action open to one. Quite clearly this takes us beyond subjective self-determination or subjective "freedom."

This range of options refers, in part, to matters external to a person. Accordingly, "positive freedom" as presented here is not merely an intrapersonal concept of freedom, i.e. exercising control over one's emotions or desires (cf. Day 1983: 17). Though an account of freedom cannot wholly neglect the role of the passions, it cannot simply focus on them. With regard to the range of options open to one, it will not do, as I have argued in Chapter 3, simply to multiply alternative courses of action in order to ensure either self-determination or freedom. The problem relates to the significance of the numbers involved.

It might seem, for example, that a counterpart to subjective self-determination would be *unrestricted self-determination* according to which a person would be self-determining only if there were a virtually unlimited range of options open to that person. However, it is wildly implausible to say that to be self-determining or free one must have such an extensive range of options open to one, let alone that they are all equally possible to realise. If this were a necessary condition for either concept, then the world would never have seen, and never will see, an example of self-determination or freedom.

Instead, self-determination (as it is relevant to freedom) requires a range of meaningful or significant options. A person is not necessarily more self-determining if she/he has greater options (even if not unlimited) than a person with fewer options. This determination also requires a number of normative and evaluative judgments. We must look to the nature and variety of those options (cf.Berlin 1969;

Norman 1987; Dworkin 1982). It is possible to multiply options in a meaningless manner. We are not more fully self-determining if the same tomato soup comes in twenty-five different cans and forty-seven different labels. Nor are we necessarily more politically free if we can choose between five candidates, when all the candidates espouse essentially the same view. Instead, some account of what constitutes a meaningful variety of options will be important to pick out that person who is more self-determining than other people.

Accordingly, self-determination requires a meaningful or significant range of options. This notion of "meaningful" (or significant) is obviously indefinite, and can be defined only within each society and historical period. In part it will also have to be measured against the ends or interests which are important to humans. But, however it is made, the extent of our freedom and self-determination depends upon it being made.

V SELF-DETERMINATION AND INFLUENCE

Self-determination does not occur in some isolated setting, but in the midst of other people. We are self-determining only within various social and political contexts, institutions, relations, and roles. As such, "self-determination" does not connote some notion of an uninfluenced influencer (Dworkin 1981: 208). Such strong definitions of self-determination are unrealistic.

What is crucial for self-determination, within such contexts, is that one's own values and desires play a primary, not a subordinate, role in one's choices and actions. If, because of the effect of various forms of subtle influence (including persuasion and manipulation), one's activities do not primarily flow from one's values and norms, then self-determination has been undercut. A person might not in such a situation feel interfered with or constrained. Nevertheless, the person's self-determination and freedom are undermined.

There are two threats to this further aspect of self-determination: particular people or institutions may impose various influences upon people which undercut the primacy of their desires and values, and (more generally) one's socialization into society seems to imply that whatever values and desires one has they are as much society's as one's own. I will consider the former threat in this section, the latter in the next section.

The primacy of one's values and interests might be subverted through the influences that other individuals and particular institutions bring to bear upon a person. For example, Benn says that:

the problem presented by propagandists, advertisers and public relations experts is quite different [from that of coercers, etc.]. They aim not at overruling contrary intentions by threats of coercion but, by persuasion, to create a willing – if possible an enthusiastic – accord. They seek to avoid or dissolve conflict, not to overrule it.

(Benn 1976: 261)

In these cases, we are not so much interfered with, as that the surrounding conditions undercut the primacy of our own values and interests. These conditions occur not simply due to "official" advertisers and propagandists, but also to other individuals and within otherwise "friendly" relations. Accordingly, we want to be able to condemn processes and situations which infiltrate and undermine one's self determination in more subtle ways. But when does this occur?

It might be argued that a person's self-determination is undercut by various forms of influence when they are non-rational rather than rational. Rational appeals direct themselves to one's reason and understanding. Non-rational appeals attempt to circumvent our understanding; they are subtle and subversive. They may occur without us knowing what they are doing. Though in some instances the distinction between forms of persuasion or manipulation may not be terribly sharp, still there is a plausible distinction here. As a result, our own values and interests are subverted.

However, Benn has persuasively argued that non-rational appeals do not, as such, undercut our self-determination or freedom. We are not less free simply because a rock star appears on television and urges us to buy "Bubbly Cola." Nor are we unfree simply because we are influenced by an advertiser, public official or friend in what we do (Benn 1967: 267). If this were the case, self-determination would be found only in hermits – even if then – and education would have to be condemned as undermining self-determination. Both these consequences indicate that we must look elsewhere.

Instead, the influences that attack self-determination prey upon one's motivational structure, e.g. one's fears, wishes, etc. For example, by attributing problems to a person, preying on that person's fears, lack of self-esteem, or psychological weaknesses, one can render a person considerably less self-determining or free. No coercion is needed. It can be a much more subtle (even apparently caring) process. This can be done by sympathetic mothers or fathers who unselfconsciously wish to keep their children around them. The child is unable to leave home as a result. The child's freedom and self-determination has been sharply restricted. It is also done by advertisers and propagandists.

This form of influence need not be self-consciously imposed, though, of course, it may be. Further, the object of this influence may or may not be aware of the influence being exercised over her. Most crucial here is the fact that the influence is effective and at odds with how the person would otherwise – in some sense – behave. But what this sense is requires some indication.

It would seem to be excessively rigorous to demand that playing on a person's fears and weaknesses undercuts his or her self-determination only when doing so would similarly cause a fully rational person to succumb. We are not always rational. Our fears and weaknesses may define who we are as much as our confidence and strengths. Some weaker standard than full rationality is needed.

Benn suggests that we appeal to a notion of "reasonableness": a person is not self-determining or unfree due to non-rational appeals when a person "could not reasonably be expected to resist, even though others might actually have resisted it in the past" (Ibid.: 267, emphasis omitted). This is an interesting suggestion.

However, according to Benn, such appeals to what is reasonable ultimately depend on the notion of a "normal" man (Ibid.: 268). He offers two kinds of criteria for the "normal" man. First, we must ask "whether a person can be aware of what is happening to him" (Ibid.: 269). Secondly, we must turn to empirical (psychological) research for other criteria for "the kinds of influence that a person of normal firmness of purpose with normal interests could reasonably be expected to withstand in a given situation" (Ibid.).

The first criterion is clearly important. However, it is unclear why this is a criterion for a "normal man." It seems more straightforward simply to refer to this as a criterion of reasonableness or reflective self-determination and leave it at that. Further, Benn's statement of this criterion is too weak. We might imagine an instance in which "a person *can* be aware of what is happening to him," but is not. Perhaps it would require a substantial effort to become aware of these matters. Perhaps the person is simply not aware that he should make the effort because he does not know what is happening to him – even though if he had some glimmer he could find out.

In these cases the person's self-determination may be variously affected even though he can be aware (but is not) of what happens to him. We do not want to say that a person must be aware of everything that is happening to him or her at every moment in order to be self-determining or free. Perhaps the point is better put negatively: people's self-determination suffers if they are not (and cannot be) aware of what is happening to them. If a person is not, but could be, then we must know why the person is not. If this is due to an effort to influence the person by keeping information from her/him, then, surely her/his self-determination suffers. Thus, movies or video programs using subliminal projection may influence a person but do not permit the person to know the nature of this influence. They undercut one's self-determination since a person is not (and cannot be) aware of what is happening. They attack the primacy of one's second order desires or reflections.

However, obviously, a person can be aware of what is happening to him and still not self-determining. Hence, the second criterion above. Benn suggests a wholly empirical approach to this criterion. But the criteria of "normality" are not something which psychological research can simply determine by itself. The notion of a "normal person" is a normative notion, not simply descriptive. This comes out if we ask who or what is the "normal" person. Is this based on the poor mountain people of Appalachia, those trapped in a large city ghetto, Indians on a reservation, refugees in a large city, or migrant farm workers? The worry, of course, is that "the normal" is constituted by members of the middle class (and usually those who are white and male). If, on the contrary, "the normal" is some non-distinct amalgam of universal features we should be concerned about its helpfulness. Thus, simply to appeal to some empirical determination of "normality" seems dangerous: it risks simply sanctioning the status quo and implicitly introducing various normative measures under the guise of science.

Instead, we must invoke normative standards concerning what a person could reasonably be expected to withstand under present conditions. That is, we must argue that within a particular situation a person could reasonably be expected to remain self-determining. These standards would indicate when certain influences were of such little significance or importance that even if they stood in the way, a person's self-determination and freedom would not be undercut. They would provide us with measures by which to know whether a person's own values and desires could be said to be primary in determining his or her actions.

VI SELF-DETERMINATION AND SOCIALIZATION

The second way in which the primacy of one's values, and hence one's self-determination, might be jeopardized is through one's socialization. We are socialized through our relations with others. Parents, peers, friends, and authorities all play a role in the development of who we are. However, beyond these individuals we develop within certain social contexts and institutions which transcend these particular individuals and through which even these individuals are to be understood. By such social contexts and institutions I refer to private property, marriage, business, churches, clubs, language, friendship, kinship, etc. Some of these are of a formal nature, others are more informal.

It is quite clear that the form our self-determination takes is structured by these institutions such that self-determination cannot be understood simply by reference to a single individual. For example, some actions are literally impossible outside of various institutions. One cannot hit a home run, let alone be a baseball hero, outside of baseball (Ryan 1980); one cannot vote outside of a social institution allowing for this kind of self-expression; one cannot commit adultery outside the institution of marriage. By far the greatest part of our lives is lived within these institutions. A person may be a member of, or partake in, some of these institutions by choice, but not always. One has no choice over one's mother language, one's parents and kin, and only little choice over the major institutions which shape the society one lives in. These institutions involve rules, rights, attitudes, emotional connections, customs, traditions, etc. Even if one chooses to move to another society, adopt other institutions and a different language, one cannot simply and completely cut oneself off from these past influences. Thus, socialization means that there are certain limits and boundaries which define both self-determination and freedom. That our lives and activities are structured in certain ways, then, is not a matter of indifference.

More than this, our very selves are defined by the various roles which we play in society and influences whereby they have been socialized (cf. Sandel 1984: 17). We do not live in society as marbles within a bag. Rather, life within society structures and determines a great deal not only of our selves but of the determinations of those selves. As such, "my" values and norms – even "my" actions – are not simply and uniquely mine inasmuch as their meaning and intelligibility stand against a social and historical dimension. One of the important tasks of philosophy is to explore these dimensions. In the sense that my values and norms are acquired by me through my induction in society, by my socialization, "my" values and norms – even with the modifications I may bring to them – are also those of society and history. This is to say that my values and norms are pursued within the relations and roles by which I am defined. The analogy often used here – an appropriate one – is that of one's language. My language is not simply mine; it is something I learn from others, something which has a history, tradition, and structure beyond me; and yet it is something I use for my own ends, and modify in various ways. Still, it cannot be understood simply by reference to me. To speak of my "linguistic self-determinations" requires understanding the nature of my language, its limits, and possibilities.

But why then consider any determination which "I" make to be mine? Why is it *my* self-determination rather than simply that of society which is made through me? Doesn't such socialization make self-determination and freedom impossible?

Just as we must avoid interpreting self-determination as requiring that one be an uninfluenced influencer, we must also avoid any view of socialization as creating a social puppet or ventriloquist's dummy. We must not only be able to allow for the social definition of the self but also that the various actions and choices which this self then undertakes can be considered to be expressive of his or her own preferences, aspirations, etc. (cf. Young 1980: 566).

The fact that I obtained my values, desires or preferences from some source is not particularly problematic. Not all socialization is manipulation or unwarranted influence. We can distinguish "my" self-determinations from those that might be said to be simply society's in the following way. First, society does not itself have some narrowly limited, relatively coherent set of values and desires such as a person might have. Society is a collection of values, desires, and preferences which will involve competition and conflict as well as coherence and interrelation.[23] This may, of course, be said of an individual as well, but society is not another person. The variation within society is inevitably greater. Accordingly, the socialization to which one is subjected is not monolithic; room is left for some maneuvering and interpretation. The strings of socialization do not function like those on a puppet.

Secondly, suppose a person simply takes over, lock, stock, and barrel, his mother's values. The person identifies with these values. This need not be problematic for self-determination to the extent that (a) this identification is not due to some psychological disposition which aims at compensating the person, or, if it is and the person became meaningfully aware of it, he would not disclaim it; (b) the person is able to reflect on, understand, and work with the implications of the values and views which he has taken over; and (c) upon reflection the person willingly accepts the consequences and implications of these values.

The self-determining person fulfills these three conditions. For the person to identify with these values is for him to claim that what he does on their basis is what *he* has done. It is for him to take responsibility for what derives from them. It is for him to take delight, pleasure, and satisfaction in their fulfilment, as well as for him to be displeased, upset, disturbed, etc. when they are not fulfilled. It is for him to seek to fulfill them, contribute to their support when appropriate and relevant, as well as seek to oppose or be hostile towards that which blocks these desires, preferences and values.

Further, if people disagree with various values and preferences into which they have been socialized, to the extent that they are self-determining they are not rigidly tied to them. Thus, they are able, if the grounds for and implications of their identification with some values and preferences are raised to consciousness, to reject those values and preferences (cf. Young 1980: 573). Still, this allows that a great deal of one's self-determination is based upon the social, political, and cultural context within which it took place.

This means that the self-determination of any person will not be intelligible simply on the basis of his or her own actions or pronouncements. The values, preferences, and attitudes which constitute the person have a social and historical dimension to them without which they cannot be understood.

As such, self-determination lies structured within the various institutions and relations that define our lives. The implication is that our freedom is also structured within certain boundaries. Nevertheless, one may remain self-determining. It may be admitted that not all our actions are part of institutions as they are in baseball, property, and political elections. Other actions are not bound up with social institutions in the preceding formal ways. People can eat, move about, and seek food without such social institutions. Nevertheless, even these actions are charged with social meaning, though not defined by it. How we eat, how and where we move, what we seek as food and how we seek it are intelligible only through the meanings we attribute to them. Their meaning derives from our institutions and history.

Thus, we can understand the particular nature of even these activities only within a social and historical context. Even the hermit is defined in relation to his separation from society. A person who is unwittingly abandoned on a desert island and who spent his years there living alone is not a hermit. All of our actions occur within social contexts or with social meanings. They are not simply "natural" acts. Though this is the case, we can remain self-determining within such contexts.

Consequently, we can identify several different forms of self-determination. *Subjective self-determination* is simply a person's acting upon his or her present desires and wants. This is an inadequate view of self-determination and freedom. It is compatible with conditions under which people are not free. Secondly, *unrestricted self-determination* requires that a person have virtually unlimited alternative courses of action available to her. This is singularly unrealistic. To be self-determining one need not have unlimited alternatives.

Thirdly, we might speak of *rational self-determination* which occurs when the person acts upon reflection and following certain rational standards beyond the minima noted above. This is the form that Kant considered. It is best viewed as an ideal, rather than the form of self-determination connected with freedom. It raises the standards of self-determination extremely high. Few might, on this view, end up being free. Further freedom is compatible with people making mistakes about themselves and others. Rational self-determination would not allow for this.

There is a final, and most important, form of self-determination that can now be distinguished. On this view, those who defend rational self-determination are correct to emphasize the importance of our ability to reflect on our actions and desires. Accordingly, if our attitude towards, or identification with, certain values was brought about by someone who circumvented our higher reflections or our second order preferences, that person would have undermined our self-determination. Secondly, a person's self-determination is diminished if there are no meaningful alternatives to what he or she does. This is not to imply that there must be a rich abundance of opportunities for self-determination, though to the extent there are one's self-determination is enhanced. Rather, if there are no meaningful alternatives at all to one's present course of action, one's self-determination is undermined. It is in this sense that the drug addict who wants to be a drug addict and could not change things even if he wanted to be otherwise is hardly self-determining.[24]

Finally, we have seen that a person can be said to be self-determining to the extent that he or she could reasonably resist the influences that surround him or her in society. On this view, that which inhibits or opposes the realization of our values or interests in an unreasonable manner interferes with our self-determination. A person might fulfill this requirement and still have false beliefs. There is no requirement that these determinations are what the person's enlightened self would supposedly say. These three features are central to a fourth form of self-determination, which I will call *realistic self-determination*. It is this form of self-determination that is bound up with freedom.

Accordingly, we must distinguish between self-determination and freedom. Ideally, we may also want to distinguish between self-determination and autonomy, reserving the latter concept simply for rational self-determination. Autonomy and freedom would, then, overlap when the realistically self-determining individual gets it right, and is also rationally or objectively self-determining. Since this may not always happen, a person could be free but not autonomous.

VII FREEDOM AND THE RIGHT TO SELF-DETERMINATION

I have argued that freedom is linked with realistic self-determination.[25] Nevertheless, the two are not the same. Instead, freedom requires that self-determination be protected or supported, rather than left simply to itself. I wish to contend that freedom is to be identified with a right to self-determination, not simply self-determination itself.

It might be argued that, simply by virtue of the fact that people are self-determining individuals, they have various rights to act or live in certain ways. Benn says, provocatively, that Locke attributed to humans "natural rights, which one might interpret as normative capacities that a person enjoys by virtue of his natural capacity as a chooser" (Benn 1982: 44).[26] What Benn means is that:

> seeing ourselves as natural persons, or makers of projects, in a world with other persons, we have developed a conception of ourselves as *moral* persons too, entitled to a degree of forbearance from any other natural person conceptually capable of grasping the nature of our self-perception.
>
> (Benn 1976: 120–1)

Accordingly, when a person proposes to do anything that will thwart someone else, one must provide "some further reason for going ahead" (Ibid.: 121). This is the justification of what Benn calls "the principle of interference."[27]

However, this is merely a "minimal or formal principle that no one may legitimately frustrate a person's acting without some reason" (Ibid.: 109). As Benn admits, this principle only locates the onus of justification. It does not determine "what is to count as a reason for interfering" (Ibid.).

Benn's proposal, then, is fairly weak. It does not, in fact, invoke rights. It does not link freedom to a general right to self-determination. Nor does it relate freedom to more particular rights to this or that kind of action. It provides little protection or support for one's self-determination. All it says, in effect, is that if someone wishes to interfere with what another proposes, that person must simply give a reason. In this way, he or she will avoid the logical oddity of contending that a person's self-determined behavior can be interfered with for no reason at all. But even if we accept this principle of non-interference, people's self-determination will remain unprotected or unsupported. As such, even if Benn's principle were fulfilled, we need not conclude that the person who is self-determining within this context is also free. Something stronger is needed.

Suppose, then, that a person seeks to be self-determining. Within various reasonable conditions, she/he determines that she/he will carry out various actions. This does not by itself wholly capture freedom for the following two reasons.

To begin with, consider whether a person would be free whose self-determinations or actions were simply not interfered with – as a matter of happenstance – by others. He or she goes about his or her way, and no one bothers them. Nevertheless, I contend, it is not enough for one to be free that others simply do not interfere with one. To believe that it is involves an abstract view of persons and the contexts in which they act. As noted above, we live amongst others. We are characterized by various relations and roles we inhabit. In our self-determination we move within this complex web. My point is that the view of freedom as simple lack of interference with one's self-determinations does not take into account the possible tenuousness of such a situation. I may be interfered with on one occasion but not on the next occasion. I may be stopped today, but not stopped tomorrow. This aspect of freedom is missed if we concentrate simply on this or that action. Perhaps I am self-determining in one context, but my self-determination is undercut in another context. Still, freedom involves something more than simply the fact that this or that action was not interfered with, or my determination to do this or that was not hindered. It involves some sense of a required non-intervention. I think this leads to rights. This stems, in part, from the fact that freedom is not simply a local concept.

Accordingly, in order to be free it is not enough that, as a matter of fact, one is simply not interfered with or threatened. Rather it must be that, with regard to this or that action, one has a right to perform it while others do not interfere because of an obligation not to do so. Such "rightful" actions do not encompass the whole of the actions we perform as free persons. However, in order to be free, not only must one not be unreasonably interfered with or threatened, but also one's self-determination must be protected. The free person has the title or "authority to determine certain sorts of things" (Hill 1979: 71). The English Lords did not seek simply King John's lack of interference with them; they sought recognition of a right to determine their own actions in accord with their values and norms. Freedom can exist only if there are guarantees that the space it requires (public as well as private) is protected. Thus, Arendt comments that "if there existed no politically guaranteed public field of activity, freedom could find no place in the world . . ." (Arendt 1961b: 192). And Hill comments that "having title to make these choices means that they have a right to expect others not to interfere with the legitimate exercise of their authority and a right to protect themselves from interference" (Hill 1979: 71).

If we think of individual actions separately, this point may be overlooked. However, if we look at people in the complexity of their relations with others this point naturally emerges. The (moral and legal) rules of society will protect some of these forms of self-determination and condemn others. The prevention or promotion of this or that form of self-determination is the point at which rights enter in. Such rights need not simply be negative rights but may also be positive rights. This corresponds, I believe, with T. H. Green's comment that by freedom we mean "a power which each man exercises through the help or security given him by his fellow-men, and which he in turn helps to secure for them" (Green 1889: 371). The "help or security" Green refers to I understand to include various negative or positive rights. In the past, with traditional society, such rights were implicitly built into society and its very structures. Today, we need to make these guarantees explicit.

There is a second way of defending this view. The obstacles which restrict social or political freedom are those which are humanly produced. One's inability to fly like the birds, a sudden snowstorm that confines one to one's house, and the like are not limitations of one's social or political freedom.

Accordingly, to say that freedom requires the lack of humanly imposed obstacles is to say that other people restrain themselves (or are restrained). Now since freedom could hardly exist where all lack of obstacles and interferences occurred because some third party was restraining a second party, some notion of self-restraint is crucial for freedom. That is, freedom can be secured through a lack of obstacles only where others restrain themselves. My freedom is (in part, but importantly) your self-restraint.[28]

But why do you restrain yourself? Does it matter? Perhaps it is enough that you do. I think not. If you restrain yourself simply whimsically or arbitrarily – now you do, now you do not – then someone might say that now you are free, but now you are not.

However, such an intermittent lack of obstacles or coercion which someone else experiences would not constitute freedom for that person. Rather, it would be a period of uncertainty and doubt. One would refrain from acting freely for fear that one might be caught off-guard. Thus, freedom is not a momentary thing. Just as Hobbes notes concerning peace, there is a temporal element to freedom. One is not free if at one moment one is not coerced, but at the next moment one is, and then at a third moment one is not. This better describes a person who is being played with by someone else, rather than a free person. It is for this kind of reason that freedom has been compared with health and said to be a virtue.[29] Freedom, I have argued, ultimately is connected with an ongoing agency, rather than simply this or that particular action. It is this underlying continuity which is important to remember when speaking of freedom.

Such self-restraint, then, must be something which continues over time. I am free, in part, because you do not interfere with me, but I do not have such freedom because you are suddenly blinded or crippled. My freedom is not your disability. This would be comparable to the desert island view of freedom. Instead, I seek freedom even though you remain fully sighted and able to interfere; I demand restraint on your part. My freedom requires your restraint.

Now this is possible only if there is some ongoing reason, some principle, or some motivation on the basis of which others continue their self-restraint. This could be due to fear. I threaten to destroy you. If I am considerably more powerful than you, if I can intimidate you completely, then you may well restrain yourself. My freedom then rests upon my suppression of you. This is the "freedom" of the super-power over the small, developing nation; it is the power of the master over the slave. But if you restrain yourself, simply because I might strike back (and vice versa), we do not have freedom so much as a balance of fear or threats.

Thus, it is not a matter of indifference how the lack of interference comes about or my self-determination proceeds. If they come about whimsically, arbitrarily, or because of a balance of threat on both sides, we can hardly say that we are free. Similarly, if we suppose that we are equally powerful and threaten each other, if our mutual threats lead us to mutual self-restraint, we do not have a situation of freedom so much as a (cold) war.

Instead, the self-restraint of others which constitutes freedom seems possible only on some principled basis, which is not to say that there is not a need for sanctions against violations of that basis. This basis is that others ought not to interfere with me; correspondingly, I claim a right that you do not interfere with me as I determine my course. In short, you restrain yourself because you believe you ought to restrain yourself; because there is an obligation to restrain yourself. In this situation, we have a significant element of what constitutes freedom. To the extent that others do not honor these obligations or threaten to break them we experience a reduction in our freedom. Such potential threats are an important reason for an agency such as the state to protect our freedom. In any case, I cannot be free if I do not have some rightful guarantee.

Your recognition of this obligation is part of your recognition of my responsibility to live my life. If I am responsible for doing something, it is part of my office or role to do so. If you stand in my way, then you are wrong to do so. Contrariwise, you have an obligation to refrain from interfering with my efforts to fulfill my responsibilities. Indeed, you might even have some positive duty to aid me in my efforts.[30]

Thus, what is important about self-determination for freedom is that to be free is for us to enjoy a right of self-determination. In this way, self-determination and freedom are not the same, though freedom and a right to self-determination are. This right is, I take it, a prima facie right or a presumptive right, but one which is utterly basic. It is not a (prima facie) right simply to the fulfillment of any impulse or desire; it is a (prima facie) right to that determination of my course within reasonable conditions. Without this right, my freedom is reduced. To this extent, my view agrees with the view of Acton who maintained that "by liberty I mean the assurance that every man shall be protected in doing what he believes his duty against the influence of authority and majorities, custom and opinion" (Acton 1985: 7).[31] Without the assurance that I will be protected, my liberty suffers. That assurance is a right to self-determination.

Thus, when liberals and conservatives speak about freedom as involving rights they are correct. Some of them, however, claim that we have a right to liberty while others speak of our right to self-determination. My argument has been that those who claim the latter are correct. The problem with those who speak of a right to liberty is that they take liberty simply to be the lack of coercion, which is, as we have seen, an overly naive and incomplete view of liberty. On the contrary, my argument has been that liberty is the right to self-determination; the right is not simply external to and indifferent towards liberty.

This gives us, however, a different response to the objection of others that we do not have a right to freedom (cf. R. Dworkin 1979; Montague 1986). For example, Montague argues that since specific rights of freedom, e.g. of religion, imply that one is "at liberty to practice the religion *of one's choice*," it follows that "if there is an exercisable right to freedom simpliciter then people are at liberty to act as they please" (Montague 1986: 73). However, he also argues that a right to freedom, as a claim right, would entail "duties not to perform *any* actions that interfere (in the appropriate way) with those of the kinds [of actions] in question" (Ibid.: 75). Accordingly, he concludes that "if there is an exercisable right to freedom simpliciter, then there is a duty to not interfere with those who are doing what they wish" (Ibid.: 76). But this, he says, implies "that one acts contrary to duty if he purchases the only copy of some book from his local bookstore, because he thereby prevents others who wish to do so from purchasing that book" (Ibid.). Since this is implausible, Montague rejects the view that there is a right to freedom simpliciter.

This argument, however, is unpersuasive. It is simply false, as I have argued above, that freedom or liberty amounts to doing simply as one pleases. Thus, it is also false that a right to freedom would be a right to act as one pleases. The problem in Montague's argument lies in his concept of freedom. If we do not accept this concept, we need not accept his conclusion.

The real problem raised by this argument concerns what we should say when the self-determination of one person interferes with the self-determination of another person – especially, when they both have a right to such self-determination. Why do we not, even on this view, get into the problem Montague raises regarding my supposed duty not to buy the last book in a bookstore, when that is the book which you were also seeking (as part of your self-determination)? Surely the answer is, all things being equal, that my freedom, my right to self-determination, is limited by a similar and equal right of yours to self-determination. The interrelation of these two rights is, however, the subject of our discussion of the second aspect of freedom as empowerment, viz. the involvement of people in the mutual determination of their own ends. But this is the topic of the following chapter.

Still, it is correct on the view here defended that we do not have a right to freedom, since freedom itself involves a right to self-determination. Thus, the views of Montague and Dworkin that we do not have a right to liberty are correct, although for reasons other than those they give.

The right to self-determination is partially decomposable. For example, it can be broken down into the rights to speech, movement, religion, and property. It contrasts, however, with rights, such as the right to property, which are fully decomposable. What has been called the "right to liberty" is here understood simply to be a right not to be interfered with or (perhaps) a right to privacy. Since self-determination, however, is an ongoing ability or disposition to undertake and maintain a certain way of acting and living which cannot be fully itemized, the right to self-determination cannot be (fully) decomposed. Underlying these individual rights traditionally associated with (social and political) freedom, is the more basic right to self-determination.[32]

This is, it should be clear, a full-blooded right in the sense that it grounds an obligation of others not to interfere with (as well as to support in various ways) one's self-determinations. Still, some of the rights into which it may be decomposed are not themselves rights in this sense. Thus, the right to self-determination is what others have called "an exercisable right" in contrast to "a non-exercisable right".[33] The former (such as the right to practice one's own religion), but not the latter (the right not to be injured or killed), ground obligations to the right holder. The latter rights do not ground obligations since they are not distinct from the obligations to which they correspond. Rather they are simply equivalent to the obligations that others have not to injure or kill the right holder (Montague 1980).

It might be objected that, to the extent that this is a moral or human right, even slaves possess this right, but they are not free. This is true, and hence we must say that a free person is one who is *effectively* able to act upon this right. This question is discussed in Chapter 7 under the third aspect of enablement.

The rights that individuals have *qua* free are multiple. An important subclass are those connected with functioning as a human being: rights to speech, self-expression, assembly, conscience, as well as not to be injured or killed. To the extent that these are political rights we have the rudiments of an account of social *and* political freedom. In this way, individual freedom and political freedom are less distantly related than liberals have tended to assume.

To the extent that all people have these within a social grouping they have them as members of that grouping. They are membership rights; they have them as members in the same moral grouping. The next chapter will explore the implications of this for freedom in a social group or community, especially when it is a political community.

The entitlement aspect of freedom, i.e. one's right to self-determination, is a form of empowerment in two senses. First, individuals *qua* free determine their own course(s) of actions. What they do is their own determination, not that of someone else. At the minimum, they have moral control and power over their lives. Their freedom is not simply a lack or an absence of constraint, but the presence of an ability or capacity to direct (or participate in directing, we shall see) the affairs which importantly impinge on their lives.

Secondly, in this determination they are not subject to arbitrary coercive forces, i.e. their determination of these courses of action is protected. Others are morally prevented from interfering in various ways. In these ways and to this extent, such persons are empowered for they have and may exercise power over other individuals who seek to meddle in their affairs. They may demand that they cease interfering. Though this may be, at this point in our argument, only a moral empowerment, it is the basis upon which more complete forms of empowerment can be built.

VIII CONCLUSION

This completes the first aspect of freedom of empowerment. The concept of freedom we need to apply to humans within a social and political context is not simply the lack of physical constraints. Though we do use what has been here called "natural freedom," such a Hobbesian view would make much of the quest for individual and political freedom unintelligible. Instead, we require a concept of freedom which is at home within a social and political context.

This view of freedom is ultimately based not on a notion of free action, but on that of the self-determining agent. There are, quite clearly, a number of different senses of self-determination. It is realistic self-determination which seems most closely linked with freedom. This form of self-determination is not undercut, as some have claimed, by the socialization processes through which people are formed. Thus, our view involves not simply the lack of various restraints but a complex of normative conditions. Ultimately, freedom is connected with such self-determination in the form of a right to self-determination, whereby one is morally (if not legally) guaranteed relief from obstacles and impediments which would hinder a reasonably self-determining agent.

This result is an important advance over ordinary negative views of freedom for several reasons. It does not allow that persons can be said to be free who are simply abandoned to their own devices. In this it explicitly recognizes the interdependence of people in society. No longer is it simply metaphorical that the loss of freedom by some is the loss of freedom by all. Further, it recognizes the importance of guarantees for freedom. This is not simply a demand for security – though freedom and security have been linked even on liberal views. Freedom is the right to exercise one's self-determination.

Further, this view responds to the criticism of rights by radical freedom as well as the attempt of liberals to reduce freedom to the lack of constraint. In these ways it is an important step beyond both views of freedom. It is true, of course, that the liberal view of freedom correctly addresses the importance of protecting individuals. But the individual it seeks to protect has been abstracted from any social or political reality. Only this explains the descriptive view of freedom at which liberals and libertarians arrive. However, whichever way we turn such a descriptive and negative view of freedom it remains unacceptable as an account of freedom. Still, it is crucial that individuals be protected. Only in this way can their (political) freedom be said to be genuine. Such freedom is a freedom as empowerment. It responds to contemporary conditions by recognizing the importance of protecting individuals from other individuals and institutions, while acknowledging the demand that people, *qua* free, set their own courses of action.

The preceding, however, is incomplete as an account of political freedom. It does not develop the implications of the social nature of individual freedom. This points to the second aspect of political freedom, viz. involvement. It is this we turn to in the next chapter.

6 Political freedom, involvement, and democracy

> Men can only *be* free with reference to one another, only, that is, in the fields of politics and of the things they do; it is only in these spheres that they come to realize that freedom is something positive and not merely a negation of compulsion.
>
> (Arendt 1961:191)

I INTRODUCTION

Freedom as empowerment is founded upon the right to self-determination. However, so far freedom has been considered largely in abstraction from political contexts. As such, our account has been one of individual freedom. Still, the implication would seem to be that politically free individuals must be able to exercise a right of self-determination in political contexts.

It is not clear, however, what this means or implies. How are we to understand our relation to others who are also seeking to exercise their rights to self-determination? We face here two problems. What is the relation of individuals exercising the same right? And, what is the relation of individual freedom and the authority of the state?

The short, but general, answer to both problems is that political freedom requires that individuals have a right to participate with other members of the political societies to which they belong in mutually determining the paths their lives will take.[1] In this way they are empowered. There are several aspects to this answer.

First, political freedom requires various rights, procedures, and structures whereby individuals may participate in the direction and control of government and state affairs in their society. Thus, political freedom is ultimately tied up with republican or democratic forms of government.[2] Accordingly, such measures as elections, recall procedures, and the rights to vote, run for office, and to assemble are inseparable from political freedom. There is empowerment here in that individuals, having a right to participate in decisions determining the direction of political affairs in a society, may demand, not simply request, that certain procedures be followed.

Secondly, to be politically free individuals must also be able to play a role in determining which issues come up for decisions before groups of which they are members. If people are excluded from such determinations, they are less self-determining. To the extent that individuals may be involved in setting the agenda for which items arise as questions requiring decision-making they are empowered. Such "agenda power" has society-wide implications. It requires that people know what alternatives they face and that small groups of elites or narrow classes cannot simply structure the situations in which decisions are made.

Thirdly, since governmental and state affairs are not identical with public and political affairs, the political freedom of individuals extends not simply to the arena of the government or state, but also to the important institutions of society, e.g. corporations, unions, and other large organizations. Thus, political freedom requires that individuals may participate in the major organizations and institutions which exercise authority over them. Through such broader participation, their right to self-determination is most adequately realized.

Political freedom, then, requires not simply a set of rights, structures and procedures of which people might take advantage for the determination of government personnel and policies. It also relates more broadly to questions of the control and influence of public and political affairs in society. Political freedom refers to one's relations with other people and institutions within a political society. It does not simply refer to one's relation to the government of one's society. It requires involvement in the direction of the public and political matters touching on the daily life of oneself and others. Such involvement is not simply instrumentally related to one's political freedom but is itself a manifestation of that freedom.

II POLITICAL FREEDOM AND THE RIGHT OF SELF-DETERMINATION

Freedom as empowerment requires individual entitlement. However, this right to self-determination is not simply an individual but also a political freedom. The sharp distinction some draw between the two, is mistaken.[3] To deny that this right extends to the political realm would require an argument that showed self-determination must stop at the backyard fence and not extend to political settings. Such an argument would leave a large aspect of one's life outside of one's own self-determination. On the contrary, the political and public realm of life are part and parcel of the lives of individuals. Indeed, the very distinction between the private and the public (or political) is itself a political decision.

But in what manner does freedom as entitlement extend into the political arena? How is it compatible with the rights of others also to be politically self-determining? After all, they will claim the same freedom and at least some of their claims will be incompatible with others. How are the various individual rights to self-determination compatible? How do individuals in a complex, diverse society remain free?[4]

There are three possible alternatives to resolving conflicts among the differing self-determinations of individuals. One could transfer the exercise of one's right to someone (or something) else, e.g. some superior person, a sovereign, or one's country. Secondly, one could simply exercise it all by oneself. That is, one might simply impose one's self-determination on others. Thirdly, one could exercise it in some form of mutual self-determination with others.

The first alternative might be realized in two different ways. People might "transfer" their right of self-determination to someone else either by simply giving it up or, alternatively, by identifying with the other and taking that person's pronouncements as one's own.

There are serious problems with each option. It is true that one may exercise one's freedom in the act of giving it up, but the consequence need not manifest that same freedom. I may, as a bachelor, wed a woman, but my actions thereafter cannot be the actions of a bachelor. Similarly, a free person may decide to become a slave, but it hardly follows that his or her actions thereafter are the actions of a free person. In this sense, the right to self-determination is not compatible with just any decision or agreement. If a person agreed, while retaining no further rights of participation for him or herself, that someone else may run the political affairs of the country then that person would have signed away his or her political freedom.

Further, on both options any number of forms of coercion might be imposed on people in their own names. People might be "freely" restricted or imprisoned – because "they" had "determined" that they would do so. Surely freedom and self-imposed restraints are compatible. However, a theory of political freedom must be able to distinguish between this and the subservience which results from simply transferring one's right to self-determination to others or adopting as one's own whatever the sovereign says. The nature of the right to self-determination must remain, even in a political context, a right of the individual self, even though there are clearly social dimensions to this self. There is not a single self into which all selves can or should be absorbed. That is the recipe for totalitarianism.

Finally, the present alternative fails to capture anything significantly political in its account of political freedom. Any sense of the determination of the forms and directions which major structures and activities take in society disappears. Any sense of the dialogue, compromises, and exchanges between individuals and those who govern or rule is lacking. Indeed, we must ask: What is *political* about such freedom? In effect, this alternative equates political freedom with freedom from politics. But one cannot be free from politics without jeopardizing the very individual freedom one seeks.

The upshot is that differences among individual self-determinations cannot be resolved simply by some single act of transfer of one's right to another, or total consent to a ruler or government. Through the wholesale subordination of one's right to self-determination to others, one might gain peace, satisfaction, or even pleasure, but not freedom.

III POLITICAL FREEDOM AND INDIVIDUAL SELF-DETERMINATION

The second alternative for exercise of the right to self-determination in a political context would be that one simply determines by oneself what takes place in one's society. One treats one's (prima facie) right to self-determination as absolute. This is the despot or divine alternative. It is hyperbolical freedom. It might be thought to be a strawman. On the other hand, it appears to be the direct implication of the view that freedom of an individual is bound up with his or her empowerment or right to self-determination. If my freedom involves the exercise of a right to self-determination, then why doesn't my political freedom simply consist in my ruling the roost? This means that I impose myself on others. But why should this matter if *I* do the imposing? Contrariwise, how can I be self-determining, when I do so in the context of others and when the results stem, even though through participation, from our conjoint self-determination? In short, why isn't the despot alternative the necessary consequence of freedom as empowerment?[5]

Freedom, I have argued, is initially characterized in terms of a right to self-determination. This right is often thought to be an utterly individual (even natural) right which a person might have independently of any and all societies. But this presupposes an asocial and apolitical view of individuals and rights which misunderstands the nature of both. One of the failings of talk about natural rights is that it characterizes rights as if they were characteristics which could be attributed to an individual even if that person fell out of society and no other individuals existed. This is a feat of heady moral imagination which gives rise to many of the problems of liberalism.

On the contrary, to speak about such rights is to speak about a system of rights and responsibilities. Some of these are specific, others are general. The rights of a parent or president are specific rights. The rights one has simply *qua* person are general. For me to have a general right, such as the right of self-determination, is not simply for someone else to have responsibility or obligation to me. Rather, it is for me to live within a moral and political system of which I am a member. In this system, other people have the same right and each of us also has corresponding obligations and responsibilities to others. Freedom is the right of self-determination not simply for me but for other people as well. We have the same right of self-determination within this common moral system.

Accordingly, having this right imposes obligations and responsibilities not simply on others, but also on oneself. Such rights and responsibilities are not separable, though we often view them as separate. This is one of the reasons why it is offensive when people "simply" stand on their rights. They thereby omit the surrounding responsibilities and connections which give meaning and significance to those rights in the first place. Views that emphasize simply the rights of individuals "forget" the moral or political community within which rights can only exist.[6] Such views attempt to isolate one part of the right–responsibility complex which constitutes freedom. However, a person, who treats his or her right to self-determination as absolute or simply outweighing all other rights and responsibilities, undermines the complex web of rights and responsibilities of which his or her right is part. Were the freedom of other persons similarly interpreted, no one would enjoy freedom. To be individually free one cannot simply impose one's self-determination on others. This would violate their rights and abrogate one's own responsibilities to them.

It follows that the freedom claims of despots – insofar as they are rights-based – undercut the very system on which they base their demands. The right to self-determination does not imply the domination of others. The person who dominates others may experience a sense of release, exhilaration, and power. However, it is mistaken to confuse these with freedom which is only a particular form of empowerment.

This conclusion stands in contrast to negative views of freedom which allow for domination. That is, if I can myself be free from coercion, by coercing others, then my negative freedom is wholly compatible with domination and tyranny of the worst sorts. Accordingly, tyrants and slave masters can genuinely proclaim their concern for freedom as they relieve coercion from themselves but impose it on others. Though their slaves and subjects are not free (even on their own view), the freedom of the tyrant is not thereby affected. Freedom as involvement is opposed to such a conclusion.

The problem of multiple rights of self-determination cannot be resolved by imposing one's self-determination on others. We must then consider whether the individual right to self-determination can be compatible with the mutual self-determination of individuals. Why isn't the most honest course simply to admit that when the rights of self-determination of individuals are exercised, there will be conflict? "Freedom for the pike is death for the minnows." Freedom is a zero-sum game in which, when I assert my right of self-determination, you may not be able to assert yours. This is why, after all, the state is deemed by many to be a necessary institution. I shall argue that this is a mistaken view of the situation. Individual freedom is compatible with conjoint empowerment.

IV THE SOCIAL DIMENSIONS OF INDIVIDUAL SELF-DETERMINATION

If we are to overcome these problems, we must reflect on how they have been formulated. The traditional way is to ask: how can this individual's freedom be preserved if his or her actions must be adjusted to the determinations of others – let alone a state? If we believe that unanimity occurs infrequently, it seems that there is little hope for a favorable answer. Aren't individual rights of self-determination inevitably incompatible?

There is, however, a different way of proceeding which draws on the preceding section. The point is *not* to begin by assuming that freedom is simply an individual affair, or that individuals who exercise their rights of self-determination are wholly separate persons unrelated and unconnected to each other. We are not isolated beings, but members of groups, institutions and societies. We are born into families, become citizens at birth, are educated in schools, and work in groups, of one sort or another. The freedom we enjoy only occurs within and is defined by a complex web of relations. It is inherently social. The freedom of separate individuals in a state of nature is a fantasy. Central to our difficulties is that we confuse independence with freedom. Individuals may be empowered or free only within a web of social (and political) relations, which also defines them as members of society. For me to be free, then, is *not* for me to have something which you do not, but for us to share a set of relations which empower us both. To be free is not to fall out of relationship with others but to have certain relations with them.[7]

These relations are constitutive, in various ways, of institutions within society. As we have seen in the preceding chapter, some of these institutions are of a formal nature, others are more informal. The former include private property, marriage, business, churches, and kinship. Individuals will be members of, or take part in, some of these institutions but not others. Their membership in some cases will be by choice while they are simply born into others. More informal relations involve how we move about, eat, and create living spaces. These too are charged with social meaning. Their meaning derives from the common values, norms, and history of the society of which we are a member. Thus, Ryan notes that "certain actions presuppose in their very descriptions a background of rights and obligations" (Ryan 1980: 491). To omit these is to commit what he calls "the State of Nature Fallacy." Only within this more complex situation can the problem of individual and political freedom be resolved.

To begin with, these institutions (both formal and informal) claim an authority over us. There is subordination. Restraint or coercion may have to be exercised on certain occasions over their members. This authority may be central and tight, or diffuse and loose. It may be the authority of an institution itself or the authority of past cultural meaning, ways of acting, habits, and etiquette.

For a society to exist, this authority cannot be wholly externally imposed. This is the point of socialization. A society which failed to socialize its children would be a failed society. Thus, in normal circumstances, substantial portions of the authority of institutions must be internally imposed, part of the nature or identity of people. It must seem "natural" to them. Further, there is nothing unnatural about this. We are neither hapless victims nor absolute agents. It is silly to think that the problem of authority and freedom arises only in the instance of the individual and the state. It is also mistaken to think that authority is wholly external to our self-determination. We are partly defined by the roles we inhabit, as well as the shared values and purposes of the society we live in. We exercise our right to self-determination within these contexts. Thus, our self-determination cannot be conceived separately from these mutual features of our lives.[8]

Secondly, these relations and institutions give our self-determination form. They create activities which would not otherwise exist. They channel and shape other activities that could independently exist, albeit in different forms. They set boundaries for our self-determination, as do the banks of a river. Within them, people may be prevented from doing various things without rendering them unfree. Thus, for example, the person who is not elected prime minister in a parliamentary system has not had her political freedom reduced. Though she attempted to become prime minister and had her efforts blocked, still she remains politically free. A person who is not allowed to yell "fire" in a crowded theater has not had his or her right to self-determination violated.[9] The same is true in non-political contexts. A centerfielder who makes a spectacular catch may prevent a batter from winning the batting title. Though something the batter has sought to achieve has been prevented, his freedom has not been diminished.[10]

These examples emphasize the importance for freedom of the institutional context, together with its implicit or explicit values, norms and rules. Many, if not most, of our activities take place within institutions, social practices, games, and roles in which it is legitimate to prevent a person from doing something so long as it is done in a certain way. As such, these institutions render the exercise of the right to self-determination by different individuals compatible. Within them we are both individually and collectively free.

Thirdly, the subordination and limitations within institutions may act as an empowerment. Such institutions and informal ways of acting do not invariably reduce one's choices or freedom. On the contrary, they may increase the number of significant choices (Cooper 1983: 133). Some actions are literally impossible outside of various institutions. These institutions partially constitute the kinds of activities through which people can be self-determining and hence free. One cannot vote outside of an institution allowing for this kind of self-expression; a person would lack security for his or her possessions without the institution of property; one cannot hit a home run outside of baseball. Mailing letters, football games, operas, and marriage are institutions which enrich our lives through creating the possibility of certain forms of action and expression which would not exist otherwise. At the same time, such institutions protect our right to self-determination in that they prevent others from treating us in various ways when we try to participate in certain activities. We may not be tripped in soccer; noisy members of an opera audience are asked to leave; we may expect that mailed letters remain unopened except by their intended recipients.[11]

Thus, we become free to act in various ways through engaging in various social relations and roles that define who we are. The mistake is simply to equate with unfreedom the constraint or subordination that such institutions require. The constrained actions referred to rest upon the basis of the institutions and forms of action themselves. The two are inseparable. Just as a river requires banks, so too human actions require limits and boundaries by which they are defined or intelligible.[12] Freedom is not possible outside institutions and social meanings. In this sense, freedom requires limits and constraints. Liberty and limitations are not inevitably opposed. Our mistake in seeking simply negative freedom is to want a part which is inseparable from a whole. A person may rebel against parts of these contexts, limitations, and some of the institutions themselves, but a person cannot rebel against the whole setting without threatening freedom itself. Similarly, the mere fact that a person must do something that she does not like on a particular occasion does not mean that, therefore, she is unfree. Rather, we must look at the context within which this requirement arises.

Still, we must look more closely at the fact that institutions and cultural forms render some choices or courses of action immoral or exceedingly difficult, if not impossible. The institution of marriage renders some acts adulterous, while the institution of property gives rise to the possibility of theft. Families and churches may impose various requirements on their members with which their members may not agree. One's language, as well as common ways of acting between males and females, may constrain one in certain ways.

For those who only partially identify with these institutions (or wholly reject them), these prohibitions and obstacles raise a question of freedom. Further, in considering an individual's freedom we must also consider the range of institutions within which a person may live, rather than simply this or that institution. Thus, we must ask: what must be true of the exercise of our right to self-determination with regard to institutions and organizations (and particularly political ones) for there to be freedom? We have seen that they may empower us by creating new, fruitful ways of acting which, nevertheless, require that we not act and even be prevented from acting in certain ways. Further, they may protect our rights in ways that we, by ourselves,

could not. However, it would also seem that they can *dis*empower us
when they make courses of action impossible or difficult (or immoral).
Thus, when do the constraints of such institutions limit or violate a
person's freedom? This is one of the most basic problems of social
and political life.

V   FREEDOM WITHIN INSTITUTIONS AND THE STATE

It might be argued that freedom is possible within a society only if we
assume that a person explicitly adopts or agrees with the values and
norms which define its relations and institutions. There is some truth
to this claim. It is the case, seemingly, with people playing baseball
or running in a political election. Only if I agree to play baseball,
will I also agree that a caught fly ball puts me out. Only if I agree
to elections will the fact that I receive fewer votes than another lead
me to believe that I am not president or prime minister. Hence, it is
essential to political freedom, some contend, that a person lives within
a framework that he or she has agreed to or chosen.[13]

The problem with this contention is that it allows that a person
who will not "choose" or agree, except on the most unreasonable
conditions, to some system within which to live has had his or her
freedom restricted. That is, to claim that one's freedom within an
institution or organization depends *solely* upon whether one explicitly
agrees to the rules, values and decisions of the institution returns us, in
effect, to the despot alternative (cf. Part III). This form of subjective
self-determination we have rejected as linked to freedom. To make
such a demand for a system within which one might live in order
to be self-determining or free implausibly stretches the meaning
of "freedom." It renders "freedom" a synonym for egoism and
self-aggrandizement. It is to suggest, falsely, that our self is wholly
independent of others.[14]

Accordingly, we might say that a person may have his *subjective*
self-determination restricted if he is prevented or restrained from
doing something by an institution whose values and norms he will not
accept except under extremely unreasonable conditions. However,
his *right* to self-determination may or may not be violated in such a
case. Hence, he might or might not thereby be rendered unfree.

Instead, whether or not we are free depends on the nature of
these institutions and their treatment of individuals. The insight
of conservatives is that we are particular beings whose lives are
not simply a matter of choice. Some of the things with which we
identify we are born into, others creep up on us. We find ourselves

identifying with them. No conscious choice was made. By being born into families, we have rights and responsibilities which are thrust upon us which we have never contemplated and chosen to undertake. They are simply ours. Unless one's parents engaged in some heinous or unjustifiable behavior, one could not morally simply decide not to fulfill these responsibilities. Our self-determination is worked out within these limits.

Similarly, to the extent that we are members of a community or citizens of a state by birth, we find ourselves having certain rights as well as responsibilities. Whether these limit or foster freedom will depend on their nature. The insight of liberals and radicals is that the institutions within which we live, and into which we are born, need not simply be taken as we find them. They must meet certain conditions in order for us to be free. Since our concern is political freedom, it is appropriate to focus upon the state.

The state is special in several ways. First, it claims an overarching authority to adjudicate certain conflicts between individuals and social institutions within its bounds and to organize the behavior of individuals and institutions in various ways. Secondly, unlike many other institutions, but like the family, one is usually born into the state of which one is a member. "Membership in a particular nation is, for most of us, one of the 'givens' of our existence, something we take for granted, except in unusual circumstances" (Johnson 1975b: 18). Thirdly, exit from the state is very difficult and costly (financially as well as otherwise). To exit one's state to find political freedom one may have to give up family, friends, culture, and language. These raise the costs of exit much higher than from other institutions (e.g. herb societies and particular businesses). These special characteristics must be kept in mind in any account of political freedom.

On the other hand, just as for individuals the despot alternative and freedom are incompatible, so too it is clear that if the authority the state claims is the right to command the citizen simply because it is the state, then political freedom and the state would be unalterably opposed. The reason is similar: under these circumstances the state might require that its citizens do simply anything. Further, this is a mistaken view of authority inasmuch as it tends to equate obedience to authority with blind subservience. (cf. Bowie and Simon 1986: 20). Thus, if we are going to be politically free within a state, the authority of the state must fulfill various conditions.

Three conditions stand out. First, the decisions and actions of the state must protect the self-determination of individuals compatible with a like self-determination of others, at least insofar as they are relevantly similar. Thus the self-determination of one individual (or group of individuals) must not be denied because of arbitrary or irrelevant considerations. To do so would violate his or her right of self-determination. As such, political freedom requires that individuals be treated as full and equal members of the state. This is one sense in which freedom and equality are interconnected.

Political freedom is one's freedom as a member of a political society. Whatever the final account, it is one's freedom *within* a group of other people. Thus, to say that the right of each individual to determine his or her course of action must be equally respected is not to say that these rights may not take certain different forms and expressions, or that individuals may not be treated differently. Children, the insane, and the senile need not be treated in an identical manner with normal adults. Still, whatever the forms political freedom takes, they must not effectively require people to give up their right to self-determination. Further, the reasons for which they are treated differently must not simply be due to matters of convenience or even simply the greater welfare of others. Though the rules of the state may require one person to subordinate him or herself to another person, they cannot require this except insofar as they thereby equally promote (albeit in various ways) the rights of self-determination of everyone. The state may then have officers, various roles and positions which different people must fill. This does not, in itself, violate rights to self-determination. Whether it does depends upon how such positions and roles are assigned, e.g. whether or not they are open to everyone.[15] Thus, my right to self-determination is neither an absolute nor an isolated right. In the end, the political freedom in the state requires that individual rights of self-determination are adjusted to each other only in ways which maximise the freedom of all individuals.

In effect, this condition reminds us that there is no such thing as absolute freedom, where this means that an individual may do simply what he or she would determine by him or herself. All social and political life involves adjustments; freedom does too. Only a person beginning with an extreme individualist view could say that a person must always do what he or she decides in order to be free. Such a view is untrue both to human nature and the nature of freedom.

Secondly, political freedom requires that the state ensure that its citizens may pursue reasonable and important human interests.[16] A state which did not arbitrarily distinguish between the rights of individuals to self-determination might nevertheless greatly confine the right of all individuals to self-determination. Thus, a state that permits all citizens to become great gymnasts, soldiers, or manual workers, but not great economists, politicians, theologians, or artists according to their own lights, inhibits political freedom. Further, states and institutions which promote short-term, arbitrary, irrational interests, e.g. those a person might seek simply as subjectively self-determining, leave people less free than institutions and states that promote more reasonable and important interests.

The preceding is not to say that political freedom allows for the strict control of trivial and indifferent matters. The small details of everyday life can be, cumulatively at least, quite important. However, a state which permitted the pursuit of trivial but not important matters would be a state which lacks political freedom. On the other hand, it remains true that in many cases trivial matters can be controlled without detriment to political freedom. Indeed, they often must be controlled so as to enhance political freedom.

Thus the overriding concern of a free state must be to permit (and to promote as necessary) the exercise by individuals of their right to self-determination which aims at reasonable and important interests.[17] This will require that the state ensure that various provisions are available (either through its own resources or privately through those of individual citizens) whereby individuals may obtain, *inter alia*, justice in their dealings with others, education, health services, and protection.

Thirdly, a politically free state cannot be one which attempts by itself to decide which interests are important and which ones are to be supported. Political freedom requires that the state not determine simply by itself how society operates or individuals live. It must acknowledge the importance of individuals creating different paths towards their various ends. This does not, on the one hand, imply that the state cannot make any of these decisions, set guidelines, or enforce standards and requirements which would enhance such self and mutual-determination. However, *qua* free these determinations must flow from the participation of its citizens to the maximum extent feasible. In this way it empowers its citizens to live as they determine.

The implications of this condition are various and many. For example, political freedom requires opportunities for those (few) individuals who seek political office as part of their right of self-determination. Though a benevolent ruler followed all the principles on which a state was legitimately founded, his or her actions would by their very nature block the self-determination of some individuals at the highest levels. Political freedom must allow the opportunity for an individual to seek and to hold political office. Very few, of course, will be successful in such attempts. However, supposing that those who achieve political office do so through fair and open elections, those who fail to obtain political office have not, as such, had their political freedom diminished.

Further, political freedom is frustrated not only when its citizens cannot become members of the government of a state by election, but also when there are few mechanisms built into the state whereby the decisions of its leaders, the rules defining the state, and its particular features can be changed through the (political) action of its citizens. That is, political freedom also requires participation that does not simply lead to office holding. Such participation may be an attempt to accomplish certain ends within the state by influencing its directions. This may be done by appealing to its members or its leaders, by installing or removing leaders, or by influencing policy decisions of the institution. On the other hand, through one's own interpretation and application of its rules, such participation can also be seen as an "enlivening" of the institution. In this latter sense, one is not simply a puppet whose strings are pulled by the institution, but, embodying the values and norms of the institution, one acts them out within one's own self-determination (cf. Scaff 1975).

Individuals who participate in both ways are free within the state to the extent that their participation is not simply something which is indulgently entertained by other members and the state's leaders, but viewed as a right of its members. Politically free individuals do not request or petition for opportunities for participation in the determinations of the state. They participate in the determinations of the state through their right to do so. This right of participation is the political version of their right to self-determination.

Finally, freedom requires not only that people may (attempt to) change the rules of an institution, but also, should those (attempts or) changes be fruitless or ineffective, that a person may be allowed (without prejudice or harm) to leave the state. East Germans and Russian dissidents have recently sought this option. To the extent that an institution or society allows its members to (attempt to) change its rules, the exit option is less important. The more difficult it is to effect these changes, the more important is the exit option to protect individual rights to self-determination.[18]

This does not make the state simply a voluntary association. In general, citizens do not, as such, choose the state so much as it "chooses" them. The costs of leaving are, for most people, prohibitively high. On the other hand, that one must be able to leave the state does open a window whereby people who believe their rights to self-determination have been systematically violated may seek relief. At times, the possibility of exit will embolden citizens to play a more active role within the state thereby ensuring greater levels of political freedom.

These conditions define a set of principles whereby a state must be organized and its agents operate if they are to respect freedom. In short, individuals are free within the state to the extent that their self-determination is protected in a manner compatible with a like self-determination of others, they may pursue reasonable and important human interests, and they can effectively participate in the determinations of the state.

Free institutions respect the right of self-determination when they allow individuals room to participate in determining the form of the institution and how that form will be carried out. Thus, free institutions must allow for rights of speech and assembly as well as for the design of structures for participation, processes for change, and the selection of leaders. As such, the above conditions set ground rules for a collective decision procedure which also defines us as free citizens. Accordingly, the state may justifiedly have authority over us. Acceptance of a state is not necessarily the abandonment of one's freedom.

However, the nature and extent of this right to participation requires further discussion. What forms must this right take so that the rights to self-determination of various people within the state can be compatible in their mutual determination of the courses of action the state takes? Further, to what extent does political freedom require that a person be successful in whatever he or she politically undertakes?

VI POLITICAL FREEDOM AND PARTICIPATION

Political freedom, I have argued, requires that individuals have a right to participate in the determinations of the state. Only in this manner can the members of a society make known the nature and scope of their interests, safeguard their own determinations, and exercise their right of self-determination.

However, more so than in most other institutions, each individual cannot participate in all (or even a great number of the) decisions of the state. Modern states are too large. Thus, government agents or political office holders are required to make decisions and see that policies are implemented which foster the interests of society's members and protect their rights. But what is the relation of these political officials and their determinations, to the politically free person? This issue is especially important because these individuals may not necessarily be particularly knowledgeable or benevolent, their determinations will require interpretation and implementation by other individuals like themselves, and the resulting state actions will conflict (at least occasionally) with the self-determinations of various individual citizens.

If the freedom of individual citizens is to be compatible with the determinations of the leaders of the state, it is clear that those who direct the government and control the implementation of its policies must be accountable to the other members of society. But in what manner? Some have argued that the determinations of political office holders can only be compatible with the right of an individual to self-determination if such persons function as that individual's (own) agent. However, this would be plausible as an account of political freedom only in the case of unanimity among all citizens. But this is highly implausible. Such agents clearly will not (and cannot) represent simply "my" interests. They will, from time to time, act against the particular interests of some individuals within the state.

Further, even if these agents were elected and represented individuals from particular districts, the problem of political freedom would not be resolved for two reasons. First, they might see themselves as accountable to the interests of the citizenry as a whole and hence act against any particular person's interests. Secondly, even if the particular representative for whom a person voted was elected and attempted to represent that person's interests, it might still be true that the state did not act in accordance with that representative's vote (and hence his or her constituent's interests). The overwhelming number of other representatives for whom a person could not vote might have opted to act for the interests of others.

Thus, the problem is not simply the relation between the individual and his or her representative, but the relation of the state's actions to one's own determinations. In order to show that democracy protects and promotes the right to self-determination, must we not "show that the individual exercises some real influence over political decisions, that the expression of his wishes and choices actually has some effect and is not an idle sideshow" (G. Graham 1983: 100). But how is this possible?

In one sense, it is not. As already suggested, it is a misconstrual of the nature of political freedom to hold that I am less free if the particular policies I advocate are not, in each case, defended by my representative and implemented by the state. It is not that my candidate wins the election, adheres to each view I have, and successfully persuades the state to adopt my views that makes me politically free. If this were the case, political freedom and tyranny would be indistinguishable. Nor must each individual be able to show that he or she "exercises some real influence over political decisions" in each particular case.

Similarly, however, in a politically free society the majority cannot simply expect to impose its self-determinations on others. The self-determinations of both the individual and the majority must be limited by various rights basic to the democratic functioning of the system. Thus, in a free state, no individual or group is always able to act simply according to its self-determinations. On the contrary, if the majority of a society could arbitrarily impose its self-determinations on minority parties and groups, we would have a formula that would undercut the dialogue and competition which democracy requires and political freedom demands.

Political freedom, then, lies in the political system having a particular character which empowers its individual citizens. It may do this even if any particular citizen is not successful on each occasion. My right to self-determination is not, I have argued, an absolute or isolated right. I have this right only as part of a web of relations in which others have a similar right. These rights and their exercise must be weighed against one another within the institution or system which gives rise to them. They are respected to the extent that the state, through its officials, promotes and protects each right to the greatest extent possible, compatible with similar treatment of others, in the pursuit of its individuals' most important interests. This means that the state does not exercise its powers arbitrarily, but rather only in accord with rules, laws, and regulations which are openly determined and promulgated, and are justified as promoting the maximum effective mutual self-determination of its citizens.

Political freedom, then, is one's freedom within such a political group. It is not simply something I have, but something I have within a group. But since others have a similar right to self-determination, political freedom is something that anyone has within a political group. This is to say that it is a quality or characteristic of the group. Individuals enjoy political freedom when the group of which they are members acts so as to maximise the effective mutual realization of the individual right to self-determination.

The question is how to accomplish this within a state. At the outset, citizens must be able to vote directly on certain issues. Though referenda carry various problems, political freedom requires the direct participation of citizens in the determination of government policies and directions through this method to the extent that doing so fosters realistic self-determination (cf. Chapter 5).

However, the vast majority of government actions will require the decisions of government officials. It is clear that these officials must be elected and that any citizen may compete for their offices. Though elected officials are not simply the sole agent of this or that citizen, they may not work wholly independently for the good of the whole.[19] Their authority rests not on them being expert agents in the sense that they have more knowledge or experience than all those they serve or represent, but on being accountable to their fellow citizens through periodic elections from various electoral constituencies.[20] Political office holders can only know what policies to work towards implementing to the extent they are periodically elected by their constituents and remain well appraised of the interests of their constituents through the participation of those individuals.[21] That is, elected representatives can only know which interests to pursue through a public process of dialogue and exchange with citizens. As suggested in Chapter 1, it is only in this process that we can identify what is rational for us to do.

Accordingly, it is crucial that the electoral process is not turned into a charade. It must be based on knowledge of the circumstances facing the electorate and of the policies of those who seek election. Morgenthau wisely comments that

> the people are being deprived of their freedom of choosing among alternative policies by choosing among different candidates for office if the different candidates for office are not identified with different policies, but compete for power as an end in itself, not as a means for a particular policy.
>
> (Morgenthau 1957: 718)

In addition, such public or political agents must be subject to recall and their political actions a matter of public record. Beyond these measures, accountability may require public financing of representative salaries and elections, as well as limiting their financial obligations (especially those not publicly acknowledged) to special interests. The techniques and conditions will vary from position to position as well as due to changes in technology and wealth of the society. Such measures, however, are means to make effective the accountability of government political office holders.

Accordingly, the right to political participation which political freedom requires goes far beyond simply protecting individuals from coercive influences in society and allowing that individuals have some say, in an hypothetical (state of nature) situation, as to the political form of one's society. Instead, it requires that we are able to vote directly on certain issues, as well as for various representatives whose stands on important issues are similar to our own. We must be able to know what government officials are doing and the nature of the issues they face. Otherwise, we cannot effectively exercise our right to participate. Thus, we must have rights to speech, assembly, and movement if we are to learn and discuss what the government does in order intelligently to vote whether directly in referenda or for government representatives themselves.

In addition, the compatibility of political freedom and elected representatives requires that individuals are able to participate in the political system in ways other than simply voting in referenda or for political officials. Bertrand Russell is mistaken when he suggests that "a common man can hope, at best, only to become a voter in a democracy" (Russell 1940: 263). Views of political freedom limited to voting in referenda or for government representatives have, in part, given rise to much scepticism about politics. Such a limited view provides people with very little power over how the agenda is set concerning which representatives vote as well as how they vote. Political freedom requires a much more robust participation on the part of citizens.

For example, it has been pointed out that one form of power is to ensure that what is momentous does not get publicly discussed. If the important issues do not arise for a vote, if certain alternative individuals cannot become candidates, then people may also be left relatively powerless. In short, one cannot be said to be self-determining, in a political context, if this only amounts to voting on preselected issues and candidates (cf. G. Graham 1983). Accordingly, issues in which blacks are crucially interested may simply not be raised in contexts within which they can participate. The result is that any participation within politics by blacks may only be distantly related to their most basic interests.

Thus, participation or involvement cannot simply be limited to voting and running for office. Political self-determination (or political freedom) requires that this agenda-form of empowerment also be addressed. Thus, for individuals to be empowered they must also – and they will have this primarily through various organisations they belong to – be able to influence the agenda which arises to the level of discussion and voting. Participation must include creating or reinforcing social and political values and institutional practices such that issues of most importance come within the political process and are subjected to public consideration.[22]

Hence, one needs also the right and power to influence the agenda which will determine which questions arise for decision. Accordingly, voter initiatives, lobbying, access to legislators, and the blocking of favored access by special interests are important for political freedom.[23] These measures will require various material resources, whose relevance as such to political freedom is discussed in the next chapter.

Only in this way can we hold public office holders accountable and work to set the agenda that comes up for decisions within the government. That is, the acceptance of the election of political officials does not imply that we need not continue to participate by way of shaping the circumstances and issues those officials consider. Hence freedom of the press, access to public officials (elected and appointed), sunshine laws and open records are crucial. The actions of the government must be revealed, even exposed, so that people may hold the government and its agents accountable in the determinations they make for society.[24]

Thus, the scope of participation must be at least threefold: (a) citizens must be able to participate in decisions whereby the basic directions of their society are determined; (b) they must be able to participate in determining who fill the posts through which the directions society takes are determined; and (c) they must be able to participate in creating or reinforcing social and political values and institutional practices that determine which issues will come within the scope of the political process and public consideration (cf. Bachrach and Baratz 1970: 7).

Within such circumstances, there is political freedom even if the activities I promote do not always succeed as a result of the elections or my activities. Still, if they never succeeded, or only rarely did so, then my political freedom would be diminished. I must be at least partly successful, in that my interests are supported and my rights protected. Otherwise my empowerment would be slight and my participation meaningless. This means that the majority may not impose restrictions and limitations which put minority groups at particular disadvantage in their attempts to exercise intellectual influence and to gain political power (cf. Morgenthau 1957: 719). Such measures delegitimize minority groups and implicitly, if not explicitly, imply that only the majority has access to political truth and wisdom. Historically, many individuals and minority groups have suffered these disadvantages and lack of success in articulating and defending their interests. Accordingly, they have suffered a lack of political freedom.

Obviously there is no simple answer to the question of how often one's participation must be successful, i.e. one's interests articulated and realised. What is clear, however, is that a person is less politically free if those who run the government do not protect his or her empowerment in the sense that a person can openly work to get the policies changed which conflict with his or her own determinations. In this sense, the system must protect one's rights.

Further, and more importantly, since one is politically free as a citizen (or member) of a society, the actions of the state must not be such that they undermine the bases upon which one is legitimately a citizen. In particular, the actions of the state must not treat one unfairly with regard to one's interests or rights. Only to the extent that the state treats its citizens justly will they continue to view themselves as citizens in the full sense required to accept that some of their particular interests are met while some are not. In this manner, political freedom rests upon a theory of justice.

VII OTHER ASPECTS OF POLITICAL PARTICIPATION

Several problems remain regarding whether, and the extent to which, individuals exercise their right to participation. For example, what of the complaint that involvement of any sort in politics is distasteful? It would seem that a *free* individual might determine that he or she will *not* participate in politics. To make one participate, it might be claimed, is to limit his or her freedom. Need the brilliant musician who is politically very retiring be less politically free than the local politician who participates in a great many political activities? How can we say that participation is (or must be) part of one's political freedom? In fact, some have defended the importance of apathy among the members of a politically free society. (cf. Jones 1954; Parry 1972: 31; Arendt 1961b: 201).

At the outset, it is important to reject the view that those who do not, or refuse to, participate have avoided being "political." Such political abstention "hides even from those people the latent politics of their passivity and acquiescence" (Walzer 1970: 210). People think, mistakenly, that their silence or lack of participation on various issues means that they are non-political. Just as sins need not simply be those of commission, but may also be those of omission, so too persons who try to remain non-political are not necessarily non-political, but simply support the present political status quo. Were they to be introduced into seventeenth-century society with their present attitudes, they might well be viewed as radicals. This is an important point, though one we also chafe at, since politics does not let us alone, but pursues us even into our solitude.

The hair stylist, for example, who professes complete indifference to politics while living in a democracy that protects his basic rights, may be said to enjoy political freedom. But he does so in a very limited sense. A great deal of what he enjoys could be found under a benevolent tyranny. Of course, he would not enjoy the right to act politically in those tyrannical circumstances. To this extent, under a politically free state, he enjoys political freedom even though he does not take advantage of it. He is like the person who "enjoys" a city with parks, libraries and concerts, but never visits or partakes of any of them. In a very limited manner, such a person may be culturally enriched through the actions of others. So too the hair stylist may be said to be politically free, but only in a very restricted sense. He could take advantage of such freedom, if he wanted, but he does not want to.[25] There is here an alienation from politics, not the least of which manifests itself in a lack of awareness of the political dimensions of his own life.

Thus, one does not escape from the political simply by inaction. In any context of individual freedom, politics will intervene to structure and shape one's life. Those who identify freedom with those aspects of their lives apart from politics are people whose lives are shaped by politics, only they are unwilling to recognize this fact. In short, they acquiesce in the political determination of their lives. Further, the avoidance of the political may itself give room for those who are less retiring but who also find the political an obstacle to their own ends.[26] In short, it may be an invitation to tyranny.

But, then, what extent of active participation by individuals does political freedom require? Quite obviously, no specific answer can be given as to the number of those who must participate or how much they must participate for political freedom to exist in a society. Even on the individual level it is not necessary, for a person to be individually free, that she or he must place his or her imprint on, or be involved in, literally everything, whether in a non-political or political context. This has already been defended above. One need not be exercising one's right to self-determination at every moment. One may yield to experts, relax and do nothing, or even take an afternoon nap.

Correspondingly, it is mistaken to suggest that, for one to be politically free, one must be wholly involved in politics or that one must participate to the full extent possible in political affairs. Freedom as involvement does not require participation in all governmental affairs by everyone – even if this were possible, which it is not. In today's large societies, direct democracy is impossible. The notion of all people equally participating in the decisions that significantly affect them is a myth (Walzer 1980). The real problem with freedom as self-determination is not to see that it extends beyond the backyard, but to see where it stops and what limits it has once it has gone beyond our private areas.

Though each citizen need not on each occasion participate in the determination of governmental or state affairs for there to be political freedom, it does not follow that political freedom is simply the opportunity for individuals to partake in government and state affairs, an opportunity which all people might simply gracefully decline. For political freedom to exist in a society there must not only be opportunities to participate, but there must also be a significant level of individual participation. At least some of us must be rowing, if the others are to reach shore. We cannot all rest on our oars if we are to enjoy political freedom. But the fact that some of us do not row, does not mean that political freedom does not require participation. Most simply the number involved must be sufficient to keep the actions of government faithful to the principles noted in the preceding sections.

Further, both the intensity and extension of participation or involvement will (and should) differ depending upon the group about which we are talking. People do not relate to the government simply on a one-to-one basis. They are members of other groups and relate to the government through these groups as well: e.g. (in the US) lawyers through the American Bar Association, doctors through the American Medical Association, and industrial workers through various unions. Participation in these groups affects the representatives of these groups who, in turn, participate at the state or province and local levels. This occurs not only through one's place of employment but also through churches and other voluntary associations. More must be said on such groups in the next section. Still, the real opportunity to participate is enlarged through the existence of a variety of institutions between those of the official government and particular individuals. One's opportunity to participate effectively in such groups is simply much larger than if citizens were left to relate to the state on an individual basis. Further, the smaller the group the more intense and extensive we may expect one's participation to be. Thus, political freedom seems to favor some form of pluralism.

The preceding does not imply that participation must include individual citizens choosing the people or leaders of the bureaucracy or even the military forces. Such individuals should be selected on the basis of competence to execute various technical tasks determined by those representative of the citizens. Such representatives are in a better position to make these determinations. Further, there is a limit to how much involvement can or should be demanded from citizens in directing various technical features within the state.

Whether citizens should choose or vote for judges will depend on the form this opportunity would take. This is not to say that such individuals ought not to be accountable to citizens as well. Further, some means of installing and removing those who emplace such people is important. However, the point of participation is not to decide every issue or problem. Only if we assumed that the involvement political freedom requires need be constant and all-encompassing would political freedom require an intensity and extent of participation that almost anyone would find impossible. Rather, participation is to ensure the respect of individual rights, the operation of mechanisms whereby conflicts between those rights are resolved in accord with the basic principles or conditions of a free society, and the understanding and appreciation of one's freedom that comes with its exercise.

Accordingly, there are multiple forms and levels of involvement or participation. People may participate through voting, lobbying, demonstrating, letter writing, public speaking, attending meetings of groups at various levels in the political process, etc. People also participate in the government by remaining informed, by placing signs on their cars, windows or lawns, debating within a public forum, discussing political issues with associates, friends, and acquaintances, contributing money to candidates, phoning in their concerns to candidates or officials, airing their grievances on radio talk shows, and placing lit candles in their windows.

The empowerment these forms of involvement provide is, assuredly, not a total empowerment. But this is neither possible nor desirable. It is an empowerment, however, which works to influence the directions one's society takes. One's right to self-determination is realized as a member of a society in which people conjointly determine their future.

Finally, the arguments in this section with regard to participation may appear to be primarily instrumental. Participation may appear to be a means whereby the decision procedure is kept faithful to principles compatible with the freedom or empowerment of this or that individual. Viewed as such it is not surprising that people do not participate in the political process when they believe that it is functioning satisfactorily. After all if a person has an instrument to accomplish some end but that end is already being realized, then there is little reason to use the instrument. If one has a garden hose to wash one's car and yet the car is shiny and clean it would be silly to use the garden hose.

On the other hand, more realistically, it is more likely today that people believe the political process is beyond correction than that they believe it to be functioning properly. Thus, it is more likely that people do not vote or participate because they are alienated. In the situation when one believes that one's car is so grimy that washing with water will hardly change anything, one would also be silly to use the garden hose.

Still, the forms of empowerment are more than simple instruments to ends outside them. Rather they constitute important forms of one's freedom as a political being, rather than simply protect something outside of them. For those who desire to partake of self-determination on this most general level, the preceding rights and opportunities are not merely of instrumental importance, but of intrinsic importance. A significant problem is that a large number of people do not seem to experience this desire. Thus, though they may need such rights instrumentally, they do not experience this need in any other measure. Accordingly, this intrinsic side of the equation has not carried as much force as it should. Without some sea change in the attitude of people towards distant government, it is unlikely that such intrinsic appeals will or can carry much weight. The government is too far, the number involved is too many, the forum is too loud, and the time commitment is too great. The importance of participation, then, must be part of the political education of the nation. This is to overcome the alienation between people, the public and the political. However, part of the difficulty here lies in viewing the political too narrowly.

VIII   THE EXTENT OF POLITICAL FREEDOM

There are two reasons why the preceding does not exhaust the participatory side of political freedom. First, though it is common to link the political to government this view is too narrow. We speak of political activity and behavior in many different contexts other than simply that of government. Political decisions are made by people in businesses, churches, unions, and even garden clubs.

There is office politics and university politics. Even on traditional views these organizations themselves may take political stances. Quite clearly, politics goes on outside state government or concerns for the public as a whole (cf. Finer 1972: 59).[27]

Secondly, other groups and organizations play an important part in our lives besides the state. We are members of some of these organizations (the business where one works; one's church, clubs, etc.), but not members of others. Some of these can (and some cannot) impose their authority on a person. A person who joins the Sierra Club or Greenpeace does not thereby come under any authority which those organizations can impose on a member. On the other hand, even though a person is not a member of certain other organizations, they may still significantly affect him or her. Their effects may alter or modify the ways in which we realize our right to self-determination. Obviously, such organizations may be either public or private.

It is particularly important to note the role that these organizations play in our lives. Many large businesses, multi-national corporations (Exxon or BP), and international organizations (ECC, IMF, etc.) transcend the state in the powers and influences which they are capable of bringing to bear on groups of people (including states, regions, etc.). Though Locke said that the state alone has the authority to impose penalties with death, this becomes increasingly irrelevant when the death penalty (or even prison) is only occasionally imposed, and economic and other penalties which other organizations can impose match those of the state. Further, the influence of these organizations plays an important role in setting the political agenda. Accordingly, if political freedom concerns the compatibility of the right to self-determination and the state (due to the influence the state can wield), it surely also concerns a similar compatibility with such large organisations.

In the remainder of this chapter, I argue that political freedom also requires a right to participate in those groups which hold authority over us. Politics and political freedom extend beyond the right to participate in governmental affairs. They apply, more broadly, to the political and public affairs of one's society. Participation in this broader sense will be much more of an ongoing affair.

The principal argument for this view is that the power, control and influence that ("private") corporations, as well as unions, exercise over their members is quite great, greater indeed than that of many states. They determine what kinds of jobs are available, how many jobs there will be and where they will be located. They provide day-care for children, restaurants, retirement funds, education, recreation centers, vacation spots, etc. Their rules regulate the rhythm and manner of life of vast numbers of individuals. They decide which regions or cities of the country will prosper and which stagnate. Their choices can alter the physical appearance of cities and the countryside. They may determine which crops are grown in third-world countries and the level of prosperity or poverty its inhabitants experience. They can bring significant financial resources and pressure to bear to alter legislative bills, government decisions, and political party policies.[28] In short, they exercise considerable power in the determination of matters of general public concern.

Such organizations are not political in the Lockean sense that they make laws which hold the power of life and death over a person. Nor are they political in the broader sense of Aristotle for whom politics was the master art whose object is the chief good. Rather they are political in the sense of governing the lives and actions of hundreds, if not thousands and tens of thousands, of members. Through complicated systems of rules and decisions, power, coercion and authority are exercised over these individuals, who, should they disobey, are subject to punishment.[29] Such power is not exercised simply by force or coercion, but primarily through discussion, persuasion, bargaining, and agreement as well as command and directives. This is yet another political element to such authority.

Finally, any political system assumes a minimum level of agreement on common values and ends. Without such agreement, there will not be political activity so much as warfare. In the last decade, Beirut (Lebanon) has been an instance where minimal common assumptions and values have collapsed and civil war has resulted. So too, corporations and large organizations assume a common enterprise, a basic level of cooperative activity, which unites the activities of their members. This is a third reason to view such organizations as political systems.

Accordingly, the age of the large-scale organization no longer allows us to limit the "political" to what goes on in state government. To the extent that we are members of a society or group which exercises authority over us through commands as well as discussion, bargaining, and agreement, and which assumes certain minimal values and ends, we are politically ruled. If we are to be politically free, our right to participation in such organizations must be recognized.

Two objections may be offered to this argument. First, it will be contended that just because an organization exercises authority over a member it is not thereby a political institution subject to the demands of political freedom. Large corporations are private organizations. They are economic, not political, institutions. Secondly, if the size and power of corporations and unions are significant because of the impact they have on their members – and it is for this reason that they are political institutions subject to demands of political freedom – then it should be recognized that the impact of a small business on its employees might also be terribly significant. It might give them less room and protection than a larger organization. However, it seems even less plausible to view these as political organizations subject to the demands of political freedom. Further, if we are concerned about the power that may be exercised over other individuals, then we should also be concerned with the effect that one individual may have upon another individual. John may have significant effects on Joe due to certain decisions that he (John) makes. Still, this does not make John a political organization or mean that Joe, therefore, can have a right to a say in what John decides.

In short, the above argument seems to lead us to extend the political realm and the demands of political freedom from large corporations and unions to small businesses and even to individuals. But surely this is a *reductio ad absurdum* of this position.

These difficulties are, however, more apparent than real. Thus, I believe that the above argument points us in the correct direction.[30] Accordingly, we must draw a number of distinctions between the effects corporations and individuals may impose, and between individual and political freedom.

To begin with, just because a person's decisions will seriously affect another person, the latter does not have a right to participate in the first person's decisions. If John and Jim are suitors for Mary's hand, they do not thereby have a right to participate in her decision.[31] Mary and her suitors do not exist in a relationship in which Mary holds authority over them. They do not exist in some common enterprise. Indeed, whether there will be such a common "enterprise" is exactly the issue. This is not to say that people such as Mary who wield significant influence over others should not listen to the people who will be affected. Still, Mary has a right to self-determination as well. She need not allow John or Jim to participate in her decision.

Conversely, to the extent that people live or work within an institution that exercises authority over them, they must (if they are to be free) have a right to participate in determining how they will be affected. Thus, when a business or union makes decisions relating to the welfare of its workers, production, or plant placement, then members of that organization should have a right to participate in those decisions. On the other hand, should an executive consider retiring, this would not be a question in which members of the business would normally have a right to participate. This is a personal decision, not a decision of the organization.

Secondly, the sharp division between political and economic realms, which liberalism has defended, has long been transcended. We do not simply have political institutions on the one hand, and economic institutions on the other. States, and their governments, are involved in the production of goods and services for vast numbers of people. Analogously, the larger instances of economic institutions are governments. They have important political effects. They are enmeshed in the political process. We speak quite intelligibly of the political clout of the National Association of Manufacturers, the United Auto Workers and large corporations such as General Motors. They are forms of political government, even though they have ends different from those of local or state governments.[32]

Further, the authority of large corporations rests upon particular political views of society. The basis of corporate activity lies in the right of private property, which is itself a fundamental political right. The exercise of this right would not entitle one to construct a city in which one simply directed all activities of its citizens. This is the point of Walzer's persuasive argument that exercise of the right of private property does not entitle one to create an organization through which one simply directs the activities of its members (Walzer 1980). Walzer's argument relies on the medieval maxim that *what touches all should be decided by all* (Ibid.: 275). The argument offered in this chapter (that freedom as the right of self-determination requires the conjoint determination of individuals involved in mutual organizations and institutions) is a variation of this maxim. The basic touchstone for political freedom is not private property, but a form of conjoint determination that renders freedom and authority compatible. This requires a right to participate in corporations and unions as well as the state. In fact, the proper division is not between the economic and the political, but between organizations which ought not to be susceptible to direct state determination and those that should.

Finally, corporations (and unions) significantly control the fate of many people. It is too simple to say that a business exercises only economic authority over its employees. Within the working day, life is circumscribed within a narrow framework of activity. Rules may govern dress codes, what activities I engage in for eight or more hours a day, relationships with others within the corporation, and associations outside the corporation. During the non-working part of one's life, the "economic" decisions of corporations may determine where I live, whether I must move to a new city, what level of income I will have, which goods I am inclined to buy (even able to or must buy) as well as the extent to which my civil rights are protected, various opportunities are secured, etc. In addition, corporations may (and do) demand that employees not smoke off the job, not take various drugs, not partake in various social activities, etc. "It should be clear by this time," Hacker has noted, "that the power of the corporate elite is not simply economic. On the contrary, its influence reaches far into society and has a deep impact on the character and personality of individual Americans" (Hacker 1969: 74).

The argument is, then, that any organization of which one is a member, which can have such effects on one, should be subject to demands of a right to participation if people are to enjoy political freedom. In effect, the corporation takes part in the political activity of the society.[33] The positions it takes will have an important impact on that society. One's contribution to that organization and its political effects are not – or should not be – simply those of some neutral instrument. Rather, one should have a say in what those impacts may be. Political freedom demands nothing less.

In addition, as these organizations and the state become even more enmeshed due to international competition, the state is in effect sanctioning the rules, conditions, etc. imposed on employees by the corporation. The argument here, however, does not rely on this further entanglement. More simply, where there are great corporations and unions, the state has permitted these powers to be exercised. It has allowed such organizations to exercise great (coercive) power over their members. But here too, as with the state, the question must arise, "who guards the guardians?" If this is a legitimate question for the state, it is a legitimate one for large institutions such as modern corporations and unions.

The answer that the market will restrain the leaders of such organizations and provide for political freedom is patently false. Great injuries can be done before the market ever has a chance to operate. With limited job possibilities, individual members of a corporation may not be able to exit the corporation without significant negative effects. One might as well argue that the pressures of world politics will guard the citizens of a country and that immigration can protect citizens from wrongdoing. In each case, the costs may be individually extraordinary. The market cannot by itself do the job. Instead, internal representation both within the state as well as within large corporations and unions is needed for the freedom that individuals require within the political sphere of society. Accordingly, demands for freedom of speech, due process, and privacy are increasingly heard within large corporations. Similarly, the demand for participation within such organizations is legitimate.

What about those organizations of which one is not a member but which affect significantly one's self-determinations? Some have argued that it is an implication of the preceding that political freedom, and hence participation, extends to questions concerning not simply government but to any enterprise which importantly affects the common good. This is mistaken in any direct sense.

In this case one does not necessarily, as an individual, have a say in their determinations. To impose involvement would be a form of distrust, interference, even paternalism, unless it is warranted by some additional factor other than having an effect. It allows for meddling and denies their own self-determination. Such other factors would include the fact that the group repeatedly harmfully affects others. Otherwise, one must be a member of the organization in order to have a right to participate. This does not imply that such groups should not be monitored or controlled by the members of the community or state. On the basis of the significant effects of such a group, governments may exercise appropriate control over their determinations.

Thus, though one's freedom is not simply against the state, but also against other people and groups, there are legitimate private groups over which neither an individual affected nor the state should have direct control. A person doesn't have a right to participate just because an organization or someone else decides something that affects her or him. We must consider the nature of the relation involved and the seriousness of the effects.

Thus, if the activities of various private groups significantly affect me, I should have some means of control through the city or state. I do not necessarily have a say in the internal determinations of this group. But the community or state of which the group is a member does have a say in the results of its determinations, and, to that extent, in the processes whereby it arrives at its determinations.

The preceding quite obviously suggests rather significant changes in society – though it is quite in line with changes that are presently going on within business as well as government. The participation which some corporations are encouraging from employees should be seen not simply as a matter of efficiency but of political freedom. If the process is not a sham, the employees thereby gain empowerment. It is on this level that political freedom may seem most meaningful to people: where their votes count and affect them, where their daily activities play a substantive role in determining their lives. In many ways, the national government is too far away, too abstract, too unrelated (except when it cracks down) to appear to many people to have anything to do with them. Or, if it does, they feel impotent and helpless.

It might be objected that the present argument leads to the politicization of organizations. But the argument here is not that such organizations should be politicized. It is that they are already political in a broader and more realistic sense of the term. Further, we should not assume that allowing such political freedom would thereby make such organizations inefficient. Indeed, it may well have the opposite effect. Managers would have to spend less time convincing people to carry out policies which they had simply imposed. Such time would have been spent in designing policies which, once enacted, would not have to be the object of a campaign to convince people to support them.

Finally, the preceding argument also suggests the desirability of forming groups closer to people in which they can have some effect. Thus, neighborhood councils, local associations, worker committees, etc. might better be able to give people a greater degree of empowerment, and hence political freedom, than they presently enjoy. Living areas might be redesigned to promote, rather than impede, the conjoint participation this chapter has defended. Indeed, if we are to reclaim a sense of political freedom it will be on this more local and immediate level, than on the national level, however, important the national level is.

IX CONCLUSION

Essential to political freedom is the right to participate in the body politic. Crucial to this notion is the individual as a full and equal member of society.

The problem of freedom, we have seen, arises on various levels: the individual, the intermediate group and the state. The problem of political freedom is *not* simply a question of the relation of the individual to the state. This is only one part of the overall question. We recognize this when we claim that people make political decisions in businesses, labor unions, and other intermediate organizations.

Further, each of these groups may also claim authority over us. Though the state may claim to be the ultimate authority (at least in some areas), this does not gainsay that there are other groups which claim a subordinate (though at times a superior, non-political) authority.[34] Solving the ultimate authority problem does not, as such, resolve the intermediate authority problem. We cannot look simply to the relation of the state and the individual. Those who begin by considering the problem of freedom as if it were simply a problem between two different individuals, or between an individual and the state, begin at an overly abstract level – even though they may believe themselves to be beginning at the most concrete level. In fact, the individual is an historical creation not to be understood independently of its relations to others.

As such, political freedom extends much more broadly than simply to the individual and the state. It involves both direct and indirect participation (through agents or representatives), in the many intermediate institutions of which we are members. Political freedom is a multi-layered fabric of societal determination which requires a complex structure.

It should be noted that just because there is participation in a political body, it does not follow that the forms that such participation takes will necessarily be humanitarian. Sparta was a polity in which participation was stressed and yet it was also an armed camp (Salkever 1977: 404). Political freedom does not exclude the possibility of an armed camp. Similarly, those who enjoy political freedom within corporations may still use that freedom to impose harmful effects on others. However, to the extent that such participation arises out of individual rights to self-determination and these are protected, these dangers will be minimalized.

In addition, the fears of legislators, managers and administrators – as well as those of the public – can be played upon and manipulated when participation is called for.[35] Even with full participation, the public may be prepared to move much more slowly than its leaders. In this sense, political freedom need not provide the most rapid or progressive manner of transforming a population. This reminds us that political freedom by itself is not the only political value or ideal. A complete political philosophy must include not only an account of freedom, but also justice, fraternity, etc.

I have argued that a person need not, in fact, participate in the decisions of governments of states. Similarly, a person need not participate in employment decisions, or in the decisions of other groups (church, club, neighborhood council, etc.) of which he or she is a member. But unless a person not only can but does participate in some of these, his or her political freedom is considerably reduced. The public arena of that person's life has shrunk to a diminishing point. *Political freedom concerns a person's self-determination within the public dimension of his or her life.* It is not limited simply to national and local governments. It extends more broadly to places of employment, neighborhood committees, etc. It is the arena in which one takes public stands, defines oneself, confronts those of differing views, defends oneself and others who are like-minded, etc.

The present account remains, however, incomplete. Specifically, we have not addressed the notion that people who are individually or politically free are *able* to exercise their right of self-determination. This incompleteness is obvious when it is noted that people may not have the money or the means to participate. This raises questions of ability and means. These remaining questions are discussed in Chapter 7.

7 Freedom, enablement, and resources

> It is . . . a sound instinct which identifies freedom with power to
> frame purposes and to execute or carry into effect purposes so
> framed.
>
> (Dewey 1963: 67)

I INTRODUCTION

Political freedom, I have argued, is a form of conjoint empowerment
in which rights protect one from other individuals, organizations,
and the state. In short, political freedom as empowerment requires
that individuals not be subjected to various forms of constraint. On
the other hand, political freedom also requires measures through
which individuals may exercise their right to participate in public
and political decision making. Together these components constitute
the right to self-determination.

It is notorious, however, that what is given with one hand may be
taken back with the other. Though their rights are legally protected,
people may remain unable effectively to exercise them. In short, their
rights may be impotent; participation may exist only on paper. They
enjoy the same "freedom" as do the rich to sleep under bridges or to
occupy a Senate seat. But for those who are unable to avoid sleeping
under bridges or to make their voice heard in political debates,
such claims of freedom mock their condition. Like blacks in the
US after the Emancipation Proclamation, their political freedom is
paper thin.

As such, we need to speak of the ability of people effectively
to exercise their right to self-determination. So far little has been
said about this aspect of freedom. However, when the rights and
participation spoken of in preceding chapters are treated as merely
formal in nature, any empowerment people gain through them is

undercut. Accordingly, political freedom requires various positive conditions, opportunities, and means. This is a criticism that radicals have repeatedly made against accounts of freedom involving rights.

In this chapter I wish to complete my account of political freedom by arguing that it also requires that people are *enabled* to act effectively in accordance with their rights (positive and negative) to participate in political and public matters. There are two general aspects to the enablement required by political freedom. First, people need material or financial resources to execute their plans. The lack of material resources "disables" rather than enables them. It fundamentally threatens political freedom, though it is disparities in material resources, as much as their simple lack, which is the real problem. Secondly, cognitive resources, including knowledge, information, and education, are also required for political freedom. How much one knows (and whether one can gain access to knowledge) about the political situations one faces is (are) important to political enablement. Thus, both cognitive and material resources are required for individuals to be empowered (or enabled).

A society in which individuals not only may participate but also are in a position to do so may be genuinely called an "open" society.[1] Though we need not completely agree with Perry – due to historical experience with the totalitarian regimes of Hitler and Stalin – certainly the general thrust of this chapter agrees with him when he suggests that "the most persistent and oppressive enemies of liberty are not external hindrances, whether physical or human, but poverty and ignorance" (Perry 1944: 525). I wish to develop and defend the philosophical basis of this claim. I oppose those who hold that material and cognitive resources are merely desirable additions to political freedom.

The general thesis of this chapter is, then, that lack of material and cognitive resources reduces one's political freedom. People are not politically free who do not have the means and opportunities to realize their right to self-determination. Any view is far too narrow that proclaims people free who are simply not being beaten over the head with truncheons. Instead, political freedom is an empowered way of living which the citizen or member of a community enjoys.

II FREEDOM, ABILITIES, AND POWER

The connection between freedom and abilities or powers has often been asserted. Jonathan Edwards claims that "the plain and obvious meaning of the words 'freedom' and 'liberty,' in common speech, is power, opportunity, or advantage that anyone has, to do as he pleases" (Edwards 1957: 163). John Dewey commented that "freedom from restriction" was "to be prized only as a means to a freedom which is power" (Dewey 1963: 64). Mortimer Adler concludes that "freedom, in any conception of it, involves an *ability* or *power* of some sort" (Adler 1958: 608). And finally, Amartya Sen speaks of "individual liberty . . . as *implying* some power of the respective individual to determine social judgments or social decisions over his or her personal sphere" (Sen 1982: 208).

On the other hand, others deny that there is such a relation at all. Liberal freedom denies that there is a conceptual connection between freedom and power or abilities. One may be free but unable to take advantage of one's freedom. For example, Hobbes claimed that a legless man has the liberty to move but not the power; whereas a man in jail (who has the power) is not at liberty to move. Hobbes's general point is that "when the impediment of motion, is in the constitution of the thing itself" it is proper to say it wants not the liberty, but rather "the power to move, as when a man is fastened to his bed by sickness" (quoted in Handlin and Handlin 1961: 17). Accordingly, freedom and enablement are two different and unrelated concepts.

Thus, the relation between freedom and powers or abilities has been sharply disputed. Those who claim that there is a connection between freedom and power claim, variously, that there are conceptual, criterial, or rational connections between the two. Opponents have denied such connections.

The relation of political freedom and enablement is a complicated relation. The quotations from writers who link the two include mention of "power," "opportunity," "advantage," and "ability." Nevertheless, these terms do not all refer to the same thing or condition. For present purposes, I will treat powers and abilities quite closely. Both powers and abilities may be "internal" as well as "external." They may both be held in occurrent and dispositional senses. That is, though the exercise of one's powers or abilities may be blocked by others on a particular occasion, it does not follow that one does not have that power or ability. Powers and abilities can be natural as well as acquired. However, since we are concerned about political freedom, we will focus on those that are acquired and exercised within society. Powers and abilities in this political sense always involve a relation between two or more beings.

The exercise of one's powers and abilities requires various means and opportunities. If one's power is one's capacity or ability to alter the behavior of individuals and conditions towards some desired end, then to have power will require various means. Of course, one need not have the means to exercise one's powers on all occasions if we view such powers or abilities in a dispositional sense. However, for a person to have the occurrent power to do something, he or she must also have the means. Further, one must also have the opportunities or the occasions within which those powers and abilities may be exercised. A person may have great charismatic power and yet no one be present over whom she or he may exercise this power.

Accordingly, I cannot have the power to influence certain decisions if I do not have the means required. Similarly, I am able to express my views only if I have the means to do so. This may require access to newspapers, as well as the financial resources that permit me to send petitions, write letters, or join with others in lobbying the legislature. More generally, I can hardly be said to have the power to determine my own life (or course of action), if I do not have the means. To have the power, in this circumstance, implies that I have the means, even though this does not imply that I must be successful. If I am not successful it may simply be that I did not apply my powers correctly. Of course, it may also be that I did not have sufficient power or means for success in this instance.

Thus, when we speak about political freedom, we are asking whether one must have certain powers or abilities (and the attendant means and opportunities) to exercise one's right to self-determination. If people are to be politically free must they also be able to exercise their right to participation and, more generally, their right to self-determination?

There are two kinds of argument that attempt to sharply separate liberty and power. One relies on a negative definition of freedom; the other appeals to ordinary language. Both arguments are mistaken.

Hobbes provides an example of the first kind of argument. He contends, for example, that freedom is simply the absence of external impediments of motion and might be applied to irrational and inanimate creatures, as well as to rational ones (Hobbes 1950: 177). However, when the impediment of motion "is in the constitution of the thing itselfe, we use not to say, it wants the Liberty; but the Power to move; as when a stone lyeth still, or a man is fastned to his bed by sicknesse" (Ibid.).

However, the implausibility of sharply separating power and freedom can be seen within Hobbes's own account of freedom.

In holding that freedom is the absence of external impediments of motion, Hobbes assumes that he can characterize the external impediments of motion independently from the inner powers of a body whereby it moves. But this he cannot do. Consider a person confined to prison. The Handlins argue, quite plausibly, that

> the capacity of the bars to hold the prisoner is not intrinsic . . . but is dependent upon the limits of his power. If he were strong enough or possessed the proper instruments he could break forth. Such restraints themselves are only a reflection of the individual's lack of power.
>
> (Handlin and Handlin 1961: 17–18)

In short, Hobbes's negative concept of freedom – the lack of constraint – cannot be formulated without implicitly recognizing the powers that a person does, or does not, have. A person can only be coerced or constrained if he/she lacks certain powers.

Suppose, for instance, that a ball and chain were fastened about a person's legs. Surely this person has been rendered unfree. But suppose further that the prisoner takes some super steroid concoction such that his leg muscles became as strong as steel coils. He might then simply walk away, the ball and chain bothering him as little as a loose thread on his trousers. That is, it is impossible to separate one's freedom from considerations of the powers or abilities one has. Thus, it is mistaken to focus simply on external restraints when this cannot be understood independently of the individual's powers. Freedom cannot be identified with only one part of this interrelated condition.

Secondly, Hobbes faces numerous problems in formulating a separation between internal and external impediments. A man might be "fastned to his bed by sicknesse" due to some virus that entered his body and robbed him of his power to move. It is rather implausible to view this impediment of motion as simply "in the constitution of the thing itselfe," as "when a stone lyeth still" (Hobbes 1950: 177). It is not part of the person's nature; it entered from the outside. Does the person, then, lack liberty due to an external impediment? This is also awkward to hold, especially on Hobbes's view, since a virus is hardly like a jailkeeper or chains.

Consequently, Hobbes cannot maintain his distinction between liberty and power. Though he claims that the absence of external impediments is liberty, while the presence of internal impediments is lack of power, we might as well say, because of the difficulties in separating external from internal impediments, that the presence of external impediments is the lack of power and that the absence of internal impediments is liberty. Better yet, Hobbes might simply claim that liberty is the absence of impediments to one's powers. Or, more positively stated, liberty is the presence of one's powers. But this would link what Hobbes sought to distinguish.

Thus, underlying the problem of Hobbes's negative view of freedom is his identification of freedom with a condition mistakenly viewed as independent and external from us. As such, it involves an alienation of freedom. What freedom we have or do not have depends, in part, upon the powers we have.

A second argument against any connection between freedom and power arises from those who appeal to ordinary language. Partridge, for example, has objected that "being free to" does not include within its meaning "having the capacity or the power to."[2] He argues that it is one thing to ask "Am I free to walk into the Pentagon" and another thing to ask "Am I free to walk across the Atlantic." The first question, Partridge suggests, will be clearly understood; to the second question, he says, the appropriate answer will be "You are free to, if you can." (Partridge 1967: 222). This linguistic fact, he says, suggests his main argument:

> The linking of "being free to" with "having the capacity or power" deprives the word "free" of its essential and unequivocal function, which is to refer to a situation or state of affairs in which a man's choice of how he acts is not deliberately forced or restrained by another man.
>
> (Ibid.)

Therefore, he concludes, "it can be said that, at least in many cases, equating freedom with possession of power, will involve a distortion of ordinary language" (Ibid.).

Partridge is correct that "freedom" and "power" do not mean the same thing. We cannot simply exchange "freedom" for "power" in any sentence. There are obviously many situations in which a person may have great power and yet not be free. I argued in the last chapter, that the powerful tyrant was not, because of his power, therefore free. The question is whether their meanings are (or should be) linked. Partridge's argument, however, begs this question.

First, our question concerns the use of "freedom." It is not settled simply by proclaiming that some other use is orthodox. The limits of an appeal to ordinary language were noted in Chapter 1.[3] There are various uses of "freedom" in ordinary language. Our task is to consider which one is theoretically most desirable and useful for a model of freedom.

Secondly, Partridge's first example clearly presupposes one is physically able to walk into the Pentagon and thus is asking about a legal condition: Will any guards stop me? It focuses, as did Hobbes, on one part of a complex situation. In his second example, we naturally assume that one is legally free to walk across the Atlantic Ocean, but question whether one has the physical ability to do so. Since physical ability may or may not accompany legal freedom, freedom and ability are said to be separate concepts.

Now surely we want to distinguish between freedom and the lack of natural ability to do certain things, e.g. walk on water (e.g. across the Atlantic) or fly through the air. However, it does not follow from this that freedom and abilities or powers are not bound up in some sense. Perry suggests this connection when he claims that "a man is not at liberty to walk unless he has sound limbs" it signifies little that no barrier prevents, or no authority forbids. . ." (Perry 1944: 513). But to have sound limbs is to have certain powers and abilities to walk. Imagine, then, a group of crippled persons, who were bussed to the Pentagon. The guard proceeds to inform them that they are free to walk into the Pentagon, but may not use wheelchairs, crutches, or be carried. Surely the guard's comment is not only insensitive but also inappropriate because they cannot take advantage of it. Lacking the ability to walk, these individuals would rightly protest that they are not free to enter the Pentagon. Accordingly, freedom is linked, at least in some minimal ways, with physical abilities and powers.[4]

Beyond this, the preceding argument is hardly conclusive since it is mistaken to suggest that political freedom is only connected to physical abilities or powers. One may be able or unable to do something in a variety of ways: economic, social, psychological, as well as legal and political. Wholly to exclude abilities and power from freedom, Partridge would have to show us that similar arguments could be made for other instances. Thus, for example, a person might be mentally crippled or socially limited such that walking into the Pentagon might be an act that that person might not be able even to consider. It wholly escapes him as something he might possibly do. Analogously, consider a primitive tribesman suddenly introduced into a modern society. It seems wholly appropriate in such contexts to say that the person involved is not free, simply because he or she might not be able to act in any number of ways, including walking into the Pentagon – it might be feared as some great menacing tomb. That is, various social and psychological conditions, e.g. fear or mental restrictions, may render one unable to act in certain ways. Contrariwise, the ability to overcome such fear or restricted understandings would render such individuals free (or more free). They would, then, be able to act on their right of self-determination. As such, one's abilities do not stand separate from one's freedom, but as necessarily part of it.

Finally, both Hobbes's and Partridge's views hold that all conditions constituting freedom are particular, occurrent, and external. These conditions take the form of constraints – people (deliberately) acting on other people to stop or hinder (directly or indirectly) them from doing something. This classically liberal view is at the heart of the problem of recognizing the connection between freedom and power. It projects freedom on to the world: freedom is the lack of obstacles or other people acting in certain ways. My argument, in the preceding chapters and this section, has maintained that there is another crucial side to freedom, viz. certain abilities and powers which allow people to act upon their right of self-determination and for the lack of which they are less free.

Consequently, the preceding arguments that freedom and power are not connected at all seem doubtful. They tend to separate what cannot be separated; they mistakenly treat freedom as simply an external matter; they tend to view individuals in merely a passive manner. They do not show that there is not some link between freedom and what one is able (in a physical and non-physical sense) to do.

III   MEANS AND POWERS AS THE VALUABLE CONDITIONS OF FREEDOM

There is a third argument which contends that, although freedom and power are conceptually distinct, one's powers (may) serve as conditions which make one's freedom more or less valuable (cf. Rawls 1971: 204–5; Gert 1972: 38). There is a normative, rather than a conceptual, connection. The means and abilities persons must have in order to enjoy freedom simply enable individuals, who are already fully politically free, to accomplish what they choose to do. Thus, one may be free without being able to enjoy that freedom. As such, freedom may be worth more to the rich man than to the poor man, since the rich man has the means to enjoy it while the poor man does not. Still, both are free.

This view is suggested by Rawls when he says that

> the inability to take advantage of one's rights and opportunities as a result of poverty and ignorance, and a lack of means generally, is sometimes counted among the constraints definitive of liberty. I shall not, however, say this, but rather I shall think of these things as affecting the worth of liberty.
>
> (Rawls 1971: 204)

The image suggested here is analogous to one in which a person owns an exquisite car but can drive it only infrequently because he or she lacks money for gas. Or perhaps a person owns a beautiful car but keeps it in storage because the roads are very bumpy or virtually non-existent. Clearly, the value and usefulness of that car would be increased if there were smooth highways to drive on and plenty of money for gas.

However, this image is misleading when we speak of freedom. Powers and means are not simply conditions valuable to freedom. One's abilities and means are part and parcel of one's political freedom. There is a conceptual connection here, not simply a normative one.

The car analogy, in fact, suggests a response to the view that Rawls and others defend. Once again, the question concerns how narrowly or broadly we conceive what we are interested in. If we take a car simply to be a piece of machinery, then surely a person can wholly own a car even if it is stored in a museum. On the other hand, if to own a car is to own a means of individual transportation – this is what people have in mind when they buy one – then when the streets are impassible or very bumpy, the object of their ownership has been diminished.

Similarly, imagine a slave immediately following emancipation. Impoverished, illiterate, an open opportunity for others to exploit, he is said to be free (theoretically no one will throw him in jail simply for wandering about), even though this freedom is of little value to him. It is unclear, however, under such circumstances what his freedom amounts to. In actuality, he might be thrown in jail simply for loitering, be run out of town, cursed and spat upon, denied any chance to voice his opinion, or participate in the political process simply because he has no means or powers to defend, let alone express, himself. It is not that he is simply not in a position to value the freedom he has, rather any freedom he might have escapes him because he does not have the requisite means or abilities. In short, he lacks an essential component of freedom.

The view at issue here corrupts freedom. By claiming that abilities and powers are valuable conditions outside of freedom, it transforms freedom into something reserved for the wealthy and the powerful. On this view, all the people of a country could be wholly free, and yet only the rich enjoy or value that freedom. Further, if the rich or powerful were lucky (and indifferent) enough, the rest of the population might remain so poor (terrible droughts reduce them to begging) that they were not able to exercise their right to self-determination in any effective manner.

Similarly, a country with no primary or secondary educational system might build fine universities, but charge so much that the poor who managed to educate themselves could never enter. Still, the wealthy might claim that there was freedom of education, since no one would be stopped who had the financial means and educational preparation for entry. Unfortunately, they note, the poor do not value this freedom very highly.[5]

On the contrary, I suggest, the preceding arguments show that for people to be free they must be able effectively to exercise their right to self-determination. Whether or not they take advantage of it must *not* depend on whether or not they can do so. It must depend on other valuations they make. *Qua* free, they must be able to do (or be), or not to do (or be), the various things they determine.

The reason that a number of philosophers have argued that distinction between the nature of something and its value is important is to allow us to weigh the value of something against other values in making various policy decisions. For example, everyone in a society might have the right to speak freely, run for office, and participate in public decision making. However, some people may not have the means or abilities to exercise some of these rights. Hence, those rights would not be terribly valuable for them. The society might then attempt to determine where to place its resources so that this or that right acquired value for additional numbers of people within the society. If we accept the proposed distinction, these decisions would not affect the freedom of any people, though they would affect the value of the particular freedoms to various individuals within the society.

Now certainly this distinction is important. But the distinction itself cannot be used to sunder political freedom and certain means or abilities which people must have in order to be politically free. Thus, in the present example above, we must assume that various rights to participate are enforced. If they were not enforced, then such a person could hardly be said to be politically free. The situation as envisioned by those above is that we might then decide upon whether we wish to commit resources to giving additional people the means to exercise their rights to participate or whether we wish to use these resources for other purposes.

However, enforcement of the above rights requires the commitment of various resources. Judges, police officers, and investigators must be hired. But this requires a prior decision that such resources will be spent for this rather than other purposes, such as giving people their own means and powers to exercise their rights. Indeed, another way of promoting the enforcement of people's rights might be to ensure that they have greater means and abilities. That is, instead of building more jails, we might use our resources to bring more people out of poverty or to improve the educational system of their children.

The underlying point here is that there is a connection between having one's rights enforced and the commitment to various means and powers, viz. the enforcement of rights requires a particular commitment of means and powers. On the other hand, those who lack various financial means and are ignorant simply do not have their rights enforced in the way that others, with such means and knowledge, have their rights enforced. It follows that they are less free. Thus, Tawney maintains that

> if . . . rights are to be an effective guarantee of freedom, they must not be merely formal, like the right of all who can afford it to dine at the Ritz. They must be such that, whenever the occasion arises to exercise them, they can in fact be exercised.
>
> (Tawney 1953: 83–4)

Abilities and powers do not simply add a gloss or a sheen to one's freedom. They are crucial for one to have freedom.

Finally, Crocker has suggested another way of viewing the relation of liberty and the worth of liberty which nevertheless does not join them conceptually. He too distinguishes between liberty and the worth of liberty, but nevertheless suggests that they be joined by means of a more general rational appeal. Thus, Crocker says

> If we take seriously the distinction between liberty and what gives liberty value or worth, we are forced to say that liberty is of no value in the absence of these other conditions. From that it would seem to follow that any policy directed towards the attainment of liberty would be irrational if it were not also directed towards the attainment of what makes liberty valuable. So if we call liberty plus what makes liberty valuable "the liberty complex," it would seem to be a rational policy to maximize (or maximize under an

equality constraint, or maximize the minimum level of) the liberty complex. And if the liberty complex plays this key role in our policy, while liberty itself does not, and if the liberty complex is, in fact, just like liberty except that it has a somewhat wider set of defining preventing conditions, then why not redeploy our terminology somewhat, renaming the liberty complex "liberty"?

(Crocker 1980: 88)

Thus, Crocker maintains that reasons are required in order to continue to speak simply of liberty and not the liberty complex. The reasons Berlin and Rawls have given, he argues, are inadequate (cf. Ibid.: 88–92). Further, in the above passage Crocker indicates that his objection with "liberty" as opposed to the "liberty complex" is that it employs too narrow a definition of preventing conditions. Certainly there is much to be said for this view.

However, we are not simply out to capture a (more complete) set of preventing conditions, but also a set of conditions which include positive conditions, such as means, abilities, and powers – conditions which are not simply the lack of preventing conditions or the absence of absences. Further, on Crocker's view the "liberty complex" is two different things he has grouped together because a rational policy would attempt to realize them at the same time. But this leaves enablement and liberty two different things. We have a mixture rather than a compound. It may be rational always to seek both health and good company, but this does not mean that they are part and parcel of each other. Consequently, it would be open to anyone to argue, in a particular instance, that it would not be rational to attempt to realize them at the same time, and that doing so would not jeopardize liberty.

In contrast, my argument has been that it would jeopardize liberty. When we speak of freedom we are (or should be) speaking about a compound of means, abilities, and rights (at least some of which guarantee us protection against various preventing conditions). However, my argument for this view has, so far, largely been a response to the views of others. The next section presents a different and more positive argument for the connection between freedom and power.

IV FREEDOM AND OPPORTUNITIES

I have previously argued that rights guarantee that certain doors remain open to people (Chapter 5) and that freedom requires protected opportunities for self-determination through participation in the political order (Chapter 6). In short, a person's right of self-determination is bound up with opportunities for its exercise. If such opportunities are denied to people, they are not free – or at least less free. By looking more closely at the notion of opportunities already built into our account, we can offer a more positive argument to accept a connection between freedom and power.

Taking this route has the added advantage that numerous negative theorists have also recognized a connection between opportunities and freedom. For example, Berlin claims that "the freedom of which I speak is opportunity for action" (Berlin 1969: xlii). Accordingly, by showing that inasmuch as freedom is linked to opportunities it is also thereby linked to the powers and abilities of the subjects of freedom, we will have strengthened our case.[6]

The problem with most accounts of opportunities – certainly those of negative theorists – is that they are viewed simply negatively, as "open doors," i.e. as passageways which are not obstructed or blocked. Thus, on this view, opportunities are separated from abilities (and means). A vivid, but misleading, image underlies this approach. Specifically, it fails to recognize that it is humans who are free – not doors. Doors may be open without people being able, or having the means, to pass through them. A door can be open, without any one being around. Supposedly after a neutron bomb attack, some doors will be open and some closed, though no people will be around to pass through them. But surely there will be no freedom in such a world.

Instead, opportunities do not exist independently of the person (and his or her abilities and powers) for whom the opportunity is said to exist. A person must be able to take advantage of the situation for it to be an opportunity. A glass of milk is not an opportunity to quench one's thirst if the person is allergic to milk. A lake is not an opportunity to swim if a person cannot swim. Suppose the person is a quadriplegic. Athletically viewed, the lake might as well be a mountain. Of course, we consider that in the normal course of things a person could learn to swim. In this sense, the lake is an opportunity for a person to learn to swim (all other things being equal).

In short, opportunities are linked to abilities to act. They presuppose that one has the relevant ability or power, or could (reasonably) acquire that ability or power. Obviously, an ability is different from an opportunity. A person may have an ability but no opportunity to use it – though if this persists long enough even the ability may decline or disappear. After years of not playing the piano, one's ability to do so diminishes. Gewirth's distinction between latent or passive powers and active or effective powers might be helpful here (Gewirth 1982: 313). Thus, if there were no opportunities to actively manifest one's abilities, one might (at least for sometime in some instances) retain the passive or latent ability.

Can't there be opportunities but individuals not have the abilities to take advantage of them? We need to be careful here. As I just argued, because there is an "opportunity" to do or be something, this does not mean that this is an opportunity for simply anyone. An advertisement in the *Wall Street Journal* announcing the position of CEO for a Fortune 500 company is not an opportunity for me – not even one I will pass by. Opportunities assume that an individual has the ability – or could reasonably acquire such – to take advantage of the opportunity. If the Empire State Building goes on sale at a drastically reduced price, again, this is not an opportunity for me to buy it and then make a large profit. It is false to assume that because something is an opportunity for someone, it is thereby an opportunity for anyone, regardless of his or her abilities or means. On the other hand, surely an opportunity may arise of which I am not able to take advantage. However, it is an opportunity for me since, if other things were equal, I could have reasonably taken advantage of it. The reason I was not able to take advantage of it was that the ability I do have was blocked or other conditions prevented me from reasonably acquiring that ability. Buying the Empire State Building, however, simply does not fit into this situation for most people.

Too often "bare" opportunities are the object of focus. Thus, a politician complains about the unemployed since there are so many job opportunities listed in the newspaper. But if the jobs advertised require training and education beyond the grasp of those unemployed, then the newspapers do not advertise any job opportunities for the unemployed. We must speak about real opportunities, not fanciful or imaginary ones. The former relate to the abilities, means, and motivation of individuals.

If we speak about real opportunities, then an opportunity involves an individual having the relevant ability or capacity. It is this that is essential to political freedom. I am not concerned with "bare" or "simple" opportunities. Put differently, bare opportunities are important for political freedom, to the extent that they become real ones. But by themselves they are not sufficient for freedom.

Thus, an opportunity is not simply the lack of an external restraint. Opportunities presuppose humans who have appropriate abilities or could reasonably acquire them.

Feinberg, however, seems to deny this connection. His account of freedom characterizes abilities and opportunities separately. Thus, he holds that the absence of an internal negative constraint (paralysis, ignorance, deficiencies in talent or skill) is "the presence of some condition [i.e., an ability] that permits a given kind of doing" (Feinberg 1973: 13). On the other hand, the absence of an external negative constraint (lack of money, transportation or weapons) is an opportunity (Ibid.). The absence of a negative interference is then said to be, depending on the point of reference, either the presence of some ability or opportunity to do something. Thus, opportunities and abilities speak to two different conditions. They are not interconnected.

It is peculiar, however, to identify the lack of external constraints with opportunity. The absence of an external negative constraint such as the lack of money is surely the presence of money. But this is hardly an opportunity for a person who does not know how to use money. The presence of transportation is not an opportunity for a person who is confined to a hospital bed. Fittingly, Dewey comments that "the mere removal of external control is no guarantee for the production of self-control" (Dewey 1963: 64). It is not simply the absence of an external absence that constitutes an opportunity and is required for freedom. Rather it is the presence of certain abilities and powers whereby one's right to self-determination may be effectively exercised – at least when some forms of social and political constraint are removed. Once again, opportunities and abilities cannot be wholly separated.

Finally, it is noteworthy that most of Feinberg's examples are material, physical, intellectual, or personal. With the exception of money, none of them include social or political conditions. Consider, then, an external negative constraint of a political nature – the denial of the right to vote. A person might not be denied this right, and still not have an opportunity to vote. On the one hand, it might be held that the person does not fall within the class of beings that either may have this right or be denied it. He or she falls into some other grouping for whom such a right is not even appropriate. On the other hand, even supposing that I am granted the right, it may be a purely formal right in that I am not in the position to use it. The voting booths may be placed too far away; I may not have the means to get to the voting booths. Once again the absence of an absence does not obviously constitute a presence.

Thus, the attempt to explicate opportunities, abilities, and freedom by means of the notion of constraint seems misguided. Feinberg's view leads us into verbal gymnastics to avoid saying that people must enjoy certain positive conditions, abilities, and powers, in order to have the opportunities crucial for freedom. Perry's comments are apropos:

> The neglect of the positive half of the meaning of liberty leads to the idea that the state promotes liberty only by removing obstacles, including itself. Or it leads to the idea that the mere absence of obstacles somehow implies the presence of capacity; as when the advocate of "free enterprise," meaning the non-interference of government, takes this to mean that the individual is "free to move about as he likes economically, socially, and politically." But the individual's freedom "to move about as he likes" can be nonexistent owing to his impotence – owing to his disease, malnutrition, ignorance, arrested development, or non-possession of the instrumentalities by which his interests are executed.
>
> (Perry 1944: 514)

There are two underlying and troubling dimensions to views that separate the opportunities freedom requires from the abilities and powers of individuals. First, failure to see the connection between opportunities and abilities is part of a tendency to project aspects of our lives onto the world outside of us: e.g. politics lies in the state; my freedom lies in the restraint of others; opportunities exist independently of the person; security lies in fences around lawns rather than people regulating themselves, etc. We must reclaim these aspects of our lives for ourselves if we are to grasp political freedom. We should reject any characterization of opportunities which separates them from the abilities of individuals.

Secondly, the view of opportunities rejected here is also troublesome because it implicitly assumes that individuals can simply gird their loins, pick themselves up by their bootstraps, and take advantage of such opportunities. It optimistically assumes that people can by themselves develop their abilities such that they can take advantage of opportunities. In making this assumption, this view has also assumed that people were roughly equal. Thus, Hobbes and Locke both comment on the rough equality of people in the state of nature. The freedom of people lies in removing obstacles to the fulfillment of individual ends. But these views fail to recognize the interdependence between people and the difficulties they face. They do not take account of the differential in means which may prevent some from developing their abilities and powers. Simple elimination of obstacles is not enough to provide the opportunities people require as part of their freedom.

Thus, in speaking of political freedom – the ability to exercise one's right of self-determination and hence to effectively participate as a member of a political society – our concern is that individuals have real opportunities instead of hypothetical or bare opportunities. To be politically free is linked with the notion of being effectively self-determining – hence empowered. And to be effectively self-determining is for a person to have the abilities and powers whereby he or she may take advantage of certain opportunities, or real alternatives.

V FREEDOM AND POWER

The preceding sections have disputed with those, such as Hobbes, who separate freedom and power, and have argued that freedom and power are connected through the notion of an opportunity. There is, however, an even more direct argument that can be made for the connection between freedom and power.[7]

The point of this argument is not to contend, it must be emphasized, that freedom and power (or enablement) are the same. When speaking of a person's powers we are not, at the same time, speaking of her or his freedom, as in speaking of widows we are speaking of women whose husbands have died. If freedom and power were the same, then the more power a person had the more free that person would be. This is not the case. To describe the powers of dictators, I have argued, is quite distinct from describing their freedom (even supposing that we wish to speak of their freedom). Though tyrants may use their power ruthlessly on their subjects, I have argued that not only their subjects are not free, but also the tyrants themselves are not free. A person who seeks to exercise his or her right to self-determination by simply dominating everyone else is not exercising his or her freedom.

Nevertheless, surely there is some direct connection between freedom and power, as is evidenced by the arguments in earlier sections. Further, it seems clear that this connection is and must be stronger than simply a practical connection. The Handlins, for example, contend that though liberty and power can be conceived separately, in some very abstract manner, the two are always practically connected. Their argument takes the following form:

> The liberty to walk to the moon or to sign a contract becomes consequential to its possessor and to others only when it is associated with the ability to use it. History which is a record of events that occurred, not of those that can be conceived, can therefore take cognizance of the development of liberty only insofar as it was capable of being used.

> (Handlin and Handlin 1961: 17)

This is, however, a rather strange argument. Though it contends that liberty and power are linked, the reason is that otherwise history cannot take cognizance of the development of liberty. A similar argument, however, might be made for a variety of concepts which we do not wish to tie together. It might be said that history cannot take cognizance of the development of democracy except through the rebellion of the poor who seek to rule. Nevertheless, this is not a good reason to link democracy and the rule of the poor, as Aristotle, for example, did. Further, this argument does not join freedom and power. Rather, it places power outside liberty. On the contrary, it seems possible that we can forge a closer bond between freedom and power. Indeed, it would seem strange that, if the realization of one concept involved another concept, they would not come to share in the meaning of each other.

Consider, then, the following. First, suppose a person had a right to self-determination, but not the power or means to exercise that right. Contrariwise, suppose a person had various powers or abilities to realize his or her desires and choices, but did not have a right to self-determination. Would a person be free in either case?

On the first alternative, for example, a person might be said to have the right to self-determination even though the authorities do not recognize it. Such claims are often made on behalf of the citizens in totalitarian countries. There are two possibilities here. The government might simply not recognize the right to self-determination of its citizens. It might physically restrain and detain any citizen who attempts to act in ways opposed to the government. In such cases, it is implausible to say that such people are free, simply because they are said to have a right to self-determination. To be free, one must not only have a right to self-determination but that right must be respected or recognized and responded to accordingly. Were we to hold otherwise, we would be forced to say that people were free even though their rights were not enforced or recognized and they were unable to exercise them. In short, we might be forced to say that slaves, serfs, and repressed peoples were free.[8] In such cases, their rights might have a theoretical status, but no real substance. The rulers might mouth their respect for such rights all the while they oppressed the individuals in question. It seems quite clear, however, that such people would not be free.

The reason that they are not free is not simply that the government treats them as it does, e.g. physically restrains them. If this were merely the case, they would become free the moment the government ceased this behavior. However, even if the government did stop physically restraining them, there might be little reason to believe that the government would continue on this path. The sudden lack of physical restraint might simply be a ploy to lure some unsuspecting individuals out into the open. Perhaps it would be a version of Mao's "Let a thousand flowers bloom" campaign. In such circumstances, people would rightly be suspicious of the claim that they are free because they might still lack the means or abilities whereby they could ensure that their right to self-determination would be respected and enforced.

Accordingly, freedom cannot simply be identified with the right to self-determination, since people may be said to have this right even though they are being trampled upon. Freedom requires that one's right to self-determination is respected. But this is to say that one can act upon it. One will be able to act upon it, however, only if others do not interfere with it and one has various resources to ensure this. It is in this sense that enablement is one aspect of freedom.

The other possibility noted above is to suppose that the government does recognize its citizens' rights to self-determination in the sense that it does not beat them or physically restrain them from engaging in actions they might rightly choose. However, most means to everyday and political life are simply not available. Perhaps the regime has cleverly arranged that people lack the resources whereby they can effectively participate in altering the present order. Food, hard currency, as well as means to travel and communicate with other citizens are in short supply. They do not have the wherewithal to print leaflets, purchase telephones, or make contacts with others of like persuasion. In general, people are unable to act upon their decisions to participate in the political affairs of the society.

It seems quite straightforward that the political freedom of such people would be considerably reduced. They would be free to the extent that they are not physically restrained. Still their political freedom would be increased if they also enjoyed various means which made their rights to self-determination and participation effective.

Suppose now that people do have various powers and abilities whereby they can realize their desires and choices. However, they lack the right to self-determination. Perhaps through sheer force they prevail. But they must exert this power or force in order to realize what they would do. For them, what they do must always be in competition with others, and at the risk that someone else will overpower them. They are, perhaps, not far from Hobbes's state of nature. Thus, though they have the power or means to accomplish their ends, their actions are accompanied with insecurity and fear. They must ever be prepared to defend themselves against encroachment by others. They dare not let down their defenses. They may form mutual protection agencies, but these are always matters of convenience and self-interest. If someone's self-interest leads in another direction, other members of the mutual protection agency may be undone without a moment's notice.

In such a situation, the freedom of individuals has shrunk almost to the vanishing point. Rather, we should speak of war, competition, the clash of power, victory and/or defeat. We do not have a realm of freedom in which people may, with some confidence (due to a protected and effective right), proceed in the determination of their lives.

Thus, for us to speak of freedom (at least in any full-fledged sense), it would seem that we must speak of the right to self-determination as well as the powers and abilities (the enablement) a person has. It is clear that freedom is not simply to be equated with abilities or power. Further, it is not claimed that whatever power or ability is connected with freedom must be a total or all-encompassing power or ability. Instead, the power or ability required must be sufficient to allow a person to effectively exercise his or her right to self-determination.

VI FREEDOM AND MATERIAL MEANS

Granted that freedom and power are linked, two forms of power particularly crucial for political freedom remain to be considered. The first is the power that comes from the possession of material means. The second is that which comes from possession of intellectual resources, access to information, etc. The direction of our argument is suggested by Thomas Leslie who held that

> every limitation of power is an abridgment of positive liberty. A man is not free to go from Shropshire to London, or from Liverpool to

New York, if the journey is too long and expensive for him; nor is he actually free to develop a powerful intellect if education lies beyond his reach.

(Leslie 1879: 19-20)

Once we recognize that freedom involves powers and abilities, the need to discuss the particular means required to realize these abilities becomes obvious and direct. Only in this manner are these abilities real ones and the persons involved enabled and hence empowered. I will discuss the question of material means in this section, and that of cognitive means in the following section.

By material means or conditions I refer to the kinds of resources required for living, such as adequate housing, health care, and (in general) resources for participating in the political process.[9] These may take the form of money, wealth, or various goods. Political freedom requires that these resources be available (to various extents) for people to take advantage of them. However, in accordance with the argument of Chapter 5, since the resources in question must be related to human action or inaction, the fact that one does not have superhuman means or resources does not count against one's freedom.

Two questions are relevant. First, what arguments show that material means are required for political freedom? And, second, how extensive must such means be in order for a person to be politically free? This latter question will be discussed in Part VIII.

It would seem fairly straightforward to claim, given preceding arguments, that material means are required in order to realize one's right of self-determination. I might have the (formal) right to do x, but be unable to do x because, lacking the means, I might not be able to acquire the appropriate abilities and powers. Since the lack of material means reduces (or eliminates) one's ability to act upon one's rights, those people who are poor are less free than those well-off. Accordingly, Arnold Kaufman claims that "Indians are made unfree by their poverty . . . They lack material resources" (Kaufman 1962: 243).[10]

Those who deny the connection between freedom and power believe that people can be free even if they do not have material resources. Liberty, for them, simply means that no one will stop them from trying to acquire such resources. However, on this view, others will not be able to acquire the same resources. Thus, the opportunity to acquire resources amounts to the opportunity to gain means by which one person may dominate others. Of course this is usually characterized as the situation in which a person can gain control of his or her fate. However, to the extent that proponents of this view see us as separate individuals, one person's control and direction of his or her fate implies that he or she directs and controls the fate of others as well. Thus, the disconnection between liberty and material conditions in liberal society seems to be captured for many people in the view that liberty is the *chance* to gain power over or to dominate others. It suggests the mentality of the gambler and is tied to a belief in luck, miracles, and good fortune. In short, it involves a magical or religious attitude. But freedom is not simply a matter of luck. Further, it ends when it is tranformed into a form of domination.

The importance of including material means in an account of freedom is not simply a negative one. Numerous "positive liberals" get material resources or means into freedom by expanding the scope of what blocks freedom (cf. Kaufman 1962; Crocker 1980). They extend the notion of what obstructs freedom from simply coercion to the broader notion of constraint, which is understood to occur deliberately as well as naturally. This is one way to link material resources (means) to freedom.

However, to take this path runs afoul of the argument of the preceding chapters. This approach does not capture a sense of empowerment so much as a sense of relief from constraint. On this interpretation, material resources are important because their lack obstructs certain ways of acting. The picture is one of individuals whose desires are blocked, though not necessarily on purpose. To receive such means or resources then does not so much empower or enable, as remove a barrier from one who could have done otherwise. In short, behind this view is an assumption of separate individuals, who themselves have powers and abilities but only need to be relieved from an obstruction. There is little sense in this view that these resources foster new abilities, create new relations and roles, and transform situations such that one can now do something. It is a non-social and non-political view of freedom that they hold. In short, on the liberal view the effect is not a positive one, but simply the elimination of a negative condition. On the view defended here, material means bestow power; they do not simply eliminate an obstruction to the exercise of a power.

Both points, the positive effect of acquired material resources and the freedom thereby experienced, are suggested in Richard Norman's example of someone who "unexpectedly inherits a fortune, and becomes aware of entirely new ways of life which are now available" (Norman 1982: 96). His point is that in such cases "one can speak quite appropriately of a sense of liberation" (Ibid.). Though I have argued that the situation is more complicated, Norman is quite correct that the provision of material resources have a positive effect on individuals and that this is part of their freedom.

It may be objected that material means are a condition of such freedom, not part and parcel of the freedom itself. But what is it to have abilities of the kinds involved in freedom? When considering the ability to play the piano, it is clear that the piano does not serve simply as a condition for this ability. The piano is integral to this ability. The ability is interdefined with piano. Similarly, the ability to determine one's own course, to exercise one's rights to speech, to associate, etc. is interdefined with determining one's own course. But to determine one's own course is not simply to select some end from among a variety of ends. It is not simply to pick a path and do nothing. It is not simply an intellectual exercise. It is a practical activity which necessarily involves the use of certain means to bring about various ends which one has set oneself. Without those means the ends cannot be reached and one cannot determine one's course.

Now some of these means must be material or economic. Without a certain level of income, for example, one can not effectively determine one's course. This is not to say that everyone must have the same level of income. People may have different ends. But it does imply that a certain minimum level is required. The possession of such means is, of course, a relative affair in that if my means remain constant and those of others grow significantly then I have less means, ability, and powers to determine my course. I will be less able to exercise my rights, when the required means to do so now exceed those I have.

Further, this is not simply an individual affair, but a social and political matter in that it must be done in the context of other people with their own rights and obligations. That is, the question of means also arises on the societal level, not simply on the individual level. Since political freedom is bound up with relations among individuals, it cannot be measured simply by what each individual has available to him or her, regardless of whether they take advantage of it. It cannot be measured simply by considering each separate individual. Rather, it must also be "measured" on the more general level of the material means for political activity available within the society itself.

Thus, figures about the level of material resources available for group and institutional activities are also important indicators of the level of political freedom. The power that any single individual can have is limited much more so than if he or she is also a member(s) of a group(s). Accordingly, Hacker correctly points out that the power that individuals have in modern society "is increasingly based on organizational position: a man has power because he has ascended to a particular chair in a particular institutional complex" (Hacker 1962: 330). Thus, we must ensure that the institutional contexts within which one lives also serve the purpose of enabling, rather than disabling, their members.

The contrary ideological function of negative freedom should be noted. If freedom is limited simply to the lack of overt, physical coercion, then the very poor may be said to be free. They cannot object to their lot at least with regard to freedom. They have failed to raise themselves materially, but since this is not related to freedom, they cannot complain about their unfreedom. "Freedom" in this sense satisfies an ideological need of the ruling classes.

Thus, Gould comments:

> If a populace . . . comes to believe that . . . freedom is a negative political matter alone, then they can well believe that their economic situation is not only natural, but also not a question of oppression at all – even when there is significant poverty and unemployment. The American people have all too thoroughly internalized the belief that liberty is a matter of negative political freedom alone. Hence, reduction or elimination of programs for the poor is not held by them to be a reduction of freedom.
>
> (Gould, 1985: 71)

If, however, freedom requires economic means and powers, then the rich cannot claim that everyone is equally free. Instead, we must ask why the poor are poor, and what significance lies in the fact that there are so many who are poor. What do the social, political and economic relations in society have to do with this? Assuming that these can be changed then the poor are simply not free.

The implications of this view are significant. It would follow that a people that would consider themselves collectively and individually free must seek ways by which to provide people with adequate material resources: housing, health care, food, and financial means. Such material means are essential to a person's ability effectively to exercise a right of self-determination. What level of such resources must be provided is the topic of Part VIII. But it is clear that freedom cannot be indifferent to poverty. There is nothing glorious about poverty, and to speak of being poor but free is only to view the situation very partially. Because those who must eke out a living are scarcely able to effectively exercise their right of self-determination, they are less free.

It has been objected that there can be no end to such implications. Freedom, it is said, will then be unreasonably extended to include paid vacations and the like. This issue I discuss below (pp. 237–41). However, just because those who defend the present view may at times extend it unreasonably it does not follow that the view itself is unreasonable (cf. Friedrich 1963: 843). Similar unreasonable extensions can be demanded of negative freedom in the form of the amount of protection or guarantees one demands from state interference. Yet few have thought that this undercuts negative freedom. Similarly, this objection does not undercut freedom as enablement.

VII COGNITIVE MEANS, RESOURCES, AND POWERS

A second form of enablement, one involving cognitive means and resources, is also required by political freedom. The importance of freedom of thought and expression to political freedom has been variously appraised. Dewey contends that "the only freedom that is of enduring importance is freedom of intelligence, that is to say, freedom of observation and of judgment exercised on behalf of purposes that are intrinsically worth while" (Dewey 1963: 61).

On the other hand, Oakeshott maintains that freedom of speech is

> beyond question . . . a great and elementary form of freedom; it may even be regarded as the key-stone of the arch of our liberty. But a key-stone is not itself the arch, and the current exaggeration of the importance of this form of liberty is in danger of concealing from us the loss of other liberties no less important. The major part of mankind has nothing to say; the lives of most men do not revolve round a felt necessity to speak. And it may be supposed that this extraordinary emphasis upon freedom of speech is the work of the small vocal section of our society and, in part, represents a legitimate self-interest.
>
> (Oakeshott 1962a: 43)

However, though its importance is variously estimated, freedom of speech is clearly recognized by all to be essential to political freedom.

Once again, if arguments in the preceding sections have been correct, crucial to freedom of thought and expression is a power or ability to exercise them. Dewey claims, for instance, that essential to freedom of thought is the "power to frame purposes, to judge wisely, to evaluate desires by the consequences which will result from acting upon them; power to select and order means to carry those ends into operation" (Dewey 1963: 64). Further, for us to have such powers or abilities, we would have to possess various means or resources. As Perry comments, "the absence of censorship . . . is not liberty except to those who possess the resources for artistic creation . . ." (Perry 1944: 513–14).

A first form of enablement here would be that one has ready access to information about one's alternatives and one's society. There are two aspects to this point. On the one hand, to determine whether a person has ready access to information we must ask to what extent such information is subject to restrictions, manipulation, or slanted presentation. The politically free require information which is subject only to minimal and justified restrictions.[11]

Some deny that access to information is a requisite for freedom. Carritt says that

> it seems clear that our freedom is not impaired by the withholding of useful information, and I am inclined to think not even by the giving of false information. That wrongs us in some other way. I should say that drugging a man, or (if that is possible) hypnotizing him against his will impaired his freedom, but I am inclined to think that propaganda, excitement by rhetoric, music and similar tricks do not.
>
> (Carritt 1967: 135–6)

Similarly, Parent claims that "someone who cannot read obscene books because his government decided to ban their sale" has had "his available options . . . limited, but we would not ordinarily use the term 'deprivation of freedom' to describe his plight" (Parent 1974a: 433). Rather, he has simply been deprived of the opportunity to do something. Accordingly, Parent claims that

> we do not say that a person who is prevented from pursuing a given activity by illness, ignorance, bias, or hatred resulting from alterable human practices has been rendered unfree in the political sense to do so. Instead we say that persons often can be deprived of the physical ability, the skill or intelligence, the fair-mindedness, and the compassion necessary for them to undertake different tasks.
>
> (Parent 1974b: 152)

These views are not only mistaken, they are also dangerous. Though Carritt's definition of liberty: "the power of doing what one would choose without interference by other persons' action" (Carritt 1967: 133), seems promising, he only allows that direct actions of violence or physical constraint, or the threats of such, constrain freedom. Part of the reason for his claim regarding information is his view that our thinking cannot be directly constrained by other persons, even though he admits it can be influenced (Ibid.: 134). Still, he holds that "thought is always free" and hence he is reluctant to hold that the influence of our thought by propaganda, or similar tricks, reduces our freedom. Like the Stoics and Spinoza, he holds "a man is 'the master of his own thoughts'" (Perry 1944: 514).[12]

But surely this view is antiquated. Perry argues, quite convincingly, that

> the Stoics neglected the fact that this liberty [of thought] . . . is no liberty at all without the capacity to think, and that it is therefore nullified by mental disease, habit, indoctrination, hysteria, or lack of education. The art of oppression has in modern times learned how to penetrate into the Stoic's stronghold.
>
> (Ibid.)

The evidence from propaganda and brainwashing strongly suggests that humans are not always master of their own thoughts. There is no inner sanctum of pure, inviolable freedom. False information and the withholding of information may seriously cripple our ability to effectively exercise our right of self-determination.

Secondly, it is strange that both Carritt and Parent, who are so solicitous of the ordinary meaning of "freedom," arrive at the above views. Ordinarily we would say that the people of a particular country were not free when their government denied them access to information. They are not as capable of exercising their right to self-determination as effectively as they would otherwise have been. But this is quite opposed to the view of Carritt and Parent.

Finally, both Carritt and Parent approach the problem of freedom simply from the level of brute individual action. Since misinformation or the lack of information do not physically impede such action, they do not limit (political) freedom. But this is to view the matter most simplistically. It equates the restriction of political freedom only with direct and brutal attacks. Though political freedom is susceptible to such attacks it is not *only* susceptible to them. Such a view might have been appropriate in the seventeenth and eighteenth centuries, but not in the twentieth century with the multiple sources of influence and conditioning to which people are subjected. The reduction of political freedom to the lack of physical attacks is analogous to the reduction of romance to sex. There is much more to both.

Thus, it is mistaken to think that freedom of thought and expression do not require at least a lack of obstacles to information, education and knowledge. However, it is quite clear that political freedom requires more than this.

It requires something positive, viz. the provision of knowledge and information. People cannot be left simply to dig out the information they require by themselves. This is the second aspect of the present form of enablement (cf. p. 230). That is, there is ready access to information when one has a real (and not simply a bare) opportunity to acquire such information. It is a question of the availability of information itself. If the rights noted in Chapter 5 are not to be empty, merely formal ones, then people must be able to know the alternatives and options they face. This requires an active and independent press, an educational system, and government accumulation and dissemination of information to the public concerning its basic interests.

This right will take different forms. It includes ensuring that information is provided not only by the government about itself but also by various non-governmental agencies. These might be private newspapers, television stations, and radio stations. It would also involve ensuring that there are no monopolies amongst these latter institutions that result only in the provision of certain views or kinds of information. On the other hand, if such private agencies were not available, the government might be required to subsidize or support some such agencies, which would act independently of its own policy directives. Thus, in addition to public radio and television, there might be public newspaper agencies. The construction of libraries is another response to this requirement for enablement. People must have access to libraries with current journals, books, and tools for the gathering of information and knowledge. The maintenance of cataloging systems which allow the use of the accumulated information and the presence of librarians trained in the use of information systems are related implications.

Further, other non-state agencies, such as large corporations, would also be required to ensure that information about them was disseminated, not only internally but also externally. Obviously there will be disputes concerning the private or public nature of the information concerned. These cannot be avoided. But for individuals to be politically free, to be able to effectively exercise their right to self-determinaton, they must know, for example, what chemicals a manufacturing plant is placing in the atmosphere. They must know the conditions under which the corporation and the city government agree to place a plant in their community. Further, individuals employed by the corporation will require an even broader range of information. The demand for access to information might require, within a corporation, not only the dissemination of information by official organs of the organization, but also by unofficial organs, e.g. what are now subterranean newspapers.

A second form of enablement political freedom requires is that individuals must be able to make deliberate and informed choices. Heaps of information in the lap of the illiterate do not constitute an opportunity or enablement. The young must be educated so that they are able to comprehend the information they must reflect on. Their intellectual development and training is crucial to political freedom. The importance of evidence and reflection, not simply emotional kinds of appeals, must be impressed on each generation. In this sense, such cognitive conditions are required not simply to make one's determinations and choices effective, but rather to develop one's ability to make such determinations at all. As Norman notes, there is a fundamental link between "the capacity for rational understanding and the capacity to make choices at all" (Norman 1982: 93).

This means that people must be educated. In a certain sense, they are being forced to be free – or at least to become capable of being free. Ritchie comments that

> if a man cannot read at all . . . or if he has no access to any public library, or if the managers of any library to which he has access refuse to permit such works on their shelves . . . or if he has not had such an education as enables him to understand what he reads, he cannot be said to get much good out of the fact that the law of the land does not prohibit him from reading [someone's] works. Thus . . . it is necessary that such forms of State interference with individual [negative] liberty – and a good many others – should be in active operation . . .. Thus, liberty in the sense of positive opportunity for self-development, is the creation of law, and not something that could exist apart from the action of the State.
>
> (Ritchie 1895: 139–40)

Though Ritchie's characterization of positive liberty should be modified, his comments on the relation of information and education to freedom is well taken. It is legitimate in developing a system of political freedom to impose cognitive conditions (education) on children and on adults (access to information) in order to secure political freedom. People are thereby enabled to be free.

Not everyone agrees with this contention. Consider a case in which various resources of a cognitive nature are denied by the government. An oligarchy deliberately attempts to keep the rest of society illiterate and ignorant by not providing schools (cf. Weinstein 1965: 161).[13]

Let us assume that there is no censorship and there are no laws against education, but the people are poor, they cannot afford schools, and the oligarchy does nothing to remedy the situation. Instead, they spend their money on fancy and outrageous armaments. After all, the people are told, their country must be defended.

Weinstein thinks that a good case can be made for accusing the oligarchy of violating men's freedom to attend school.

> In any case where one man is deliberately weakened or "conditioned" (as in brain washing) by another, the resemblance to coercion is so close that we may be justified to speak of the former as less "free", and not merely as being less "capable" of using his freedom.
>
> (Weinstein 1965: 161)

Others, such as Parent, think that this is mistaken: such cases "do not entail threats to freedom properly conceived" (Parent 1974b: 164). "The oligarchy is attempting to deny the rest of society, not the freedom, but the opportunity to receive an education; Y deprives X only of the ability to think for himself" (Ibid.).

But, contrary to Parent's claim, a government can reduce or undercut political freedom in more ways than one. Parent mistakenly ties questions of freedom simply to coercion. His approach is representative of an erroneous reductionism that seeks to define all of political freedom in terms of coercion or constraint. This monomania interferes with our understanding of political freedom.

On the contrary, I suggest, "the opportunity to receive an education" is connected with "having political freedom." Parent simply rejects this since he sticks with a narrow meaning of "freedom." He can thus agree that the oligarchy is denying people the opportunity to receive an education but insist that it is not reducing people's political freedom.

However, suppose we allow that the people in this society, though not imposed upon by others physically are nevertheless quite ignorant (through psychological conditioning or institutional arrangements) of what occurs in their society, whether in the government or the large public institutions. As a result, they do not understand the few pieces of information that are available. The argument I have defended is that their inability (their ignorance) to use this information undermines their political freedom. This should not be understood absolutely. Of course, they enjoy political freedom to a minimal degree. The information is available. But their effective ability to exercise their right to self-determination is unmistakably reduced by their inabilities.

The correctness of this conclusion is suggested if we ask why the oligarchy does not provide people with the means and resources to understand available information. It is quite clear that if it does not, people will be less inclined or able to assert themselves or demand what is theirs. If kept quite isolated they will be less inclined to demand that they take part in decisions affecting themselves and the whole of society. In such cases, their political freedom is curtailed.

Thirdly, political freedom requires that people have access (and the means for such access) to the sources of information. This is crucial due to the unilateral power that newspapers, radio and television possess. Perry nicely brings this to our attention when he comments that

> with the radio [and television!], and to a considerable extent the press, persuasive communication is unilateral, and inflammatory utterance is not even neutralized by resistance or counter-attack. A wide public is then defenseless against the potent influence of rhetoric, which may be used with mendacious intent, and which in any case will obscure the facts and short-circuit the reasoning faculties.
>
> (Perry 1944: 544)

The unilateral nature of the media renders access to them extremely important. Quite obviously, as in many cases already, this aspect of political freedom cannot be something that each person might demand on the same occasion. Rather it is a requirement that holds more generally for society. The various forms of the communications media must allow a voice to the various segments of the community. It is a strange use of the word "communications" that allows us to attach it to newspapers, radio, and television, when the flow of discourse, information, and influence is primarily one-way. Two people do not communicate when only one does all the talking. Hence, it is terribly important that different groups have access to the media. This must encompass not simply the inclusion of letters in newspapers, but also commentaries and responses in newspapers, radio, and television. These and other forms yet to be invented are crucial for political freedom. Each of the present forms of media must give greater access to members of the community or the representative groups of those community members.

Finally, so that the government and political bodies may disseminate the information required, they must keep records of their proceedings, decisions, and policies. These must be made available at normal (or modest) costs to people. The availability of this information must itself be advertised and publicized. The widest possible provision of information is crucial here. This is true, it should be noted, not simply on the national, but also on the state and local levels.

This is also true not simply of what are ordinarily considered political bodies. As I maintained above, such political groups as large corporations must also provide means of access to information concerning themselves. For example, the availability of information can be especially crucial for individuals on whom corporations maintain records which are then used for various corporate purposes.

Thus, political freedom requires that individuals have the resources and means whereby they may be reasonably well-informed. This implies that they have reasonably accurate information available to them, and that they be educated and trained to make use of that information, and that that information not be manipulated in ways of which they cannot be aware. To be reasonably well-informed is required for realistic self-determination and for participation in the public and political affairs of one's society. Individuals who are politically free are people who have various cognitive means at their disposal so that they are able effectively to exercise their right of self-determination.

More generally, I have claimed, political freedom concerns the participation of individuals in the political societies of which they are a member. Any restriction of information directly impedes this and thereby restricts one's freedom. There is a shift of perspective here that leads us to see political freedom as something arising from the bottom up (through participation), rather than the top down (lack of government coercion). This shift of perspective is crucial for seeing the importance of information and education to political freedom.

VIII   FREEDOM AND THE LEVEL OF RESOURCES: LIBERTY AND EQUALITY

If freedom and power were independent of each other, then people might be very rich or very poor and yet be equally free. The difficult question concerning the level of resources required for people to be free would not arise. But because freedom and power are interconnected, something must be said about the resources people must have in order to be free.

It should be clear from earlier discussion that political freedom does not require that each person have resources that would enable his or her opinions to be heard and accepted on each occasion by others in his or her society. If we built such a condition into political freedom, we would create an absurdly strong view, one which few could realize. Instead, political freedom requires that a person have the resources and means such that he or she may participate effectively in the political process. This implies that on different occasions that person's views and actions may or may not be successful. As in a game, one can be an effective player and self-determining even if one does not dominate the game and all other players. Obviously, if a person's views were never effectively represented in the electoral process, we would say that person lacks the relevant powers. Thus, the extent of one's power must be understood within one's social and political context.

What this amounts to, however, remains very vague. It is impossible to specify exactly what the level of means must be. The ultimate answer must come through the participation of individuals in the political processes within their societies. However, the direction of the argument in this and the preceding chapters has been that liberty requires some rough equality, with departures (or inequalities) only to the extent that they maximally enhance the ability of each person subject to them to determine his or her own life. The argument for this view is severalfold.

First, freedom requires, as we have seen, that all those who are capable of being self-determining enjoy the right to self-determination. Exceptions are to be made only in cases in which the individuals lack the competence to exercise such a right. Accordingly, Tawney claims that "the rights which are essential to freedom must be such as to secure the liberties of all, not merely of a minority" (Tawney 1953: 84). In this sense, freedom requires strict equality. The presupposition is that all individuals equally possess the right to self-determination.

Secondly, in order for one's self-determinations to be effective, we have seen, a person requires various resources, both cognitive and material. That is, certain means are required to give one the ability or power to exercise one's right to self-determination. However, possession of power, means or resources is itself a relative phenomenon. I have a certain amount of resources with $100 when you have $200. But if you had $2,000, the significance and power of my $100 would be meaningfully diminished. As a consequence, the differential in powers and means in getting one's voice and views heard may be so extreme as to reduce, if not negate, those who are among the least well off. Accordingly, if the poor of a rich country earn $20,000 a year but the rich earn $2 million there is still a problem of freedom. To the extent that resources are distributed extremely unequally, the capacity or ability to make effective personal choices is also unequally distributed and, hence, so too freedom. As Dahl comments: "To the extent that the capacity to make personal choices effective is unequally distributed, then freedom and opportunity are also unequal" (Dahl 1970: 106).

It might be contended that only a rather strict egalitarian distribution of powers and resources will produce the greatest amount of political liberty in a society. For example, Richard Norman contends that

> power . . . is essentially a relation between persons. If some people have more power than others, they necessarily have it at the expense of others, because it is power over those others. Therefore it would be contradictory to suppose that by distributing power unequally we could increase the power of the least powerful.
>
> (Norman 1982: 107)

However, this is mistaken inasmuch as by extending special powers and resources to some (e.g. in various organizations and institutions) the powers of all may be increased through the activities of the organization. In this sense, though Norman is correct that liberty requires a strong measure of equality, still it does not demand strict equality. Differences in powers and resources among people can be allowed, but only to the extent that they maximally promote the freedom of all people subject to such differences. Still, since freedom requires effective participation in the major institutions to whose authority one is subject, this will mean that the resources that freedom requires must be roughly comparable to that of others.[14] Thus, in contrast to claims frequently made, liberty and equality are positively, rather than negatively, connected.

In fact, in most contemporary societies material resources are subject to considerable disparities. In American society both material and cognitive resources are distributed in extremely unequal fashion. Thus, the opportunity to make effective personal choices, and hence the degree of individual freedom and opportunity, are markedly unequal in the United States. Certainly, the financial means to meet the extravagant costs of campaigning are among the crucial inequalities in political resources (cf. Dahl 1970: 106, 114). More generally, "the freedom and opportunities available to human beings at birth depend not on differences in inherited abilities . . . nor on any special contribution the one has made . . . but, rather, on the accident of birth," e.g. one is born into a wealthy family (Dahl 1970: 112). Thus, some have more and some have less freedom depending on the amount of resources (means) which they have.

Similar implications follow for cognitive resources. Roughly equal access to education and information is crucial for political freedom. Otherwise not only will this or that individual lack the cognitive means to exercise effectively his or her right to self-determination, but also we face the underdevelopment of this or that class or race. Both results undermine political freedom.

Nevertheless, opportunities for education and access to information and knowledge remain widely disparate. Entire school systems receive significantly different amounts of state and federal (or national) money. Accordingly, the effective abilities that children and people develop or can exercise are seriously affected. Freedom suffers, apart from any questions of equity or justice.

There is another way in which to portray the level of resources required for freedom. This is to recall that an important part of having such power involves membership in groups or classes which can successfully elect political officials, gain access to information, education, etc. That is, political freedom also pertains to the level and kind of power that groups and classes have, rather than simply to this or that individual. In short, there is a social level to our evaluation of the opportunities and means promoting the material and cognitive resources required for political freedom. We cannot simply measure the situation from the level of each particular individual.

Thus, though I have argued that each person need not have exactly the same means or resources to obtain information and knowledge, they must also not be part of a class, on the other hand, which is systematically unable to obtain the information and knowledge needed for effective participation in political activities. In general, there must be a sufficient level of resources for informedness across society. It is this general level that brings our attention to different races and classes and their role in political freedom.

It might be objected that if the resources that people must have to exercise their right to self-determination must be roughly comparable, achieving or maintaining this situation would greatly restrict the liberty (and power) of people who already have more resources or those who are more inventive or energetic and can obtain greater resources. Thus, the present proposal actually promotes unfreedom (Hume 1965: 45).

Some reply to this objection by simply admitting that limitations on the freedom of some is the price that must be paid for the greater freedom of all. Freedom is not to be an elite privilege. The idea of a free society requires equal freedom and this implies that some will have their freedom reduced (Norman 1982: 186).

This reply, however, essentially relies on an appeal to justice or quality, rather than freedom. We can, I believe, give a better answer that relies on an appeal to freedom itself. First, the view of (negative) freedom currently popular (and assumed by many who raise the above objection) permits the unlimited accumulation of means and resources by the few. Thus, it justifies, and practically assumes, significant differences in the abilities of people to determine their activities. Some will be effectively able to exercise their rights to self-determination; others will not. As a result, some will consistently prevail over others in the political determination of society's course of action. Thus, the resources of the few place others at a disadvantage.

On the negative view of freedom everyone might remain equally free in such a situation, as long as those with extensive resources do not impose constraints or coercion upon others. However, to take resources from some (by confiscation or taxation) so as to provide them to others, according to those who share this view, is to coerce them. It reduces their freedom without any gain of freedom to others. Equality has replaced freedom. On the other hand, those who simply link freedom with power will also see a reduction in the freedom of individuals with special resources and powers, though this may be compensated by the increased freedom (powers) of those who thereby acquire additional resources.

However, if my argument in the second part of this book is correct, both views of freedom are inadequate. Political freedom is not simply the lack of constraint (negative freedom) or the simple possession of powers and abilities, but the effective ability to exercise one's right to self-determination in conjunction with others. If the possession of extensive resources by some places others at a disadantage in the conjoint determination of their mutual activities, this implies that their greater resources and abilities undermine the conjoint determination in which they participate and on which their freedom is based. That is, if we take seriously the view that the liberty any person can have is dependent on living and acting cooperatively with others, and that the freedom of anyone is his or her ability to effectively exercise a right to self-determination within this context, then such limitations on some people not only promote the mutual freedom of all but also are required by their very own freedom. This is not to say, I have contended, that some differences in resources and powers cannot be allowed. But beyond those levels which promote the abilities of individuals to mutually determine their lives according to their rights, such differences undermine the liberty of all involved.

Thus, it is true that, in the sense of political freedom defended here, we are obliged, on behalf of the freedom of all, to tax the wealth and resources of all people, though some more heavily than others. But freedom cannot be allowed to imply that a few may fly high only because many others sink quite low. As T. H. Green noted, "we are right in refusing to ascribe the glory of freedom to a state in which the apparent elevation of the few is founded on the degradation of the many" (Green 1889: 372)

Finally, to what extent can a society realize higher levels of political freedom due to higher levels of economic development, or is the level of economic development independent of the level of political freedom in a country?

Once again we must say that the two are positively linked. Nevertheless, it does not follow that simply because a society is highly developed economically it will therefore be, or have, higher levels of political freedom. The material and cognitive resources available within any country are only one part of the political freedom equation.

On the other hand, a country may have to use material resources in ways which do not promote political freedom, at least in the short term. Thus, for example, "the net national product may be so small that the community may attempt to consume the greater part of it. Economic growth, then, might require that consumption be restrained in the interests of preserving the investment surplus" (Schweinitz 1957: 170). Any full sense of political freedom might have to remain hostage to the development of an adequate material basis.

Because of the connections drawn out above between political freedom and cognitive and material resources, we are better able to explain why certain countries have greater difficulties than others in sustaining political freedom. We should not simply hold, as some have held, that when a constitution is drawn up, a parliament built, and various laws passed protecting simply negative rights, political freedom has been achieved. Surely an important step has been taken. But a step is not a journey.

IX FREEDOM AS EMPOWERMENT: CONCLUSION

The preceding three chapters have argued for political freedom as a form of empowerment. There are three aspects to such empowerment: entitlement, involvement, and enablement. My intention in developing this model of freedom has been to build upon the views offered in the first part, while avoiding their problems. This has required constructing a new concept and model of political freedom.

Though this concept is broader than other concepts of political freedom, I do not think that it is simply equivalent to self-realization. Much more would be required for an account of self-realization than is discussed above. For example, we would not simply have to speak of rights to participation or self-expression, but the actual ways in which each individual participated or expressed him or herself. It may well be that an account of political freedom is part of any account of self-realization. But this is not to say that the two are the same.

I have tried to draw out a few of the implications of this model as it was developed. I do not claim that the meaning I have attributed to "freedom" is exactly the one that everyone will immediately recognize. This is not to be hoped for inasmuch as so many different meanings have been attributed to "freedom." On the other hand, I do not claim that the view of political freedom defended here is wholly new. Quite clearly it has deep roots in the past. Further, we see movement towards this view of freedom not only in government but also in corporations to the extent that workers and employees demand rights of participation and protection as well as the means to realize both. That is, to the extent that such demands are raised in the daily lives of citizens and workers, this view of freedom becomes recognized as the one required for our time.

Notes

1 Political freedom and political philosophy

1   I do not pretend or believe that the preceding examples accurately represent the views of all conservatives, liberals or radicals. I simply wish to offer a number of examples of some of the different practical positions that people take because of their different views on political freedom.

2   Various emotivists have held this view (cf. Ayer 1946). More recently, Alasdair MacIntyre argued that our moral (and political) language has suffered a breakdown such that moral dispute is not longer possible (cf. MacIntyre 1981).

3   The rejection of emotivist views has been quite general. Among those critical of emotivism: Hare 1961; Frankena 1973. The following chapters may also be viewed as part of the argument against emotivist views and those of MacIntyre.

4   Patrick Day says that "the unique, true definition of the *meaning* of 'free' is, as Bentham says, 'unrestrained'" (Day 1986: 121).

5   Gerald Dworkin seems to hold a similar view with regard to autonomy: "It is very unlikely that there is a core meaning which underlies all these various uses of the term ['autonomy']" (Dworkin 1988: 6). Instead, he argues that "it will be necessary to construct a concept given various theoretical purposes and some constraints from normal usage" (Ibid.). This is what I do in Part 2 of this book.

6   Various authors speak openly of different concepts of freedom. H. J. McCloskey claims that there are several concepts of liberty (1965). Arnold Wycombe Gomme entitles one of his essays "Concepts of Freedom" (cf. Gomme 1962). V. J. McGill claims that "in the world today two concepts of freedom are locked in struggle" (McGill 1948: 515). Note that Berlin's famous article is called "Two Concepts of Liberty" — that is, not "Two Conceptualisations of Liberty" (Berlin 1969).

   On the contrary, the following contend that there is a single concept of freedom: Benn 1988; Steiner 1975.

7   Why, then, do different traditions insist on the same word? How can I speak of different conceptions of freedom, rather than simply different freedoms? My answer is developed in the following section (pp. 7–12). It

has to do with a certain logical or conceptual space within our lives that freedom fills, even if it does it in distinct ways. With Wittgenstein we must look to see whether our various words have the self-same meaning in all their different uses. John Hardwig has urged the importance of these objections on me.

8   Others who hold this view: Connolly 1974: 17–22; Swanton 1985. Dorothy Emmet also holds that Gallie's notion of an exemplar must be rejected; cf. Emmet 1979: 13.

9   Even in the natural sciences it has been held that "there is not a finite and determinate set of necessary and sufficient conditions which determine the application of a concept (Waismann) or a word (Putnam)" (MacIntyre 1973: 2). And though they allow that "in normal circumstances and in standard conditions we can behave *as if* there were such a finite and determinate set and we do indeed so behave," MacIntyre claims that in social inquiry there are not such temporary and provisional settlements: "debate remains open about which the central, standard, and paradigmatic instances of the phenomenon are" (Ibid.).

10 John Stuart Mill says that his discussion of liberty concerns "the nature and limits of the power which can be legitimately exercised by society over the individual" (Mill 1956: 3). This is fairly close to what I am suggesting as a characterization of the "logical space" of freedom. Surely what Mill says does not define "freedom," since his own definition of freedom is along the lines of "doing what one desires."

11 Here I draw on Gallie's third characteristic of an essentially contested concept: "Any explanation of its worth must therefore include reference to the respective contributions of its various parts or features; yet prior to experimentation there is nothing absurd or contradictory in any one of a number of possible rival descriptions of its total worth" (Gallie 1956: 172).

12 I draw here on a similar approach to politics taken by Connolly (cf. Connolly 1974: 12–13).

13 This is not to say that the logical space for freedom is defined by inconsistent ingredients. These ingredients do not collectively define the logical space of freedom. Rather they are historically and philosophically available interpretations or formations of this space. The space is amorphous without one or more of these ingredients.

We might think of people having various building blocks that they can use to construct a house of freedom. Some blocks will nicely fit together; others will not. Thus, some of the latter group have to be discarded if the rest are to be used. Together or (in some cases) separately they form (and fill) the space we call freedom. Still, all are building blocks which can be used to build houses.

14 For example, submission to one's leader, recognition of necessity, and action in accord with a rational rule are additional ingredients of "freedom." Cf. Saint Paul's statement that "I feel most free precisely when I am a slave."

15 This means that even those ingredients which have been used to construct Nazi or Fascist views of freedom are included here. To exclude them would simply be conceptual legislation. Instead, we must substantively argue against those views or interpretations of freedom which Fascists

have held.

16 Gray characterizes such a view: "answering the question where a man is free to do something does not involve making an evaluative judgment of any sort. The question is an empirical question" (Gray 1980: 77).

17 It is for this reason, I believe, that Stanley I. Benn is correct when he asserts that "freedom is very closely connected with other concepts, such as authority, rights, will, autonomy, and so on, such that the sense one ascribes to any one of these is going to affect the meaning of freedom itself" (Benn 1988: 307).

18 A model, as I use the term, is not the same as a theory. A model attempts to portray a particular view of freedom, whereas a theory would abstract from any particular model and discuss, for example, various commonalities among the various models. The presentation of a model of freedom will seek to portray both its theoretical and practical aspects. However, it attempts to focus on something more particular than a theory. Clearly, there could be a theory about the nature of models of freedom. Theories tend to be explicit and conscious, whereas models need not be.

19 I do not imply that such past thinkers spoke to exactly the same issues as we confront. Obviously they did so only in part. My point here is that in formulating our own present view of political freedom it is important to look to this "past." Still this problem is one of the reasons I concentrate on modern thinkers on this book.

20 By "essentially contested concept" Gallie refers to concepts of the kind at issue in this chapter. That is, concepts over which we seem endlessly to dispute.

21 Of course not all normative theorists would agree with this. Intuitionists argue that, though our criteria for political concepts may be multiple and evaluative, and even though "there is no decision procedure for specifying in advance what [the] right answer is" (Swanton 1985: 821), still there is a right answer. I cannot argue against such a view here, but will simply assert that any claim to "the right answer" without being able to specify what the decision procedure is for specifying what a right answer would be must be held in great suspicion.

22 Similarly, Connolly suggests that because of "more basic and partly shared ideas" disputes may go on with essentially contested concepts and rationality be part of them (Connolly 1974: 191–8).

23 Thus, I agree with Bernard Williams' rejection of the assumption some hold about rationality that "two considerations cannot be rationally weighed against each other unless there is a common consideration in terms of which they can be compared" (Williams 1985: 17). "This assumption," he says, "is at once very powerful and utterly baseless" (Ibid.).

24 I will include libertarians under liberals. Since these terms are used variously in the United States, Britain, and other countries, the meaning I attribute to them must be gathered from the text. Suffice it to say here, that "liberal," as I use the term, refers to what some would today call "classical liberals" or libertarians. I do not apply it as such to contemporary American liberals who represent a mixture of liberal and socialist (radical) views.

2 Conservative freedom

1   In the following, I concentrate on conservatives such as Burke, Lord
    Cecil, Tocqueville, Lippman, Oakeshott, and Kirk. I pay scant attention
    to more reactionary conservatives such as de Maistre and Bonald. For
    this reason it might be objected that I am painting an unduly favorable
    picture of conservatism. There may be some truth to this objection.
    On the other hand, the more moderate form of conservatism is the
    predominant form of conservativism today. Further, the works of the
    more moderate conservatives seem to have had much greater influence
    than those of the more reactionary. Finally, there is not a total gulf
    between the two conservatisms. On rival brands of conservatism cf.
    Viereck 1956. William R. Harbour takes the same approach in his *The
    Foundations of Conservative Thought* (cf. Harbour 1982: 1–3).
2   Oakeshott's comments are actually made with reference to Henry C.
    Simons whose views Oakeshott is discussing in "The Political Economy
    of Freedom." It is clear, however, from this article that Oakeshott shares
    Simons' views. Other conservatives also speak highly of freedom, e.g.
    "Liberty has always been the American conservative's favorite topic"
    (Rossiter 1955: 359).
3   By "classical liberal" I refer to those who today would be called
    "libertarians." Essentially, they are those who hold to the views of
    liberals of the eighteenth and nineteenth centuries. In the following,
    whenever I speak of liberals or liberalism, I refer to this classical
    formulation. On this view, as we shall see in chapter 3, freedom is
    simply the lack of constraint. This view of freedom is quite generally
    referred to as "negative freedom" inasmuch as freedom consists in a
    lack or absence (the negation) of constraint.
4   Scruton claims that freedom *cannot* occupy a central place in conservative
    thinking (Scruton 1980: 19). On the other hand, William Harbour says
    that freedom is one of the conservative's highest values (Harbour 1982:
    101). Cowling argues that "it is not freedom that conservatives want; what
    they want is the sort of freedom that will maintain existing inequalities or
    restore lost ones, so far as political action can do this" (Cowling 1978:
    9).
5   Rossiter argues that "the conservative should give us a definition of
    liberty that is positive and all-embracing, not negative and narrow"
    (Rossiter 1955: 361).
6   For example, in Russell Kirk's book, *A Program for Conservatives*
    (1954), there is discussion of justice, fraternity, etc. etc. but no
    mention of liberty or freedom. Samuel Huntington lists six points
    which constitute, he says, the major components of the conservative
    creed, but does not mention liberty or freedom once in these six points
    (Huntington 1957: 456). William Aylott Orton lists "twelve leading
    attributes of conservatism" but freedom or liberty is not mentioned
    once (Orton 1945: 13–14). The same is true of Lord Cecil's account
    in *Conservatism* (Cecil 1912: 48).
    On conservative reluctance to formulate the principles or philosophical
    bases of their views see Lewis 1953: 728, 729; Wilson 1941: 29.

7 Lord Cecil distinguishes between political or modern conservatism and natural conservatism. Natural conservatism is "a natural disposition in the human mind" which is averse to change, distrusts the unknown, and prefers experience over theory (Cecil 1912: 8–9; cf. also 9–17).

8 Oakeshott adopts this view quite explicitly (cf. Oakeshott 1962a:39). On the other hand though Tocqueville does not himself offer a definition of freedom, he does approvingly quote Mather's definition:

> But there is a civil, a moral, a federal *liberty*, which is the proper end and object of *authority*; it is a *liberty* for that only which is *just* and *good*; . . . This *liberty* is maintained in a way of *subjection to authority*; and the *authority* set over you will in all administrations for your good be quietly submitted unto, by all but such as have a disposition to *shake off the yoke*, and lose their true *liberty*
>
> (Tocqueville 1969: 46).

Quite clearly, this is neither a liberal nor a radical definition of freedom. The other views that Tocqueville holds, as noted in the following, plausibly place him in the conservative camp.

9 Speaking of English conservatism, John Casey claims that "it has not sought to base itself upon allegedly universal principles claiming a validity that transcends national frontiers, particular traditions, religious beliefs, institutions, loyalties, pieties and customs" (Casey 1978: 82).

Burke himself comments that "nothing universal can be rationally affirmed on any moral or any political subject. Pure metaphysical abstraction does not belong to these matters" (Burke, 1901b: 80–1). Cf. Tocqueville 1969: 617.

10 Harbour notes that "Burke is not so much concerned with any abstract definition of freedom as he is with the possible moral substance that might be given to the acts of free men" (Harbour 1982: 102).

11 One can find other meanings attributed to freedom by other conservatives. In general, these other meanings are much less plausible. For example, Cowling claims that "control by individuals and families over a larger proportion of their earnings . . . is what freedom means" (Cowling 1978: 15).

12 Jeffrey Hart's comment is relevant: "I think the best way of stating Burke's fundamental objection to the [French] Revolution would be to say that it turned on a definition of 'freedom' – that for Burke, freedom was a concrete and historical thing, the actual freedoms enjoyed by actual Englishmen" (Hart 1967: 224).

13 Accordingly, Tocqueville holds, according to Hereth, that it would not "be possible to acquire the concept of freedom, if one does not know it through practice . . . For him [Tocqueville] freedom was a practical matter, which could be described in theoretical discourse only with the greatest difficulty" (Hereth 1986: 16).

14 Cf. Hart on Sartre (Hart 1967: 227).

15 Thus, Cowling claims that conservatives believe that "a nation has to be stratified and that stratification entails privilege; and they assume this not as a matter of principle but because it is something to which they are accustomed" (Cowling 1978: 10). He does go on, however, to say that "the conservative conception of a social structure not only assumes

that marked inequalities are inevitable but also declines to justify them because their inevitabilty makes justification unnecessary" (11).

16 Accordingly, conservatives do not necessarily believe that they can draw on the experience of other countries and societies. For example, Maurice Cowling simply dismisses the importance of Solzhenitsyn for British conservatism: "he is a Russian, bearing on himself the marks of the Russian experience. There is no common ground between him and us or between his experience and ours" (Cowling 1978: 1).

17 Nisbet says that "there is no principle more basic in the conservative philosophy than that of the inherent and absolute incompatability between liberty and equality" (Nisbet 1986: 47). Cowling argues that the kind of freedom conservatives want is "the sort of freedom that will maintain existing inequalities or restore lost ones, so far as political action can do this" (Cowling 1978: 9). Tocqueville is also sceptical regarding the compatibility of freedom and equality (cf. Tocqueville 1969: 57, 689). However, he allows that conceivably the two might be compatible (503).

18 Actually he speaks variously of the relation between the dispersion of power and freedom. For example, he also says that it is a criterion (Oakeshott 1962a: 40), a principle (Ibid., 48f), and a basis (Ibid., 53) of freedom. Rossiter also speaks to the importance of the dispersion of power (Rossiter 1955: 363).

19 "Our tradition . . . running back through Adams and Madison and Dickinson and Otis to Coke and the British common law, is a tradition of imposing limitations upon the arbitrary exercise of power" (Evans 1964: 70–1). Nisbet notes that Burke viewed the American colonists as working for "freedom from 'arbitrary power'" (Nisbet 1986: 5).

20 Both liberal and radical freedom reject (in different ways) the political realm. This is one of several ways in which their models of freedom differ from the conservative model of freedom.

21 "It is not exercise of power or habits of obedience which deprave men, but the exercise of a power which they consider illegitimate and obedience to a power which they think usurped and oppressive" (Tocqueville 1969: 14).

22 Oakeshott says, however, that the duty not to deny others of their rights to voluntary association is "merely the negative definition of the right" (Oakeshott 1962a: 44). He claims that every right is "self-limiting." Thus, the right of private property "proscribes slavery, not arbitrarily, but because the right to own another man could never be a right enjoyed equally by every member of a society"(45).

   Huntington claims that one of the essential elements of Burke's views and of conservatism is that "the rights of men derive from their duties" (Huntington 1957: 456).

23 Thus, Ortega y Gasset agrees that "political freedom cannot be defined as absence of pressure [constraint]" (Ortega y Gasset 1946: 34). His reason, however, is that in human society there simply cannot be a lack of "pressure." "A society is not a man-made institution, as eighteenth-century philosophers thought, but a condition in which man finds himself irremediably and without any hope of true escape" (Ibid.).

24 Conservatives believe in "the existence of universal, absolute moral

standards"; there exists "some kind of objective moral ordering to the universe" (Harbour 1982: 83). Cf. Parkin 1956: 121. Tocqueville seems to express such a view when he claims that "there are some universal and permanent needs of mankind on which moral laws are based; if they are broken all men everywhere at all times have connected notions of guilt and shame with the breach" (Tocqueville 1969: 616–17).

25 Kirk says that "Burke's premise in all moral and juridical questions" is that "God has given man law, and with that law, rights" (Kirk 1951: 441). It is hard to see why this would not amount to the view that man therefore has natural rights. Indeed, Kirk goes on to cite a passage from Burke in which Burke speaks positively of natural rights, though Kirk notes Burke's "reluctance to embrace abstract and undefined rights" (442)!

26 Lippmann too claims that "All rights are ultimately a creation of the state and exist only where they are organized by the government" (Lippman 1934: 107).

27 Kirk claims that Burke accepts natural law (Kirk 1951: 441). Canavan also links Burke and natural law (Canavan 1959); so too does Harbour (Harbour 1982: 87).

28 Huntington notes that Leo Strauss makes "the point that Burke differed from previous thinkers precisely in that he did not judge the British constitution by a standard transcending it" (Huntington 1957: 459).

29 Burke indicates how he moves from talk of natural rights to talk of "the chartered rights of men" in his "Speech of Fox's East-India Bill" (cited in Kirk 1951: 441–2).

30 Casey suggests another route that conservatives might take to account for the validity of institutions. On his (Hegelian) view, the validity of institutions would derive "from some sort of consonance with the expressive possibilities of an age" (Casey 1978: 87). What this seems to amount to is that those institutions and customs are valid which permit the most complete expression (which is compatible with the ability of people to bring this expression or description within their own self-consciousness) of the particular historical nature of a people (cf. Casey 1978: 95–6). Formulated in this manner, however, Casey's suggestion borders on a form of self-realization. This is, of course, a possible answer to the conservative problem, but one that involves a host of other problems.

31 A more positive characterization of this natural conservatism is to say that it reflects a notion of "pietas," of respect, for the institutions, customs and traditions which have formed one (cf. Casey 1978: 85, 99). However, Casey also seems to gloss such "pietas" as simply "an instinctive attachment" (85).

32 Thus, Babbitt refers to Burke's distrust of the intellect and connects it to Burke's Christianity (cf. Babbitt 1924: 106). Babbitt reminds us of Burke's view that "we know, and what is better, we feel inwardly, that religion is the basis of civil society, and the source of all good and comfort" (quoted in ibid.: 101).

33 This seems to accord with Babbitt's account of Burke on change: "Burke would admit innovations in the existing social order only after a period of severe probation" (Babbitt 1924: 105).

34 Thus, I am sympathetic to Hayek's claim that "the decisive objection to any conservatism which desires to be called such . . . is that by its very nature it cannot offer an alternative to the direction in which we are moving" (Hayek 1960: 398). In his view, conservatism simply is an attitude that resists change. It is what Cecil calls "natural conservatism." My argument has been that though they have a method to determine that direction, that method has fundamental problems.

35 Dispute over these two supposed forms of conservatism has gone on for several decades (cf. Meyer 1964).

36 Harbour suggests this view of conservatives (Harbour 1982: 98, 101–12). Still he is sensitive enough to the nature of freedom to note that the discussion of the relation of traditional and libertarian conservatives importantly arises due to "the influence that liberal thought has had on Conservatism. . . . [M]any Conservatives have borrowed from the liberal view of freedom when it comes to discussing economic and political questions" (105).

3 Liberal freedom

1 I develop the liberal model of freedom drawing principally on the work of John Locke, J. S. Mill, and Isaiah Berlin. I choose to build the liberal model on the backs of these three philosophers quite simply because they are three of the most prominent liberal philosophers.

2 For ease of reference, I will refer to sections in Locke's *Second Treatise* rather than pages.

3 By the "political nature of humans" I mean that for humans (collectively and even for large numbers of people individually) politics is not simply an instrumental feature of life which might indifferently be abandoned for some other method of coordinating the life of a community or society. Rather, politics, of some form or other, is a uniquely human and valuable way by which people may organize the manner in which they live together. By "politics" I refer to the attempt to resolve disputes by discussion and compromise, rather than simply by force. It is, however, a process that necessarily involves the possibility of coercion and sanctions.

4 What I have identified as central to liberal freedom is what has been called "negative freedom." To identify such freedom with liberals does not capture the complexity of the views which actual liberals have held. Locke did not center his views on negative freedom. Even J. S. Mill did not wholly and strictly stick to negative freedom. Still, the lack of constraint was crucial to their views of freedom. Thus, Isaiah Berlin claims that there is a special relation between negative freedom and the intellectual traditions of liberalism.

5 Though Mill does not hold Locke's view, there is some suggestion of it in Mill. Thus, for example, Mill comments that "the only freedom which deserves the name is that of pursuing our own good in our way, so long as we do not attempt to deprive others of theirs or impede their efforts to obtain it" (Mill 1956: 16–17. If this is the case, then we cannot say that those people who pursue their own good at the expense of others exemplify freedom.

6 This is not to say that the loss of some freedom might not be balanced by the gain of other freedom such that, on the whole, there is greater freedom (fewer constraints) through the imposition of some constraints. Still, even in this situation there is a loss of freedom since some constraints are imposed (cf. Berlin 1969: 123, 148).

7 Section VIII discusses the liberal view of reason and justification.

8 Still, many liberals have held it (cf. Steiner 1974–5).

9 Though Berlin uses "prevent" on some occasions (Berlin, 1969, xxxviii, 122), he also speaks in ways as noted in the text which allow for hindrances and impedance (130).

10 Mill even allows that in England the yoke of opinion is heavier than that of the law (Mill 1956: 11).

11 "Thus we have the first and greatest paradox of freedom: restraints restrict freedom, but without restraints there can be little or no effective freedom, at least not for most men" (Spitz 1964: 117; emphasis omitted).

12 One might think that the only condition would be when one's own acting freely (without restraint) placed a restraint on someone else – since they are then less free (cf. Hayek 1960). But since restraint has been so broadly interpreted problems arise on this suggestion.

13 Honderich holds a similar interpretation of Mill's basic principle in *On Liberty* (Honderich 1974: 466–7).

14 Other examples include competitive examinations and free trade (Mill 1956: 115).

15 I will use "injury" hereafter to include those forms of harm and offense for which liberals would permit the imposition of constraints and/or coercion on an individual who caused them.

16 Wolin argues that Locke solves the problem of specifying the law of nature by appealing to the Christian ethic (Wolin 1960: 335). Even if this were true of Locke, it certainly has not been true of Mill and Berlin. On the other hand, it seems more straightforward to see Locke's solution simply to be that of constructing a political process whereby the law of nature is made more specific. This is, afterall, what Locke says rather straightforwardly in his *Second Treatise* (1982).

4 Radical freedom

1 I develop my account of radical freedom by drawing principally on the works of Karl Marx, Friedrich Engels, Vladimir Lenin, and Herbert Marcuse. This is justified, I believe, due to the vast influence that Marx and those he inspired have had. Inasmuch as the present account is anchored in Marx's views, it focuses on what might be called "classical radical freedom." It does not attempt to take into account all the differences and modifications which those who might also characterize themselves as radicals have most recently defended. Some of these more recent radicals' views are incorporated in Part 2 of this book.

2 Lenin complains that attempts are made to convert views of revolutionaries such as Marx "into harmless icons, to canonize them, so to say, and to surround their names with a certain halo for the 'consolation' of the oppressed classes and with the object of duping them" (1966a: 272).

In short, Lenin complains about "de-radicalizing" the views of Marx and other revolutionaries. I concur with Lenin's complaint. If radical freedom needs revising because of its radical nature, then we should be candid enough to say so, and hence to say (if we do at all) that we advocate a revised Marxism or Leninism, not the original thing. Lenin at least had the courage to go after the original, radical thing. Lenin's criticisms against reformism and revising Marx ring throughout *The State and Revolution* (e.g. Lenin 1966a: 286, etc.).

3   This characteristic was suggested to me by Scott Arnold.

4   I use "radical" rather than "socialist" or "communist" because the last two terms carry very different and conflicting connotations for many people. Even Marx refers to himself some times as a socialist and some times as a communist. Further, others upon whom it is legitimate to draw in formulating this model of freedom might not accept one or the other of these two labels. By using "radical" I hope to circumvent some of the discussions which these terms unavoidably raise.

5   I use the word "communal" here, rather than "social," to remind the reader that the society (and its members) radicals envision have been dramatically altered. The word "social" might be used in such cases. However, inasmuch as the word "social" is also used by liberals to contrast with "political" features of a society and since radicals do not propose that we bring about a social system in this sense, I think it is better to use the word "communal" whenever possible.

6   This is not a simple or accidental terminological difference, but signals the breadth, the complexity and the communal nature of radical freedom. The radical language of freedom indicates a rather different way of looking at things, one which cuts across boundaries which the concepts of liberty, rights, and constraint tend to preserve. Marcuse also emphasizes the need for new categories (Marcuse 1969a: 7f).

7   Those who claim that radical freedom is a negative freedom include: G. A. Cohen 1981a; Lukes 1985b. Lukes explicitly denies that freedom for Marx is rational self-determination (Lukes 1985b: 75). Lloyd Easton attributes to Marx a view of freedom as self-determination (Easton 1981: 194).

8   Cf. Kant 1956; Green 1941; Hegel 1967; McCloskey (1965) discusses both self-determination and "reasonable" self-determination.

9   Berlin is known for this separate identification: negative freedom is simply the lack of obstacles to possible choices, while positive freedom is self-mastery or self-control (Berlin 1969: 121–34). I reject his view and the claims of those such as Walicki who maintain that Marx's view of freedom is a perfect example of Berlin's positive freedom (Walicki 1984: 226). Others, however, such as Agnes Heller claim that Marxian freedom has both positive and negative aspects (Heller 1981: 349).

10 The default for empiricists, we might say, is that they are not connected. For radicals, it is that they are connected.

11 For sophisticated interpretations of Marx as an empiricist see Little 1986 and Shaw 1978. In contrast, Marcuse's account of Marxian dialectic is one of many reasons to believe that radicals are not empiricists (Marcuse 1967).

12 Lenin insists on these points. He pointedly notes that he does not hold that the state conciliates classes; rather it is an organ for the oppression of one class by another (Lenin 1966a: 274). It may moderate this collision and struggle; but it does not overcome or conciliate it (Ibid.).

13 In his early writings, Marx held that full freedom can be realized in a communist society. In his later writings, Marx held that such full freedom can be realized in a communist society only outside the realm of necessity. Within the realm of necessity, a lesser freedom must be realized (Marx 1967b: 818–20). Still, full freedom can be realized in some form.

14 Radicals are rather reticent about detailing the structure of a future society. This is understandable. Marx objected to any attempt to dogmatically prefigure the future even before he was a communist (Marx 1975b: 141–51). On the other hand, radicals must tell us enough so that we are able to understand and evaluate the kind of freedom they defend. The following sketch is drawn from their writings. Marcuse argues that radicals must begin to speculate on the utopian possibilities blocked by present society (Marcuse 1969a). Still, even Marcuse says that "the true positive is the society of the future and therefore beyond definition and determination" (Marcuse 1969c: 87).

15 Marx indicates that the Commune of France in the 1870s was a "working, not a parliamentary body [it embodied] executive and legislative [functions] at the same time" (Marx 1968: 57). Cf. Lenin 1968: 115.

16 Marx obviously believes that most other conflicts, metaphysical and moral, will also be solved by communism. Thus, he comments on how communism (the realm of freedom) involves overcoming conflicts between existence and essence, objectification and self-confirmation, freedom and necessity, individual and species (Marx 1975c: 296).

17 Heilbroner contends that "it is not the content of the ideas themselves that contains this danger [of oppression and domination] . . . Instead, the danger lies in the feelings of a select discipleship generated among those who have accepted the ideas" (Heilbroner 1980: 144). I think the preceding sections (pp. 114–27) show that there are dangers in radical ideas – at least dangers in the ways in which they have been classically developed. There may be others that are more benign – though perhaps also less radical.

5 Political freedom as empowerment

1 By "social" I do not intend to imply a realm that is wholly distinct from the political. I intend simply that individuals cannot be understood in and by themselves. We must make reference to other individuals and relations between them.

2 After arriving at this threefold account, I discovered Friedrich's article in which he distinguishes three dimensions of political freedom: those of independence, participation, and creation (Friedrich 1963: 850). These three dimensions roughly correspond to what I talk about. The third dimension is the least similar to the three I propose.

3   This mistake has been particularly damaging in Western attempts to foster political freedom in various developing countries.

4   Hobbes offers such a definition: "Liberty, or Freedom, signifieth (properly) the absence of Opposition; (By Opposition, I mean external Impediments of motion;) and may be applied no less to Irrational, and Inanimate creatures, than to Rationall" (Hobbes 1950: 177). Day explicitly links negative freedom and a physical view of liberty (Day 1983: 19).

5   It should be noted that "natural freedom" as I use the phrase here is different from that of Locke, Rousseau, and others who also use the same (or a similar) phrase.

6   I do not deny that there is some connection between the various uses of "free." The sense of "freedom" towards which I argue includes the idea of a lack of certain kinds of physical interference. Thus, the word "free" does not wholly and completely refer to different conditions. Still, even though there is (to a certain extent) overlap amongst different uses, the differences remain significant.

7   It might be objected that we do not have to appeal to some other good, but can simply appeal to the greatest reduction of physical interferences. But this would permit that human freedom takes second place to that of the rest of nature: e.g. tigers, cattle, and fish. That is, this approach might mean that the greatest freedom (absence of physical interference) requires interference with humans rather than the rest of creation. I suppose that this is a possible view. However, its very statement suggests that some other value or good, e.g. the sacredness or importance of all creation, lies behind it and it is *for this reason* that it is acceptable. That is, even this view presupposes an appeal to some other good.

8   A similar argument, it will be recalled, was used against liberal freedom in Chapter 3.

9   J. P. Day claims that Hobbes created the negative concept of individual liberty. He "formed it by analogy with the concept of freely moving bodies. It is an essentially physical concept, and its introduction was causally connected with the then rapidly rising science of dynamics" (Day 1983: 19).

10   For example, Steiner holds that "an individual is unfree if, and only if, his doing of any action is rendered impossible by the action of another individual" (Steiner 1975: 33).

11   This fits with Gert's claim that "only someone with the ability to will can act freely or can act under coercion, that is, only voluntary actions are done freely or under coercion" (Gert 1972: 32).

12   Thus, the thesis I defend is related to one defended by Benn and Weinstein: "we shall argue that underlying and presupposed by the concept of freedom of action there is another but related concept, that of autonomy – of the free man as chooser" (Benn and Weinstein 1971: 194).

13   Dworkin holds that freedom is a local concept, whereas autonomy is a global one (Dworkin 1981: 211). This is, I believe, mistaken.

14   There is an interesting analogy with health here. Wendell Berry protests against "our narrowed understanding of the word *health*." By health, he complains "we mean little more than how we feel . . . By health,

in other words, we mean merely the absence of disease. Our health professionals are interested almost exclusively in preventing disease . . . and in curing disease . . . But the concept of health is rooted in the concept of wholeness. To be healthy is to be whole. The word *health* belongs to a family of words, a listing of which will suggest how far the consideration of health must carry us: heal, whole, wholesome, hale, hallow, holy. And so it is possible to give a definition of health that is positive and far more elaborate than that given to it by most medical doctors and the officers of public health" (Berry 1986: 102–3).

15　Thus, I reject MacCallum's view that freedom is a triadic relation of someone (or thing), from something, to do something (MacCallum 1967). Similarly, I reject Bayles' claim that "freedom always involves being free from something to do something" (Bayles 1972: 24).

16　Cited by Cooper 1983: 132. Others also hold this view. Hobhouse is said to hold that freedom is the ability to do what one wants to do, whether good or evil (Nichols 1962: 126).

17　This is a problem, it should be noted, not because Epictetus speaks of wants or desires. The same problem would arise for wishes, intentions, undertakings, etc.

18　Oscar Wilde's claim that a man can be totally free even in prison is an instance of such a view (cf. Cooper 1983: 131).

19　T. H. Green, however, goes on to add that this power or capacity is linked to "doing or enjoying something worth doing or enjoying" (Green 1889: 371). I do not follow Green in this further step.

20　My characterization of this sense of self-determination draws on Berlin's description of positive freedom (cf. Berlin 1969: 131).

21　The examples are from S. I. Benn (Benn 1976: 113).

22　Virginia Held argues that to be coerced "the person coerced must in some sense be doing what he is doing against his will" (Held 1972: 50).

23　Richard Norman has pointed out that this may be less true for tribal and primitive society. Still, even such "simple" societies are not monolithic in the values they defend.

24　The example comes from H. Frankfurt (1971); it is cited in Dworkin who also gives his own view (G. Dworkin 1981: 211).

25　Recall that realistic self-determination does not require that the determinations of this or that self are necessarily morally right or correct, or even simply prudent. Rather, it is to say that a person can be said to be self-determining even though he or she faces obstacles, challenges, etc. insofar as these do not require an unreasonable amount of effort or skill to overcome them. In this section I will speak, hereafter, simply of self-determination. When I do so, however, it should be understood in this sense of realistic self-determination.

26　Unfortunately, Benn does not elaborate on what he means by interpreting Locke's natural rights as "normative capacities." On the face of it, one would think that a person might have any number of "normative capacities" that did not involve rights.

27　Another route that Benn has also taken is to argue that "the principle of interference" arises out of "normative talk" concerning freedom. This appears to give this principle a semantic foundation, rather than one in the nature of persons.

28 The irony here in speaking of one's freedom consisting in the lack of restraint by others deserves notice. Quite ordinarily for a person to lack restraint is for that person to do anything that comes to mind, which usually means impinging on others. In this context, it means exactly the opposite. The lack of restraint I enjoy from you is exactly your self-restraint.

Hill says that the right of self-determination implies that one has a right to expect others not to interfere (Hill 1979: 71). But what is the nature of this expectation? This is what I try to address here.

29 Malinowski compares freedom to health (Malinowski 1944: 74). Pennock claims that "freedom" is a virtue word (Pennock 1972: 2).

30 Thus, we may agree with T. H. Green when he says that "we rightly refuse to recognise the highest development on the part of an exceptional individual or exceptional class, as an advance towards the true freedom of man, if it is founded on a refusal of the same opportunity to other men" (Green 1889: 371).

31 Edmund Leach suggests another way of linking freedom and rights. He contends that we can best formulate the concept of freedom by formulating its antithesis, servitude. Servitude is then defined as the lack of various rights: "In any given social system particular conditions of servitude can be precisely specified: 'If an individual in servile status X lacks rights *a, b, c, d* . . . which are available to other members of the same society, then in *this* context, and in relation to *this* particular servile status we might define a *free* man as a person in status Y who possesses rights a, b, c, d'" (Leach 1963: 74).

32 Thus I agree with Arnold Wycombe Gomme who argues that freedom (individual or political) "is the right or sum of rights belonging to the individual in relation to the ruling body" or belonging to the individual *qua* citizen (Gomme 1962: 139). I disagree with him to the extent that he holds that freedom is simply a sum of rights, to which we can refer without taking notice of a more basic, underlying right of self-determination.

C. J. Friedrich notes that "the right of self-determination is a paramount right which by many persons today is placed ahead of all personal rights" (Friedrich 1963: 843). He is correct to note the primacy of the right to self-determination, but he is mistaken to see this as in conflict with other "personal" rights, e.g. to life, speech, or movement. The latter are, partially, the contents of the former.

33 Cf. Montague 1980, 1986. It is worth noting that Montague suggests that one interpretation of the right to liberty is that it is an exercisable right "to act autonomously in matters affecting the course of one's life" (Montague 1980: 383). Though I do not agree with this way of formulating the matter, I think that the spirit of Montague's suggestion is in line with my own argument.

Sharon Bishop Hill claims that the right of self-determination means that one has "the authority to determine certain sorts of things." She elaborates: "having title to make these choices means that they have a right to expect others not to interfere with the legitimate exercise of their authority and a right to protect themselves from interference" (Hill 1979: 71). Thus, the right to self-determination involves, on her account, both a non-exercisable right and an exercisable right. This is quite in line with the proposal I am making.

6 Political freedom, involvement, and democracy

1 The notion of politics, it should be remembered, originates from the Greek word *polites* which refers to one who is a citizen, i.e. a member of a particular form of social organization or society.
2 Frank H. Knight is one of many who note the connection between political liberty and "the popular, everyday conception of democracy" (Knight 1947: 184).
3 Thus, T. H. Green's comment is quite appropriate: "every usage of the term ['freedom'] to express anything but a social and political relation of one man to others involves a metaphor" (Green 1941: 2).
4 In raising the question in this manner I do not start by asking about the compatibility of individual entitlement with the state (cf. R. P. Wolff 1970). On the other hand, I am not presupposing some state of nature. I assume that the individuals involved are real individuals to be found within a society with its various historical and governing institutions, practices, and the like.
5 Hans J. Morgenthau identifies two contradictory meanings of freedom. One of them is the freedom to dominate others. Thus he claims that the absolute ruler is free to govern as he sees fit (Morgenthau 1957: 717). Similarly, Bertrand Russell claims that "complete freedom is . . . only possible for omnipotence" (Russell 1940: 251). It is because of such views that discussion of the present alternative is not frivolous. Both Russell and Morgenthau arrive at the preceding statements because they adopt a negative concept of freedom. Such a view of freedom was rejected in the preceding chapter.
6 Rights require a community for their existence: "if there is no community . . . there can be no rights" (Salkever 1977: 398). For others who share this view, see Harman 1983; Baker 1975; Green 1941.
7 In spite of Sartre's various existential musings on individual freedom, I take it that this is what his character Mathieu learns in *The Age of Reason*.
8 Connolly claims that "to see oneself as a free, responsible agent, as a person whose position in life is merited by the skills, energy, and self-discipline exercised at home and at work, one must identify with some of the practices within which one is implicated" (Connolly 1981b: 163). Sandel also argues that we are partly constituted through the roles and relations we occupy (Sandel 1984).
9 Likewise, the right to exercise one's religion is not violated if one is stopped from sacrificing children.
10 Cf. Ryan 1980: 482. Similarly, a defensive soccer player who stops another player from scoring a goal has prevented the other person from acting in a certain way, but it seems silly to say that he has limited his freedom (cf. Oppenheim 1981: 54). His freedom would have been diminished if someone had tripped him, but legitimately to block his shot is within the rules of the game; it does not diminish his freedom.

258   *Notes*

11   Bertrand Russell notes, for example, that "no one protests against [traffic regulations] in the name of liberty" since they are required for the safety of each person (Russell 1940: 251). Charles Taylor gives a similar example (Taylor 1979).

12   This does not, of course, mean that all constraints or limits function in this way.

13   Obviously, there are a variety of institutions and organizations that might be in question here. Some are purely voluntary: herb clubs and soccer teams. Others are less voluntary: unions and professional groups. Yet others appear involuntary – the family and one's state – at least in the sense that one is born into them, even supposing that one might renounce both one's family and state and seek to live elsewhere among other people. I deal with institutions and organizations generally here since the problem of being asked or required to do something one does not want to do may arise in any one of the preceding kinds of organizations.

14   Contrariwise, on the present proposal – which simply requires that a person explicitly choose the institution or organization within which he or she lives – a person might choose an institution that enslaves him. But this would neither make that person free nor be a free institution!

15   Institutions inhibit freedom or self-determination to the extent that they do not treat people equally, unless and except when differentiations are needed in order to promote the like freedom of others. In these cases, the positions, roles, etc. which are treated differently, and unequally, must be open to all to obtain. A person's freedom is not violated by playing in a game such as soccer since who fills what position is open equally to all with the requisite talents. Institutions such as marriage, however, which differentiate roles based merely on historical prejudice may well stifle the freedom of some.

16   This should be understood to include not simply not standing in the way, but also fostering and promoting in certain cases.

17   This does not mean that institutions whose aim is entertainment (e.g. sports) or diversion (e.g. herb clubs) are freedom restricting. They promote occasions when people may exercise their rights of self-determination. Further, other important interests may be fulfilled within them (e.g. camaraderie, development of physical and mental skills, etc.). It is to say, however, that if all the institutions in which we could participate were limited to these kinds, we would be less free than if we were also able to participate in institutions and organizations whose aim was political, economic, or religious.

18   Obviously the possibility of exit will vary from institution to institution. One might easily exit from herb societies and soccer clubs, though even within these other members may make such exiting very difficult. Marriages and families may be harder, or even much harder, to opt out of. In part this will depend upon the decision of the society within which they are found and the extent to which freedom is thought desirable within these relations and/or institutions. Exit from a society or country may also be quite easy or very difficult depending on laws, one's financial status, one's emotional attachments, etc.

19   This is the manner in which Burke conceived the role of a representative

(cf. Arblaster 1987).

20 A practical problem is the size of the constituencies and the number of representatives. The smaller the constituency the greater the accountability; however, the larger the number of representatives, the more difficult the deliberations and proceedings within the governing body. Other matters of concern include designing constituencies to exclude minority groups, or advocating at-large elections to overwhelm minority groups. The tricks and problems are many.

21 In speaking of interests here, rather than opinions, I allow that a representative, through further acquaintance with the facts of the situation and reflection of their implications, might vote against what his or her constituents give expression to as their opinions. Such opinions may fluctuate and be the very temporary result of media hype, fear etc. This is not a Burkean view of representation since the interests of a particular locality may differ from the general interests (cf. Arblaster 1987: 83).

Further, representatives from one district might be approached by citizens of another district so as to present their views to him or her. We should not think that participation is limited simply to that between a representative and his or her constituents in the district from which one is elected.

22 It follows that questions of the equality of power are also important.

23 Still, we must be aware of the limitations of participation. For example, increased use of referenda carry definite limitations and dangers. Part of this has to do with voter information. Numerous cases can be cited in which information has been manipulated such that the public vote on the basis of patently irrelevant concerns. We should have no illusions that the results of such votes will always be the most rational.

In addition, we should be wary that demands and expectations for greater participation may produce even lower levels of participation (Steed 1972: 99). People are subject to ballot weariness. Indeed, the arguments are well known that high participation is a sign of unhealthy electoral conditions (Ibid.: 100). Still, the thrust of the above argument is against such views.

24 Needless to say the means used to implement these decisions (e.g. the bureaucracy) must be streamlined so as to impede as little as possible the legitimate aims of the state. I speak little of the bureaucracy here, and yet much of the success of political freedom will depend on its operations.

25 His abstention may be due to a variety of reasons. Quite commonly people even despise the opportunity and those who do pursue it – "they are all crooks." There is a moral purism here which abstracts from the kinds of decisions and compromises which are part and parcel of public life and which structure one's life.

26 Cf. Bernard Crick: "The person who wishes not to be troubled by politics and to be left alone finds himself the unwitting ally of those to whom politics is a troublesome obstacle to their well-meant intentions to leave nothing alone" (Crick 1982: 16).

27 Dewey speaks of government in the family, business, church, etc. (Dewey 1937: 459). Walzer suggests that when citizens begin to complain

to one another "they have established or begun to establish a *political* tie not readily encompassed by the first view of citizenship" (Walzer 1970: 208). The first view of citizenship is one defended by Hobbes and Locke in which individuals have ties simply vertically to the state, which serves instrumentally to protect them.

28   I draw many of these examples from Andrew Hacker (Hacker 1969: 70–4).

29   Michael Walzer argues that "the capitalist economy proliferates what are plausibly called private governments. [The] . . . process of decision making [within them] . . . has the crucial characteristics of a political regime" (Walzer 1980: 277). The characterists Walzer lists and those noted in my text are essentially the same.

30   Among the many others who view corporations as having a political nature are: Pateman 1970; Lindblom 1977; Walzer 1980.

31   The example is Nozick's (Nozick 1974).

32   Robert Dahl has defined a political system as "any persistent pattern of human relationships that involves to a significant extent power, rule or authority" (Dahl 1963: 6).

33   I am assuming that corporations engage in a broad spectrum of political activities and that this involvement is corporate activity "rather than merely the independent undertakings of individual managers" (Epstein 1969: 12).

34   Is the authority of a church less than that of the state when it can condemn one to eternal damnation, while the state may "merely" execute a person?!

35   For example, participation in the form of referenda may carry dangers of the public being manipulated. In October, 1955, the Swedes had proposed to them a switch from left-hand driving. Opponents raised fears of increased deaths due to the change. The measure was defeated by a vote of 84.3 to 15.7. "Twelve years later without a further referendum but with agreement reached through the normal organs of representative democracy Sweden switched to right-hand driving; the death-rate from road accidents dropped, almost certainly reflecting the greater care taken by drivers in the aftermath of the change" (Steed 1972: 94).

7   Freedom, enablement, and resources

1   Dorothy Emmet claims that "the first use of the term 'open society' . . . [was by] Max Weber . . . who used it to refer to a society which can be entered by anyone 'who wishes to participate and is actually in a position to do so' " (Emmet 1963: 91).

2   Partridge is not considering the view that "freedom" and "power" are the same, but simply considers whether the meaning of the latter must be included in the meaning of the former.

3   Many philosophers have noted the limits of appeals to ordinary language. For example, J. Gould correctly argues that "ordinary usage, however, is not the proper test in this matter" (Gould 1985: 69). He proceeds to reject views that are based "upon language analysis rather than explicating freedom situations to determine the meaning of freedom" (Ibid.).

4   Perry argues that "the opening of prison doors does not make a man free unless he chooses to walk, and has the necessary leg power; unless he has somewhere to go and is able to get there" (Perry 1953: 125). Similarly, a tyrant, who ruled over a country of citizens uable to walk, would hardly have extended the freedom of the citizens of that country by rescinding the laws opposing physically walking out of the country.

5   Of course it makes sense to speak of things that people possess which they do not value highly because they cannot use them. A person might not value her television set because she has moved to the mountains where there is no electricity. A person who is blind might not value the books that his father leaves to him. My contention is that freedom is not like television sets or books that people cannot use and hence do not value. For a person to be free is for that person to be able to use that freedom, whether or not he or she values it.

6   Bernard Gert admits that "there is a sense of freedom in which a person is free to do x if and only if he has the voluntary ability to do x, a reasonable opportunity to do it, and there are no unreasonable incentives influencing his will either to do or not to do it" (Gert 1972: 37). However, he proceeds to read such an ability out of freedom so that he can "keep the distinction between liberty and power" (Ibid.). The argument of this chapter is that we ought not to follow Gert's suggestion. Gert does not give us an argument for this move, but rather an account of coercion and freedom without power being linked to freedom. It is striking, then, that Gert himself goes on to note "the close relationship between freedom and ability [inasmuch as] . . . it would be the sickest kind of humor to say to a person whom you know to be physically unable to dance, "You are free to dance" (Ibid: 38).

7   It might be objected that, inasmuch as I have linked freedom and empowerment, I have identified freedom and power. The answer is that "empowerment" refers to a normative condition which includes different things: rights (entitlement), participation, and enablement. The concepts of freedom and power or ability are also connected, but not the same thing. Put differently, to be empowered and to have power are not, as I use the terms, the same thing.

8   Martin comments that "if a man has not the means to defend his rights in a court of law, he practically has no rights of which he may not be deprived" (Martin 1930: 243).

9   Crocker (in speaking about Berlin) mentions health (though he must mean the material conditions to foster health) and economic sufficiency (Crocker 1980: 87–8). Kaufman speaks generally and vaguely of "material resources," "material welfare," "poverty." He also speaks of dams, flood prevention, electrical power, capital, and food (Kaufman 1962: 242f).

10 Martin notes the claim of critics of liberalism that a person who lives in poverty is never free to do what he wants:
    He must endure all sorts of petty tyrannies on the part of his employer and overseers. . . In theory, his labor is not forced labor because he is presumed to have contracted freely with his employer; but a contract which is not entered into freely is theoretically null and void, and if the person signing

it is not in a position to accept or reject its terms, he is not free. Yet he who must find work immediately, or starve, has little choice in the matter.

(Martin 1930: 243)

11 This raises complicated subsidiary issues of the free press: e.g. control of newspapers, restrictions on advertising, the relation of commercial speech and free speech, etc.

12 D. G. Ritchie also holds such a view: "Freedom of thought in . . . the strictest sense of the words . . . every one has, and nobody can restrict" (Ritchie 1895: 148). Nevertheless, Ritchie goes on to admit that "indirectly, if not directly, even this sad privilege of freedom of thought is destroyed by systematic repression of freedom of utterance" (Ibid.).

13 The case is mentioned and discussed by Parent 1974b: 164.

14 Another suggestion would be that I must have that amount of power or ability which enables me to compete fairly with you. This suggests a fairness criterion.

References

Acton, J. (1985) *Essays in the History of Liberty*, 3 vols, J. R. Fears (ed.), Indianapolis: Liberty Classics.

Adler, M. J. (1958) *The Idea of Freedom*, 2 vols, Garden City, New York: Doubleday & Co.

—— (1961) *The Idea of Freedom*, 2 vols, Garden City, New York: Doubleday & Company.

Arblaster, A. (1984) *The Rise and Decline of Western Liberalism*, Oxford: Basil Blackwell.

—— (1987) *Democracy*, Minneapolis: University of Minnesota Press.

Arendt, H. (1961a) "What is Freedom?," in *Between Past and Future*, New York: The Viking Press.

—— (1961b) "Freedom and Politics," in A. Hunold (ed.), *Freedom and Serfdom*, Dordrecht: Reidel.

Ayer, A. J. (1946) *Language, Truth, and Logic*, New York: Dover Publications.

Babbitt, I. (1924) *Democracy and Leadership*, Boston: Houghton Mifflin Co.

Bachrach, P. (1967) "Corporate Authority and Democratic Theory," in D. Spitz (ed.), *Political Theory and Social Change*, New York: Atherton Press.

Bachrach, P. and Baratz, M. S. (1970) *Power and Poverty*, New York: Oxford University Press.

Baker, C. E. (1975) "The Ideology of the Economic Analysis of Law," *Philosophy and Public Affairs* 5: 3–48.

Bakunin, M. (1950) *Marxism, Freedom and the State*, London: Freedom Press.

Barry, B. (1975) "The Obscurities of Power," *Government and Opposition* 10: 250–4.

Bayles, M. D. (1972) "A Concept of Coercion," in J. R. Pennock and J. W. Chapman (eds), *Coercion*, NOMOS XIV, Chicago: Aldine and Atherton.

Benn, S. I. (1967) "Freedom and Persuasion," *The Australasian Journal of Philosophy* 45: 259–75.

—— (1976) "Freedom, Autonomy and the Concept of a Person," *Proceedings of the Aristotelian Society* 76: 109–30.

—— (1982) "Individuality, Autonomy and Community," in E. Kamenka (ed.), *Community as a Social Ideal*, London: Edward Arnold.

—— (1988), *A Theory of Freedom*, Cambridge: Cambridge University Press.

Benn, S. I. and Weinstein, W. L. (1971) "Being Free to Act, and Being A Free Man," *Mind* 80: 194–211.

Berlin, I. (1969) *Four Essays on Liberty*, London: Oxford University Press.

—— (1979) *Russian Thinkers*, Harmondsworth: Penguin Books.

—— (1981) *Concepts and Categories*, Harmondsworth: Penguin Books.

Berry, W. (1986) *The Unsettling of America*, San Francisco: Sierra Club Books.

Bowie N. E. and Simon, R. E. (1986) *The Individual and the Political Order* (2nd edn), Englewood Cliffs, NJ: Prentice-Hall.

Burke, E. (1901a) "A Letter to John Farr and John Harris, Esqrs., Sheriffs of the City of Bristol, on the Affairs of America," in *The Writings and Speeches of Edmund Burke*, II, Boston: Little Brown & Co.

—— (1901b) "An Appeal from the New to the Old Whigs," in *The Writings and Speeches of Edmund Burke*, IV, Boston: Little Brown & Co.

—— (1964) *Speech on Conciliation with the Colonies*, Chicago: Henry Regnery Co.

—— (1973) *Reflections on the Revolution in France*, Garden City, NY: Anchor Books.

—— (1982) *A Vindication of Natural Society*, Indianapolis: Liberty Classics.

Canavan, F. P. (1959) "Edmund Burke's Conception of the Role of Reason in Politics," *Journal of Politics* 21: 60–79.

Care, N. S. (1973–4) "On Fixing Social Concepts," *Ethics* 84: 10–21.

Carr, C. (1983) "The Problem of Political Authority," *The Monist* 66: 472–86.

Carritt, E. F. (1967) "Liberty and Equality," in A. Quinton (ed.), *Political Philosophy*, London: Oxford University Press.

Casey, J. (1978) "Tradition and Authority," in M. Cowling (ed.), *Conservative Essays*, London: Cassell.

Cecil, L. H. (1912) *Conservatism*, London: Thornton Butterworth Ltd.

Clarke, B. (1979) "Eccentrically Contested Concepts," *British Journal of Political Science* 9: 122–6.

Cohen, G. A. (1981a) "Freedom, Justice and Capitalism," *New Left Review* 126: 3–16.

—— (1981b) "Illusions about Private Property and Freedom," in J. Mepham and D.-H. Rubin (eds), *Issues in Marxist Philosophy*, Sussex: Harvester Press.

Cohen, M. (1960) "Berlin and the Liberal Tradition," *The Philosophical Quarterly* 10: 216–27.

Connolly, W. E. (1974) *The Terms of Political Discourse*, Lexington, MA: D.C. Heath & Co.

—— (1977) "A Note on Freedom Under Socialism," *Political Theory* 5: 461–72.

—— (1981a) *Appearance and Reality in Politics*, Cambridge: Cambridge University Press.

—— (1981b) "Personal Identity, Citizenship, and the State," in *Appearance and Reality in Politics*, Cambridge: Cambridge University Press.

Cooper, D. E. (1983) "The Free Man," in A. P. Griffiths (ed.), *On Liberty*, Cambridge: Cambridge University Press.

Cowling, M. (1978) "The Present Position," in M. Cowling (ed.), *Conserva-*

tive Essays, London: Cassell.

Cranston, M. (1967) "Liberalism," in P. Edwards (ed.), *Encyclopedia of Philosophy*, IV, New York: Macmillan Publishing Co. and The Free Press.

Crick, B. (1955) "The Strange Quest for an American Conservatism," *Review of Politics* 17: 359–76.

—— (1982) *In Defense of Politics*, 2nd edn, Harmondsworth: Penguin Books.

Crocker, L. (1980) *Positive Liberty*, The Hague: Martinus Nijhoff Publishers.

Dahl, R. (1963) *Modern Political Analysis*, Englewood Cliffs, NJ: Prentice-Hall.

—— (1970) *After the Revolution*, New Haven: Yale University Press.

Daniels, N. (1975) "Equal Liberty and Unequal Worth of Liberty," in N. Daniels (ed.), *Reading Rawls*, New York: Basic Books.

Dauenhauer, B. P. (1982) "Relational Freedom," *Review of Metaphysics* 36: 77–101.

Dawson, G. W. (1975) "Man in the Marxian Kingdom of Freedom: A Critique," *Archiv fur Rechts und Sozialphilosophie* 59: 357–73.

Day, J. P. (1983) "Individual Liberty," in A. P. Griffiths (ed.), *Of Liberty*, Cambridge: Cambridge University Press.

—— (1986) "Is the Concept of Freedom Essentially Contestable?" *Philosophy* 61: 116–23.

Devlin, P. (1965) *The Enforcement of Morals*, London: Oxford University Press.

Dewey, J. (1937) "Democracy and Educational Administration," *School and Society* 45: 457–62.

—— (1963) *Experience and Education*, New York: Collier Books.

Diamond, C. (1988) "Losing Your Concepts," *Ethics* 98: 255–77.

Doppelt, G. (1984) "Conflicting Social Paradigms of Human Freedom and the Problem of Justification," *Inquiry* 27: 51–86.

Dowty, A. (1989) "The Right of Personal Self-determination," *Public Affairs Quarterly* 3: 11–24.

Dworkin, G. (1970) "Acting Freely," *Nous* 8: 367–83.

—— (1976) "Autonomy and Behavior Control," *Hastings Center Report*, 6: 23–8.

—— (1981) "The Concept of Autonomy," in R. Haller (ed.), *Science and Ethics*, Amsterdam: Rodlopi.

—— (1982) "Is More Choice Better Than Less?," in P. A. French, T. E. Uehling, and H. K. Wettstein (eds), *Midwest Studies in Philosophy*, 7, Minneapolis: University of Minneapolis Press.

—— (1988) *The Theory and Practice of Autonomy*, Cambridge: Cambridge University Press.

Dworkin, R. (1977) *Taking Rights Seriously*, Cambridge: Harvard University Press.

—— (1979) "We Do Not Have a Right to Liberty," in R. Cunningham (ed.), *Liberty and the Rule of Law*, Texas Station: Texas A & M University Press.

Easton, L. (1981) "Marx and Individual Freedom," *The Philosophical Forum* 12: 193–213.

Edel, A. (1969) "Metaphors, Analogies, Models, and All That," in S. Morgenbesser, P. Suppes, M. White (eds), *Ethical Theory*, New York:

St. Martin's Press.

Edwards, J. (1957) in P. Ramsey (ed.), *Freedom of the Will*, New Haven: Yale University Press.

Eliot, T. S. (1962) *Notes Toward the Definition of Culture*, London: Faber & Faber Limited.

Emmet, D. (1963) "The Concept of Freedom with Reference to Open and Closed Societies," in D. Bidney (ed.), *The Concept of Freedom in Anthropology*, The Hague: Mouton & Co.

—— (1979) *The Moral Prism*, New York: St. Martin's Press.

Engels, F. (1939) *Anti-Duhring*, New York: International Publishers.

—— (1975) "Speeches in Elberfeld," in *Marx–Engels Collected Works*, IV, New York: International Publishers.

—— (1978) "On Authority," in R. C. Tucker (ed.), *The Marx–Engels Reader* (2nd edn), New York: W. W. Norton & Co.

Epstein, E. M. (1969) *The Corporation in American Politics*, Englewood Cliffs, NJ: Prentice-Hall.

Evans, M. S. (1964) "A Conservative Case for Freedom," in F. S. Meyers (ed.), *What is Conservatism?*, New York: Holt, Rinehart and Winston.

Ewing, D. W. (1977) *Freedom Inside the Organization*, New York: McGraw-Hill.

Exdell, J. (1981) "Liberty, Equality, and Capitalism," *Canadian Journal of Philosophy* 11: 457–71.

Feinberg, J. (1973) *Social Philosophy*, Englewood Cliffs, NJ: Prentice-Hall, Inc.

Finer, S. E. (1972) "Groups and Political Participation," in G. Parry (ed.), *Participation in Politics*, Manchester: Manchester University Press.

Fishkin, J. S. (1984) *Beyond Subjective Morality*, New Haven: Yale University Press.

Frankena, W. K. (1973) *Ethics* (2nd edn), Englewood-Cliffs, NJ: Prentice-Hall.

Frankfurt, H. (1971) "Freedom of the Will and the Concept of a Person," *Journal of Philosophy* 68: 5–20.

Freeman, M. (1980) *Edmund Burke and the Critique of Political Radicalism*, Chicago: The University of Chicago Press.

Friedman, M. and R. (1981) *Free to Choose*, New York: Avon Books.

Friedrich, C. J. (1963) "Rights, Liberties, Freedoms: A Reappraisal," *The American Political Science Review* 57: 841–54.

Frost, R. (1955) *Robert Frost*, Harmondsworth: Penguin Books.

Fuller, L. L. (1955) "Freedom – A Suggested Analysis," *Harvard Law Review* 68: 1305–25.

Gallie, W. B. (1956–7) "Essentially Contested Concepts," *Proceedings of the Aristotelian Society*, new series 56: 167–98.

—— (1956) "Liberal Morality and Socialist Morality," in P. Laslett (ed.), *Philosophy, Politics, and Society*, Oxford: Basil Blackwell.

Gellner, E. (1967) "The Concept of a Story," *Ratio* 9: 49–66.

Gert, B. (1972) "Coercion and Freedom," in J. R. Pennock and J. W. Chapman (eds), *Coercion*, New York: Atherton Press.

Gewirth, A. (1982) "Civil Liberties as Effective Powers," in *Human Rights*, Chicago: The University of Chicago Press.

Gilbert, M. (1981) *Churchill's Political Philosophy*, Oxford: Oxford University Press.

Gildin, H. (1964) "Mill's *On Liberty*," in J. Cropsey (ed.), *Ancients and Moderns*, New York: Basic Books.

Gomme, A. W. (1962) "Concepts of Freedom," in D. A. Campbell (ed.), *More Essays in Greek History and Literature*, Oxford: Basil Blackwell.

Gould, C. C. (1988) *Rethinking Democracy*, Cambridge: Cambridge University Press.

Gould, J. (1985) "Negative Freedom: Constraints and Opportunities," *Journal of Value Inquiry* 19: 67–72.

Graham, G. (1983) "What is Special About Democracy?," *Mind* 92: 94–102.

Graham, K. (1982) "Democracy and the Autonomous Moral Agent," in K. Graham (ed.), *Contemporary Political Philosophy*, Cambridge: Cambridge University Press.

Gray, J. (1980) "On Negative and Positive Liberty," *Political Studies* 28: 507–26.

—— (1986a) *Liberalism*, Minneapolis: University of Minnesota Press.

—— (1986b) "Marxian Freedom, Individual Liberty, and the End of Alienation," *Social Philosophy and Policy* 3: 160–87.

Gray, J. N. (1977) "On the Contestability of Social and Political Concepts," *Political Theory* 5: 331–48.

—— (1978) "Liberty, Liberalism and Essential Contestability," *British Journal of Political Science* 8: 385–402.

—— (1980) "Freedom, Slavery and Contentment," in M. Freeman and D. Robertson (eds), *The Frontiers of Political Theory*, New York: St. Martin's Press.

Green, T. H. (1889) "Lecture on Liberal Legislation and Freedom of Contract," in R. L. Nettleship (ed.), *Works*, III, London: Longmans, Green & Co.

—— (1941) "On the Different Senses of 'Freedom' as Applied to Will and to the Moral Progress of Man," in *Lectures on the Principles of Political Obligation*, London: Longmans, Green & Co.

Greenleaf, W. H. (1972a) "Hobbes: The Problem of Interpretation," in M. Cranston and R. S. Peters (eds), *Hobbes and Rousseau*, Garden City, NY: Anchor Books.

—— (1972b) "Theory and the Study of Politics," *British Journal of Political Science* 2: 467–77.

—— (1973) "The Character of Modern British Conservatism," in R. Benewick, R.N. Berki, and B. Parekh (eds), *Knowledge and Belief in Politics*, London: George Allen & Unwin.

Gutmann, A. (1982) "Moral Philosophy and Political Problems," *Political Theory* 10: 33–47.

Hacker, A. (1962) "Freedom and Power: Common Men and Uncommon Men," in C. J. Friedrich (ed.), *Liberty*, NOMOS IV, New York: Atherton Press.

—— (1969) "Power to do What?," in W. E. Connolly (ed.), *The Bias of Pluralism*, New York: Atherton Press.

Handlin, O. and Handlin, M. (1961) *The Dimensions of Liberty*, Cambridge: Harvard University Press.

Harbour, W. R. (1982) *The Foundations of Conservative Thought*, Notre Dame: University of Notre Dame Press.

Hardwig, J. (1973) "The Achievement of Moral Rationality," *Philosophy* and *Rhetoric* 6: 171–85.

Hare, R. M. (1961) *The Language of Morals*, Oxford: Clarendon Press.

Harman, J. D. (1983) "Rights and Social Freedom," *Metaphilosophy* 14: 209–24.

Hart, J. (1967) "Burke and Radical Freedom," *The Review of Politics* 29: 221–38.

Hayek, F. (1960) *The Constitution of Liberty*, Chicago: The University of Chicago Press.

Hegel, G. W. F. (1967) *Philosophy of Right*, trans. T. M. Knox, New York: Oxford University Press.

Heilbroner, R. (1980) *Marxism: For and Against*, New York: W. W. Norton & Company.

Held, V. (1972) "Coercion and Coercive Offers," in J. R. Pennock and J. W. Chapman (eds), *Coercion*, New York: Atherton Press.

Heller, A. (1981) "The Legacy of Marxian Ethics Today," *Praxis International* 1: 346–64.

Hereth, M. (1986) *Alexis de Tocqueville*, trans. G. Bogardus, Durham: Duke University Press.

Hill, S. B. (1979) "Self-determination and Autonomy," in S. Bishop and M. Weinzweig (eds), *Philosophy and Women*, Belmont, CA: Wadsworth Publishing Co.

Hobbes, T. (1950) *Leviathan*, New York: E. P. Dutton and Company.

Hoffman, R. J. S. and P. Levack (1949) *Burke's Politics*, New York: Alfred A. Knopf.

Honderich, T. (1974) "The Worth of J. S. Mill *On Liberty*," *Political Studies* 22: 463–70.

Horkheimer, M. (1966) "On the Concept of Freedom," *Diogenes*, 53: 73–81.

—— (1974) *Critique of Instrumental Reason*, New York: Seabury Press.

Hume, D. (1965) "An Enquiry Concerning the Principles of Morals," in A. MacIntyre (ed.), *Hume's Ethical Writings*, New York: Collier Books.

Huntington, S. P. (1957) "Conservatism as an Ideology," *American Political Science Review* 51: 454–73.

Johnson, K. (1975a) "A Note on the Inapplicability of Olson's Logic of Collective Action to the State," *Ethics* 85: 170–4.

—— (1975b) "Political Obligation and the Voluntary Association Model of the State," *Ethics* 86: 17–29.

Jones, W. H. M. (1954) "In Defense of Apathy: Some Doubts on the Duty to Vote," *Political Studies* 2: 25–37.

Kant, I. (1956) *Critique of Practical Reason*, trans. L. W. Beck, Indianapolis: The Bobbs-Merrill Co.

Kaufman, A. (1962) "Professor Berlin on 'Negative Freedom'," *Mind* 71: 241–3.

Kekes, J. (1988) "Self-direction: The Core of Ethical Individualism," in K. Kolenda (ed.), *Organizations and Ethical Individualism*, New York: Praeger.

Kirk, R. (1951) "Burke and Natural Rights," *The Review of Politics* 13: 441–56.

—— (1952) "Burke and the Principle of Order," *Sewanee Review* 60:

187–201.

—— (1954) *A Program for Conservatives*, Chicago: Henry Regnery Co.

—— (1956) *Beyond the Dreams of Avarice*, Chicago: Henry Regnery Co.

—— (1964) "Prescription, Authority, and Ordered Freedom," in F. G. Meyer (ed.), *What is Conservatism?*, New York: Holt, Rinehart & Winston.

—— (1986) *The Conservative Mind*, 7th edn rev., Chicago: Regnery Books.

Knight, F. H. (1943) "The Meaning of Freedom," in C. M. Perry (ed.), *Philosophy of American Democracy*, Chicago: University of Chicago Press.

—— (1947) *Freedom and Reform*, New York: Harper & Brothers.

Kristeller, P. O. (1985) "Philosophy and its Historiography," *The Journal of Philosophy* 82: 618–25.

Ladenson, R. F. (1972) "Legitimate Authority," *American Philosophical Quarterly* 9: 335–41.

Lakoff, S. A. (1969) "Private Government in the Managed Society," in J. R. Pennock and J. W. Chapman (eds), *Voluntary Associations*, New York: Atherton Press.

Leach, E. (1963) "Law as a Condition of Freedom," in D. Bidney (ed.), *The Concept of Freedom in Anthropology*, The Hague: Mouton & Co.

Lenin, V. I. (1934) *The Emancipation of Women*, New York: International Publishers.

—— (1966a) "The State and Revolution," in H. M. Christman (ed.), *Essential Works of Lenin*, New York: Bantam Books.

—— (1966b) "What is to be Done?", in H. M. Christman (ed.), *Essential Works of Lenin*, New York: Bantam Books.

—— (1966c) *The Emanicipation of Women*, New York: International Publishers.

—— (1968) "Writings on the Commune," in Karl Marx and V. I. Lenin, *Civil War in France: The Paris Commune*, New York: International Publishers.

—— (1971a) "The Socialist Revolution and the Right of Nations to Self-Determination," in *V. I. Lenin: Selected Works*, New York: International Publishers.

—— (1971b) "Economics and Politics in the Era of the Dictatorship of the Proletariat," in *V. I. Lenin: Selected Works*, New York: International Publishers.

Leslie, T. E. C. (1879) *Essays in Political and Moral Philosophy*, Dublin: University Press.

Lewis, G. K. (1953) "The Metaphysics of Conservatism," *Western Political Quarterly* 6: 728–41.

Lindblom, C. (1977) *Politics and Markets*, New York: Basic Books.

Lippman, W. (1934) *The Method of Freedom*, New York: The Macmillan Company.

Little, D. (1986) *The Scientific Marx*, Minneapolis: University of Minnesota Press.

Locke, J. (1955) *A Letter Concerning Toleration*, Indianapolis: The Bobbs-Merrill Company.

—— (1959) *An Essay Concerning Human Understanding*, New York: Dover Publications, Inc.

—— (1982) *Second Treatise of Government*, R. Cox (ed.), Arlington Heights, IL: Harlan Davidson, Inc.

Loenen, J.H.M.M (1976) "The Concept of Freedom in Berlin and Others:

An Attempt at Clarification," *Journal of Value Inquiry* 10: 279–85.

Lukes, S. (1974a) *Power*, London: The Macmillan Press.

—— (1974b) "Relativism: Cognitive and Moral," *Proceedings of the Aristotelian Society* (supplementary volume) 48: 165–89.

—— (1977) "A Reply to K. I. Macdonald," *British Journal of Political Science* 7: 418–19.

—— (1985a) "The Future of British Socialism?", *Dissent* 32: 197–206.

—— (1985b) *Marxism and Morality*, Oxford: Clarendon Press.

McCloskey, H. J. (1965) "A Critique of The Ideals of Liberty," *Mind* 74: 483–508.

—— (1974) "Liberalism," *Philosophy* 49: 187, 13–32.

MacCallum, G. C. (1967) "Negative and Positive Freedom," *Philosophical Review* 76: 312–34.

Macdonald, K. I. (1976) "Is 'Power' Essentially Contested?", *British Journal of Political Science* 6: 380–2.

Macfarlane, L. J. (1966) "On Two Concepts of Liberty," *Political Studies* 14: 77–81.

McGill, V. J. (1948) "Two Concepts of Freedom," *Philosophy and Phenomenological Research* 8: 515–21.

MacIntyre, A. (1973) "The Essential Contestability of Some Social Concepts," *Ethics* 84: 1–9.

—— (1977) "Utilitarianism and Cost/Benefit Analysis," in K. Sayre (ed.), *Values in the Electric Power Industry*, Notre Dame: Philosophic Institute of the University of Notre Dame.

—— (1981) *After Virtue*, Notre Dame, IN: University of Notre Dame Press.

Macpherson, C. B. (1968) "The Social Bearing of Locke's Political Theory," in C. B. Martin and D. M. Armstrong (eds), *Locke and Berkeley*, Garden City, NY: Anchor Books.

—— (1972) *Real World of Democracy*, New York: Oxford University Press.

—— (1973) "Berlin's Division of Liberty," in *Democratic Theory*, Oxford: Clarendon Press.

Malinowski, B. (1944) *Freedom and Civilization*, New York: Roy Publishers.

Maneli, M. (1978) "Three Concepts of Freedom: Kant – Hegel – Marx," *Interpretation* 7: 27–51.

Mannheim, K. (1953) *Essays on Sociology and Social Philosophy*, P. Kecskemeti (ed.), London: Routledge & Kegan Paul.

Marcuse, H. (1964) *One-Dimensional Man*, Boston: Beacon Press.

—— (1967) "Dialectic and Logic Since the War," in E. J. Simmons (ed.), *Continuity and Change in Russian and Soviet Thought*, New York: Russell and Russell.

—— (1969a) *An Essay on Liberation*, Boston: Beacon Press.

—— (1969b) "The Realm of Freedom and the Realm of Necessity: A Reconsideration," *Praxis* 5: 20–5.

—— (1969c) "Repressive Tolerance," in *A Critique of Pure Tolerance*, Boston: Beacon Press.

—— (1970) *Five Lectures*, Boston: Beacon Press.

—— (1972) "Freedom and the Historical Imperative," in J. De Bres trans; *Studies in Critical Philosophy*, London: New Left Books.

Martin, E. D. (1930) *Liberty*, New York: W. W. Norton & Co.

Marx, K. (1967a) *Capital*, I, New York: International Publishers.

—— (1967b) *Capital*, III, New York: International Publishers.

—— (1968) *The Civil War in France*, New York: International Publishers.

—— (1975a) "Contribution to the Critique of Hegel's Philosophy of Law," in *Collected Works*, III, New York: International Publishers.

—— (1975b) "Letters from the *Deutsch-Franzosische Jahrbucher*", in *Collected Works*, III, New York: International Publishers.

—— (1975c) "On the Jewish Question," in *Collected Works*, III, New York: International Publishers.

—— (1975d) "Comments on James Mill, *Elemens d'economie politique*," in *Collected Works*, III, New York: International Publishers.

—— (1975e) "Economic and Philosophic Manuscripts," in *Collected Works*, III, New York: International Publishers.

—— (1975f) "The Holy Family," in *Collected Works*, IV, New York: International Publishers.

—— (1976) "Theses on Feuerbach," in *Collected Works*, V, New York: International Publishers.

—— (1978a) "The Class Struggles in France, 1848–1850," in *Collected Works*, X, New York: International Publishers.

—— (1978b) "Critique of the Gotha Program," in R. C. Tucker (ed.), *The Marx–Engels Reader* (2nd edn), New York: W. W. Norton & Co.

—— (1979) "The Eighteenth Brumaire of Louis Bonaparte," in *Collected Works*, XI, New York: International Publishers.

Marx, K. and Engels, F. (1976a) "The German Ideology," in *Collected Works*, V, Moscow: Progress Publishers.

—— (1976b) "Manifesto of the Communist Party," in *Collected Works*, VI, Moscow: Progress Publishers.

Meyer, F. S. (1964) "Freedom, Tradition, Conservatism," in *What is Conservatism?*, New York: Holt, Rinehart & Winston.

Mill, J. S. (1851) *System of Logic*, II, London: J. W. Parker.

—— (1956) *On Liberty*, Indianapolis: The Bobbs-Merrill Company, Inc.

—— (1957) *Utilitarianism*, Indianapolis: The Liberal Arts Press, Inc.

—— (1962) *Considerations on Representative Government*, South Bend, IN: Gateway Editions, Ltd.

—— (1964) *Autobiography*, New York: The New American Library.

Millar, M. F. X. (1941) "Burke and the Moral Basis of Political Liberty," *Thought* 16: 79–101.

Montague, P. (1980) "Two Concepts of Rights," *Philosophy and Public Affairs* 9: 372–84.

—— (1986) "Is There a Right to Freedom?", *Philosophical Studies* 49: 71–81.

Morgenthau, H. J. (1957) "The Dilemmas of Freedom," *American Political Science Review* 51: 714–23.

Morley, J. V. (1946) *On Compromise*, London: Thinker's Library.

Morriss, P. (1980) "The Essentially Uncontestable Concepts of Power," in M. Freeman and D. Robertson (eds), *The Frontiers of Political Theory*, New York St. Martin's Press.

Nicholls, D. (1962) "Positive Liberty, 1880–1914," *American Political Science Review* 56: 114–28.

Nisbet, R. (1986) *Conservatism: Dream and Reality*, Minneapolis: University of Minnesota Press.

Norman, R. (1982) "Does Equality Destroy Liberty?", in K. Graham (ed.), *Contemporary Political Philosophy*, Cambridge: Cambridge University Press.
—— (1987) *Free and Equal*, Oxford: Oxford University Press.
Nozick, R. (1974) *Anarchy, State, and Utopia*, New York: Basic Books.
Oakeshott, M. (1962a) "The Political Economy of Freedom," in *Rationalism in Politics*, New York: Basic Books.
—— (1962b) "Political Education," in *Rationalism in Politics*, New York: Basic Books.
—— (1962c) "On Being Conservative," in *Rationalism in Politics*, New York: Basic Books.
—— (1962d) "The Tower of Babel," in *Rationalism in Politics*, New York: Basic Books.
Ollman, B. (1977) "Marx's Vision of Communism: A Reconstruction," in Z. Brzezinski (ed.), *Radical Visions of the Future*, Boulder, CO: Westview Press.
Oppenheim, F. (1981) *Political Concepts*, Chicago: University of Chicago Press.
Ortega y Gasset, J. (1946) "Concord and Liberty," in *Concord and Liberty*, trans. H. Weyl, New York: W. W. Norton & Co.
Orton, W. A. (1945) *The Liberal Tradition*, New Haven: Yale University Press.
Pagano, F. N. (1983) "Burke's View of the Evils of Political Theory: or, A Vindication of Natural Society," *Polity* 16: 446–62.
Parekh, B. (1972) "Liberalism and Morality," in B. Parekh and R. N. Berki (eds), *The Morality of Politics*, New York: Crane, Russak & Co.
—— (1973) "Social and Political Thought and the Problem of Ideology," in R. Benewick, R. N. Berki, and B. Parekh (eds), *Knowledge and Belief in Politics*, London: George Allen & Unwin.
—— (1983) "Review Article: The Political Thought of Sir Isaiah Berlin," *British Journal of Political Science* 12: 201–26.
Parent, W. A. (1974a) "Freedom as the Non-Restriction of Options," *Mind* 83: 432–8.
—— (1974b) "Some Recent Work on the Concept of Liberty," *American Philosophical Quarterly* 11: 149–66.
Parkin, C. (1956) *The Moral Basis of Burke's Political Thought*, Cambridge: Cambridge University Press.
Parry, G. (1972) "The Idea of Participation," in G. Parry (ed.), *Participation in Politics*, Manchester: Manchester University Press.
—— (1982) "Tradition, Community and Self-Determination," *British Journal of Political Science* 12: 399–419.
Parry, S. (1964) "Reason and the Restoration of Tradition," in F. S. Meyer (ed.), *What is Conservatism?*, New York: Holt, Rinehart, & Winston.
Partridge, P. H. (1967) "Freedom," in P. Edwards (ed.) *Encyclopedia of Philosophy*, III, New York: Macmillan Publishing Co.
Pateman, C. (1970) *Participation and Democratic Theory*, Cambridge: Cambridge University Press.
—— (1975) "Sublimation and Reification: Locke, Wolin and the Liberal Conception of the Political," *Politics and Society* 4: 441–67.
Pennock, J. R. (1972) "Coercion: An Overview," in J. R. Pennock and J. W.

Chapman (eds), *Coercion*, Chicago: Aldine & Atherton.
Perry, R. B. (1944) *Puritanism and Democracy*, New York: Vanguard Press.
—— (1953) "What Does It Mean To Be Free?," *The Pacific Spectator* 7: 124–41.
Peters, T. J. and Waterman, R. H. (1982) *In Search of Excellence*, New York: Warner Books, Inc.
Rawls, J. (1971) *A Theory of Justice*, Harvard: Harvard University Press.
Raz, J. (1986) *The Morality of Freedom*, Oxford: Clarendon Press.
Ritchie, D. G. (1895) *Natural Rights*, London: Swan Sonnenshein & Co.
Rossiter, C. (1955) "Toward an American Conservatism," *Yale Review* 44: 354–72.
Russell, B. (1940) "Freedom and Government," in R. N. Anshen (ed.), *Freedom: Its Meaning*, New York: Harcourt, Brace & Co.
Ryan, C. (1980) "The Normative Concept of Coercion," *Mind* 89: 481–98.
Salkever, (1977) "Freedom, Participation and Happiness," *Political Theory* 5: 391–413.
Sandel, M. J. (1982) *Liberalism and the Limits of Justice*, Cambridge: Cambridge University Press.
—— (1984) "Morality and the Liberal Ideal," *The New Republic* 190: 15–17.
Sartre, Jean-Paul (1961) *The Age of Reason*, Harmondsworth: Penguin Books.
Scaff, L. A. (1975) "Two Concepts of Political Participation," *The Western Political Quarterly* 28: 447–62.
Schneewind, J. B. (1983) "Moral Crisis and the History of Ethics," in P. A. French, T. E. Uehling, H. K. Wettstein (eds), *Midwest Studies in Philosophy*, VIII, Minneapolis: University of Minnesota Press.
Schweinitz, K. D. (1957) "Economic Growth, Coercion, and Freedom," *World Politics* 9: 166–92.
Scruton, R. (1980) *The Meaning of Conservatism*, Totowa, NJ: Barnes & Noble Books.
—— (1983) "Freedom and Custom," in A. P. Griffiths (ed.), *Of Liberty*, Cambridge: Cambridge University Press.
Sen, A. (1982) "Liberty as Control: An Appraisal," in P. French, T. E. Uehling, H. K. Wettstein (eds), *Midwest Studies in Philosophy*, VII, Minneapolis: University of Minnesota Press.
Shaw, W. H. (1978) *Marx's Theory of History*, Stanford: Stanford University Press.
Skillen, A. (1982) "Freedom of Speech," in K. Graham (ed.), *Contemporary Political Philosophy*, Cambridge: Cambridge University Press.
Smith, G. W. (1977) "Slavery, Contentment, and Social Freedom," *The Philosophical Quarterly* 27: 236–48.
—— (1982) "Marxian Metaphysics and Individual Freedom," in G. H. R. Parkinson, *Marx and Marxisms*, Cambridge: Cambridge University Press.
Spitz, D. (1961) "The Nature and Limits of Freedom," *Dissent* 8: 78–85.
—— (1964) *The Liberal Idea of Freedom*, Tucson: University of Arizona Press.
—— (1965) "A Liberal Perspective on Liberalism and Conservatism," in R. A. Goldwin (ed.), *Left, Right and Center*, Chicago: Rand McNally & Co.

Steed, M. (1972) "Participation Through Western Democractic Institutions," in G. Parry (ed.), *Participation in Politics*, Manchester: Manchester University Press.

Steiner, H. (1975) "Individual Liberty," *Proceedings of the Aristotelian Society* 75: 33–50.

Stephen, J. F. (1967) *Liberty, Equality, Fraternity*, London: Cambridge University Press.

Swanton, C. (1985) "On the 'Essential Contestedness' of Political Concepts," *Ethics* 95: 811–27.

Tawney, R. H. (1953) "We Mean Freedom," in *The Attack*, New York: Harcourt Brace & Co.

Taylor, C. (1979) "What's Wrong with Negative Liberty," in A. Ryan (ed.), *The Idea of Freedom*, Oxford: Oxford University Press.

Ten, C. L. (1980) *Mill on Liberty*, Oxford: Clarendon Press.

Tocqueville, A. de (1969) *Democracy in America*, Garden City, NY: Anchor Books.

Tully, J. (1984) "Locke on Liberty," in Z. Pelczynski and J. Gray (eds), *Conceptions of Liberty in Political Philosophy*, New York: St. Martin's Press.

Tussman, J. (1960) *Obligation and the Body Politic*, London: Oxford University Press.

Viereck, P. (1956) *Conservatism: from John Adams to Churchill*, Princeton, NJ: D. Van Nostrand Co.

Walicki, A. (1984) "The Marxian Conception of Freedom," in Z. Pelczynski and J. Gray (eds), *Conceptions of Liberty in Political Philosophy*, New York: St. Martin's Press.

Walzer, M. (1970) *Obligations*, Cambridge, Massachusetts: Harvard University Press.

—— (1980) "Town Meetings and Workers' Control: A Story for Socialists", in *Radical Principles*, New York: Basic Books.

—— (1984) "Liberalism and the Art of Separation," *Political Theory* 12: 315–30.

Weinstein, W. L. (1965) "The Concept of Liberty in Nineteenth Century English Political Thought," *Political Studies* 13: 145–62.

Williams, B. (1985) *Ethics and the Limits of Philosophy*, Cambridge: Harvard University Press.

Wilson, F. G. (1941) "A Theory of Conservatism," *American Political Science Review* 35: 29–43.

Wolff, R. P. (1970) *In Defense of Anarchy*, New York: Harper & Row.

Wolin, S. (1960) *Politics and Vision*, Boston: Little, Brown & Co.

—— (1968) "Paradigms and Political Theories," in P. King and B. C. Parekh (eds), *Politics and Experience*, Cambridge: Cambridge University Press.

Wood, E. M. (1972) *Mind and Politics*, Berkeley: University of California Press.

Young, R. (1980) "Autonomy and Socialization," *Mind* 89: 565–76.

Index

Adler, M. J. 207
administration 115–22, 136
agency 145–9, 165, 166; agents
 144, 145, 149, 177
Archimedean point 25
Arendt, H. 164
Aristotle 197, 222
authority 6–8, 59, 60, 115–24,
 128, 133, 171, 172, 177, 181,
 185, 188, 196–9, 203; command
 authority 122, 123, 128; focal
 authority 123; radical authority
 122, 123; respect authority 122,
 123
autonomy 46, 104, 112, 140, 162

Bakunin, M. 115
Benn, S. I. 154–7, 162, 163
Berlin, I. 1, 3, 5, 6, 28;
 ch. 3 *passim*; 141, 148, 151, 216,
 217
Burke, E. 28, 31, 33–5,
 37–9, 41, 43–57, 59–63

Carritt, E. F. 230, 231
Casey, J. 55
Cecil, Lord 63
children 68, 71, 80, 91, 133,
 155, 177, 182, 197, 215, 233,
 239
citizen 126, 176, 181–8, 190,
 191, 193, 206, 222
civil society 54, 89, 102
classes 77, 98, 99, 108, 111,
 112, 132, 172, 228, 239

coercion 4–6, 13, 28, 33, 47, 66,
 71, 77–80, 83, 104, 111–13,
 119, 120, 134, 141, 144, 145,
 153, 155, 165, 166, 173, 176, 177,
 197, 226, 228, 234, 240; physical
 coercion 78, 228
cognitive resources 206, 238,
 239, 241
community 25, 46, 53, 63, 78–80,
 93, 100, 105, 118, 124, 134, 168,
 175, 181, 201, 206, 232, 235, 241
conservatives 1, 2, 13, 16, 28;
 ch. 3 *passim*; 71, 94, 101, 102,
 110, 112, 113, 133, 135, 166,
 180; libertarian conservatives 72;
 traditional conservatives 16, 63
constraints: external constraints
 94, 95, 219; inner constraints 94;
 internal negative constraints 147
core meaning 3–7, 11
corporations 134, 172, 196–201,
 203, 232, 236, 242
Cowling, M. 51, 52
Crocker, L. 215, 216
customs 28, 39–42, 46, 48–60,
 77–9, 94, 95, 131, 158

Dahl, R. 237
democracy 4, 13, 41, 81, 98, 101,
 115, 171, 186, 187, 189, 192, 193;
 direct democracy 193
Dewey, J. 207, 219, 229
dialectics 106; contradiction(s) 33,
 58, 66, 103, 107, 108, 110–14,
 124, 132

domination 8, 44, 66, 103, 108, 109, 112, 113, 118, 129, 135, 148, 175, 176, 226

Edel, A. 16
education 103, 155, 183, 195, 197, 206, 214, 218, 225, 231, 233, 234, 236, 238, 239
Edwards, J. 206
elections 41, 111, 112, 160, 171, 180, 184, 198, 199
elite 41, 117, 119, 200
emancipation 102, 105, 107, 126, 205, 213; human emancipation 105, 107, 126; political emancipation 105, 107
empowerment 139–41, 144, 167, 169–72, 174, 176, 178, 189–91, 194, 195, 202, 205, 206, 241
enablement 140, 168, 205–7, 216, 221, 223, 224, 229, 230, 232, 233, 241
Engels, F. 101, 106, 108, 110, 116–18, 120, 123, 124, 127, 130, 132, 136
entitlement 5, 139, 141, 169, 172, 173, 141
Epictetus 149, 150
equality 4, 41, 44, 101, 182, 216, 220, 236–40
exemplar 3, 6, 20, 21

Feinberg, J. 73, 75, 82, 219, 220
freedom: absolute freedom 100, 182; "freedom from" 37, 47, 49, 147, 148, 174, 198, 207, 209, 226; freedom of the press 39, 40, 190; hyperbolical freedom 174; material means 5, 224–8; nature freedom 141–5, 169; negative freedom 5, 14–16, 32, 46, 49, 50, 70, 92, 105, 137, 147, 176, 179, 209, 228, 229, 240; ontological freedom 45; ordered freedom 43; perfect freedom 76, 78, 80, 92, 94; positive freedom 5, 46, 74, 105, 137, 147, 153; radical freedom 28, 54, ch. 4 *passim*, 140, 163; right to freedom

167; subjective freedom 150; wild freedom 45
French Revolution 48

Gallie, W. B. 4, 20, 24
Glorious Revolution 58
Gould, J. 228
government 28, 31, 35, 37, 49, 51, 56, 65, 66, 71, 72, 76, 78, 84, 97, 99, 100, 112, 113, 118, 171, 172, 174, 184–6, 188–91, 193–7, 199, 201, 202, 220, 222, 223, 230–6, 242
Gray, J. N. 18
Green, T. H. 150, 164, 241

Hacker, A. 200, 227
harm 84–8, 90, 146, 153, 184; harm principle 86, 87; physical harm 146, 153; psychological harm 85
Hart, J. 38, 50,
Hayek, F. 78, 79
Heller, A. 115
Hill, S. B. 164
Hobbes, T. 14, 143, 165, 207–12, 220, 221, 224
Horkheimer, M. 131
Hume, D. 96
Huntington, S. P. 55

ideology 82, 93, 104, 111
injury 75, 76, 87–90, 95, 97, 99
interests 9, 84–6, 88, 89, 92, 99, 108–13, 116–21, 123–6, 129, 132, 154–6, 161, 182, 183, 185–91, 220, 232, 241; human interests 182, 185; irrational interests 183
involvement 13, 139, 167, 170–2, 176, 189, 191, 193, 194, 201, 241

John, King 164
justice 5, 12, 39, 43, 61, 65, 67, 83, 97, 183, 191, 203, 239

Kant, I. 46, 161
Kirk 53, 54, 56, 59

lack of constraint 12, 14, 15, 32, 47, 63, 66, 67, 69, 71, 72, 81–3, 100, 139, 140, 145, 147, 170, 209, 240
law 8, 21, 28, 31, 39, 56, 62, 67–72, 78, 79, 84, 87, 89, 91, 94, 104, 112, 115, 233
Lenin, V. I. 28, *see* ch. 4
Leslie, T. E. C. 224
liberal freedom 11, 15; ch. 3 *passim*; 101, 103, 113, 120, 137, 140, 141, 207
liberalism 28, 40, 66, 78, 79, 92, 93, 130, 137, 175, 199
liberation 102, 132, 150, 227
libertarians 16, 134, 170; libertarian conservatives 63
liberty: absence of constraint 75, 83, 169; lack of interference 12, 28, 145, 147, 148, 163–5; natural liberty 72; rational liberty 43
license 42, 68
Lippman, W. 6
Locke, J. 28; *see* ch. 3; 162, 196, 220

McCloskey, H. J. 5
Macfarlane, L. J. 72
Mannheim, K. 55, 56
Marcuse, H. 28; *see* ch. 4
market 77, 78, 94, 104, 109, 122, 134, 200, 201
Marx, K. 28, *see* ch. 4
material means (resources) 2, 5, 17, 39, 140, 188, 190, 204, 206–8, 212–30, 233, 235–40, 241, 242
Mill, J. S. 28; *see* ch. 3; 150
model(s) ch. 1 *passim*; 38, 42, 66, 70, 91, 106, 139–41, 211, 241
Montague, P. 167
Morgenthau, H. J. 188
moral law 55, 68

natural law 8, 54–8, 68, 69, 89, 98
Norman, R. 226, 227, 233, 238

Oakeshott, M. 28; *see* ch. 2; 229
obligations 40, 42, 47–9, 113, 166, 168, 175, 177, 227
objectivity 19, 24

offense 86–8; offense principle 87
opportunities 4, 9, 70, 140, 161, 183, 184, 193, 195, 200, 206–8, 213, 216–21, 238, 239; bare opportunities 218, 221; real opportunities 218, 221
oppression 1, 59, 79, 108, 113, 228, 231
options 69, 70, 73–7, 80, 153, 154, 173, 230, 232
order 21, 28; ch. 2 *passim*; 67, 71, 83, 102, 111, 112, 123, 134, 220, 223
Ortega y Gasset, J. 40, 49, 58

Parekh, B. 22
Parent, W. A. 230, 231, 234
Paris Commune 115, 119
participation 1, 4, 13, 90, 98, 102, 114, 117, 119–21, 140, 172–4, 183–5, 188–97, 200–3, 205, 208, 217, 224, 236–9, 242; right to participation 185, 191, 197, 200, 208
Partridge, P. H. 210–12
Perry, R. B. 206, 211, 220, 230, 231, 235
planning 13, 31, 115, 116; central authority 115, 122, 130, 133; central direction 116, 121, 132–5; centralism 116
political philosophy 1, 19, 25, 47, 67, 203
poverty 134, 196, 206, 213, 215, 225, 228
power: arbitrary power 43, 44, 47, 55; agenda power 172; charismatic power 208; dispersion of power 43–5, 47, 51; occurrent power 208
prescription 56, 57, 59
privacy 66, 80, 86, 89, 91, 92, 168, 201
private 65, 66, 75, 80, 81, 89–95, 97, 100; ch. 4 *passim*; 164, 173, 193, 196, 198, 199, 201, 232; private domain 90; private realm 28, 66, 80, 81, 89, 90, 92, 93, 95, 100, 113

private property 39, 42, 92, 104,
    108–10, 112, 117, 158, 177, 199
Procrustes 27
proletariat 101, 128
Prometheus 135
public 41, 75, 86, 89–93, 99,
    118, 132, 172, 173, 188, 195, 196,
    203, 204, 232, 235, 236; public
    realm 89–91, 93, 173

radicals 1, 2, 13, 16, 24, 27, 28, 51,
    59, 60, 63; ch. 4 *passim*; 181, 206
rationality 20, 21, 25, 26, 28, 45,
    59, 103, 104, 109, 114, 121, 126,
    130–2, 134–6, 156
Rawls, J. 213, 216
reason: light of reason 56, 58;
    practical reason 60, 61; radical
    reason 131–3, 135; theoretical
    reason 59
referenda 187, 189
representative(s) 117, 119, 186,
    188, 194, 235
restraint(s) 47–9, 65, 71, 83,
    84, 86, 87, 89, 94, 129, 209
revolution 101, 104, 124
right(s): civil rights 200; exercisable
    right 167, 168; individual rights
    40, 42, 44, 47, 81, 168, 173, 176,
    182, 184, 194, 203; natural rights
    85, 162, 175; prescriptive rights
    40; prima facie right 166; right to
    poverty 42, 168; rights of man 39,
    46, 55, 56; specific rights 167, 175;
    worker rights 140
Ritchie, D. G. 233
Russell, B. 189
Ryan, C. 177

Scruton, R. 52
security 28, 56, 57, 65, 67,
    85, 97, 109, 164, 170, 178, 220
self-determination: conjoint self-
    determination 174; lack of self-
    determination 146, 153; rational
    self-determination, *passim*; realistic
    self-determination 162, 169, 188,
    236; right to self-determination
    102, 139, 141, 162, 166–9,
    171–6, 178, 179, 180, 182–4,

186, 187, 192, 194, 196, 198,
    205, 206, 208, 214, 219, 221–4,
    231, 234, 237, 239, 240; social self-
    determination 139; subjective self-
    determination 150, 153, 161, 180;
    unrestricted self-determination
    153, 161
Sen, A. 207
slave(s) 44, 68, 150, 151, 165,
    168, 173, 176, 213; slavery 23, 38
Smith, G. W. 127
social contract 33, 34, 123
state 12, 14, 15, 31, 34, 43–5,
    52, 56, 57, 61, 67, 78, 83, 89, 94,
    97, 98, 100–2, 104, 111–13,
    115–18, 122, 166, 171, 172,
    176, 177, 180–7, 191–4, 196,
    197, 199, 200, 201–3, 205,
    220, 229, 232, 233, 236, 239, 241
state of nature 34, 76, 78,
    94, 98, 115, 177, 189, 220, 234
"State of Nature Fallacy" 177

Tawney, R. H. 215, 237
Taylor, C. 151
threats 76, 78, 142, 146, 155,
    165, 166, 230
Tocqueville, A. de 28, 31
totalitarianism 141, 174
tradition 28; ch. 2 *passim*;
    78, 79, 84, 94, 95, 97, 131, 159
trial by jury 39

umbrella term 11, 15
unions 172, 193, 195, 196,
    198–202
universal suffrage 112, 116, 117

virtue 28, 31, 62, 63, 165
voluntary association 48, 184

Walzer, M. 191, 193, 199
Weinstein, W. L. 234
welfare 31, 87, 88, 90, 103, 140, 182
"wisdom of the species" 39, 51
Wolin, S. 97